OXFORD READINGS IN POLITICS
AND GOVERNMENT

PARLIAMENTARY VERSUS
PRESIDENTIAL GOVERNMENT

OXFORD READINGS IN POLITICS AND GOVERNMENT

General Editors: Vernon Bogdanor and Geoffrey Marshall

The readings in this series are chosen from a variety of journals and other sources to cover major areas or issues in the study of politics, government, and political theory. Each volume contains an introductory essay by the editor and a select guide to further reading.

OTHER TITLES IN THIS SERIES

Communitarianism and Individualism

Edited by Shlomo Avineri and Avner de-Shalit

Marxist Theory

Edited by Alex Callinicos

The West European Party System

Edited by Peter Mair

Ministerial Responsibility

Edited by Geoffrey Marshall

Liberty

Edited by David Miller

Legislatures

Edited by Philip Norton

PARLIAMENTARY VERSUS PRESIDENTIAL GOVERNMENT

EDITED BY
AREND LIJPHART

OXFORD UNIVERSITY PRESS

Oxford University Press, Walton Street, Oxford OX2 6DP

Oxford New York

Athens Auckland Bangkok Bombay
Calcutta Cape Town Dar es Salaam Delhi
Florence Hong Kong Istanbul Karachi
Kuala Lumpur Madras Madrid Melbourne
Mexico City Nairobi Paris Singapore
Taipei Tokyo Toronto

and associated companies in
Berlin Ibadan

Oxford is a trade mark of Oxford University Press

Published in the United States by
Oxford University Press Inc., New York

First published in hardback and paperback 1992
Paperback edition reprinted 1993, 1994, 2000

British Library Cataloguing in Publication Data
Data available

Library of Congress Cataloging in Publication Data
Parliamentary versus presidential government / edited by Arend Lijphart.
—(Oxford readings in politics and government)
Includes bibliographical references and index.
1. Comparative government and representation.
I. Lijphart, Arend. II. Series.
JF11.P36 1992 320.3 – dc20 91–27651

ISBN 0–19–878043–5
ISBN 0–19–878044–3 (Pbk)

Printed and bound in Great Britain
on acid-free paper by Biddles Ltd
www.biddles.co.uk

For Anna and Brian

ACKNOWLEDGEMENTS

I owe my greatest debt of gratitude to the authors whose works are represented in this book of readings. It is the quality of their thinking, their insights and originality, that largely account for the value of this compilation. Almost all of the readings are excerpts from longer works, and this means that I also owe the authors an apology for doing at least some violence to the integrity of their writings. However, my aim throughout has been to choose excerpts that highlight and are genuinely representative of the contributors' arguments and analyses. And the obvious advantage of including excerpts, instead of entire articles and chapters, is that a much greater variety of materials, viewpoints, and perspectives can be included—a special advantage for so controversial a subject as parliamentary versus presidential government. The one selection that is not an excerpt from an already published work is Bolívar Lamounier's chapter on Brazil, which he prepared at my request for inclusion in this book. The chapter by José Batlle y Ordóñez appears here in a new translation by John M. Carey which was also prepared expressly for this volume. I am especially grateful for these two original contributions.

I have benefited a great deal from the advice and knowledge of many people, scholars as well as politicians, who have been concerned with the question of parliamentary versus presidential government. It was a special privilege to meet with the Council for the Consolidation of Democracy in Buenos Aires in November 1987, to serve on the International Forum of the Israel-Diaspora Institute which met in Tel Aviv and Caesarea in March and April 1989, and to testify before the Special Study Commission on the Chilean Political Regime of the Chamber of Deputies in Valparaiso in September 1990. I am also grateful for the many excellent comments I received during lectures and seminars on democratization and alternative models of democracy that I gave at the Catholic University of Valparaiso, the Centro de Estudios de la Realidad Contemporánea in Santiago, and the University of Buenos Aires in November 1987, and at Yonsei University in Seoul, the Institute for National

Policy Research in Taipei, the National Taiwan University, the University of Hong Kong, the Chinese University of Hong Kong, the University of the Philippines, and the Philippine Council for Foreign Relations in May 1990.

During the last few years I have participated in two comparative and collaborative research projects on presidential government: the project on 'Democracy: Presidential or Parliamentary: Does it Make a Difference?' directed by Juan J. Linz and Arturo Valenzuela, and the Brookings Institution project on comparing the US presidential system with selected parliamentary systems, directed by R. Kent Weaver and Bert A. Rockman. I have learned much from my interaction with the directors and the other participants in these projects, especially Ronald Rogowski.

Finally, I should like to express my appreciation for the advice and assistance I have received from Milton I. Vanger of Brandeis University, Jorge Otero Menéndez, editor of *El Día* in Montevideo, my colleagues at the University of California, San Diego, Matthew S. Shugart, Mathew D. McCubbins, and John M. Carey, and Oxford University Press editors Janet Moth and Henry Hardy.

La Jolla, California   A.L.
January 1991

CONTENTS

PART II

PRESIDENTIALISM IN LATIN AMERICA

PART III

SEMI-PRESIDENTIALISM AND OTHER
INTERMEDIATE FORMS

PART IV

PARLIAMENTARISM AND PRESIDENTIALISM IN AFRICA, ASIA, AND EUROPE

PART V

SYSTEMATIC EVIDENCE: BROADLY COMPARATIVE AND MULTIVARIATE ANALYSES

INTRODUCTION

Democracies can be organized in a variety of ways. This book focuses on what is probably the most important institutional difference among them: the relationship between the executive and the legislature. The two principal alternative models are parliamentary and presidential government. The relative merits of these two forms of democracy have been debated for a long time—considerably longer than the existence of modern democracy itself, which was not fully established anywhere (if we take the requirement of universal suffrage seriously) until the beginning of the twentieth century. There have been ups and downs in the intensity of the debate. The current great interest in the question of parliamentarism versus presidentialism coincides, not surprisingly, with the wave of democratization—and the writing of new democratic constitutions—that has swept the world since the mid-1970s, beginning in southern Europe and spreading to Latin America, East Asia, eastern Europe, the Soviet Union, and South Africa. Indeed, the debate has never been as spirited or as truly worldwide as it is today.

The authors represented in this volume are from all parts of the world and range from eighteenth-century classics to modern, late twentieth-century advocates and analysts. The chapters are organized into five parts on the basis of geographical and conceptual criteria. Part I deals with the debate as it originated and developed in Great Britain and the United States, the two countries that have served as the main models of parliamentary and presidential government respectively and from which these models have spread to many other parts of the world. The US model was especially influential in Latin America, where presidentialism has become deeply rooted—the topic of Part II. Part III treats intermediate democratic forms such as French-style semi-presidential and Swiss-style collegial government; the semi-presidential model has been especially influential—it was also adopted in Portugal and Sri Lanka and has been proposed in several Latin American countries—and therefore receives the greatest attention. The chapters in Part IV are examples of proposals and arguments concerning the parliamentary and presidential alternatives in other parts of the world—Africa, Asia, and Europe. Finally Part V contains several broadly comparative and multivariate analyses that attempt to evaluate the available evidence as systematically as possible.

The main subject of the debate has been the respective advantages and disadvantages of parliamentary and presidential government, and almost all of the chapters in this volume deal with this topic in one way or another. The second important (albeit less controversial and hence less frequently discussed) subject is the origins and causes of these alternative forms of government. And the third question—which logically should be the first question—concerns the exact definitions of parliamentary and presidential government as well as the definitions of forms of government that appear to be intermediate between parliamentarism and presidentialism: can these various systems of government be clearly and unambiguously distinguished from one another?

DEFINITIONS

Douglas V. Verney's eleven 'propositions' concerning parliamentary and presidential government, published in 1959, represent the most thorough statement on the differences between these forms of democracy (see Chapter 1). His first proposition concerns their origins and growth—a subject to which I shall return later in this introduction—but the remaining ten are definitional criteria. Most authors use broader definitions based on just two of Verney's criteria: numbers 7 and 10.

The first distinction to be made is that, in parliamentary governments, the head of the government—for whom there are various different official titles such as prime minister, premier, chancellor, minister-president, and taoiseach—and his or her cabinet are dependent on the confidence of the legislature and can be dismissed from office by a legislative vote of no confidence or censure; in presidential forms of government, the head of government—almost always called president—is elected for a fixed, constitutionally prescribed term and in normal circumstances cannot be forced to resign by the legislature (although it may be possible to remove a president by the highly unusual and exceptional process of impeachment).

The second crucial difference is that presidential heads of government are popularly elected, either directly or via an electoral college, and that prime ministers are selected by the legislature; I use the general term 'selected' deliberately because the process of selection can range widely from formal election to the informal emergence from inter-party bargaining in the legislature followed by an official appointment by the head of state. It is interesting to note, however, that Walter Bagehot does not hesitate to use the term 'election' in its broad meaning even for the British case where formal election never occurs: 'a cabinet is *elected* by a legislature' (Chapter 6, emphasis added). These two differences are based on the distinction between the principle of separation of executive and legislative powers, first expounded by Montesquieu in 1748 (see Chapter 2), in presidential systems and the principle of non-separation or, in Bagehot's words, 'fusion' of powers in parliamentary systems.[1]

A third fundamental distinction is also often used: parliamentary systems have collective or collegial executives whereas presidential systems have one-person, non-collegial executives; this is Verney's proposition number 5. The prime minister's position in the cabinet can vary from pre-eminence to virtual equality with the other ministers, but there is always a relatively high degree of collegiality in decision-making; in contrast, the members of presidential cabinets are mere advisers and subordinates of the president. As we shall see, this distinction plays an important role in the debate on the advantages and disadvantages of the alternative forms of government.

The classical writers also insisted on the unipersonal character of the executive as an important adjunct of the separation-of-powers system they proposed. For Montesquieu, this meant the

---

[1] It should be emphasized that the term 'separation of powers' means not just having separate executive and legislative branches of government but their mutual *independence* or non-subordination. Moreover, both separation and fusion of powers refer exclusively to the relationship between the executive and the legislature—not to the judicial branch of government, which is substantially independent in all democracies, regardless of whether they are parliamentary or presidential.

monarch: 'The executive power . . . is better administered by
one than by many' (Chapter 2). Both Alexander Hamilton and
Simón Bolívar argued at length in favour of a one-person president (Chapters 4 and 11). And, more than a century and a
half later, the Nigerian drafters of a presidential constitution
followed the same line of reasoning (Chapter 25). Robert A.
Dahl relates that the possibility of a plural executive was discussed at the American Constitutional Convention in 1787,
but that there was very little support for it (Chapter 5). It
is worth noting that this third characteristic of presidential
government is not logically linked to the principle of separation
of powers, and that it may even be argued to be philosophically
at odds with it: separation of executive from legislative power
means the limiting of power and the need for sharing power,
but the unipersonal president means the concentration of
power *within* the executive—the very opposite of limited and
shared power.

In addition to the above three criteria, several writers have
used additional distinctions, especially that presidents are both
heads of government and heads of state whereas prime ministers
are mere heads of government, and that presidents cannot
simultaneously be members of the legislature whereas prime
ministers and other members of their cabinets usually are
(Verney's propositions 2 and 6). These additional criteria raise
two problems. One is that there are serious empirical exceptions: for instance, Dutch and Norwegian legislators have to
give up their legislative seats when they join the cabinet, but this
requirement does not appear to have any significant effect on the
basically parliamentary operation of the government in these
countries. Second, even when there are no empirical exceptions,
as in the case of presidential executives being the heads of both
state and government, this characteristic does not appear to be
logically necessary. Indeed, the proposals for a 'directly elected
prime minister' in The Netherlands and in Israel (Chapters 27
and 28) entail the establishment of presidential government
according to all three of the above crucial criteria; it would be
hard to argue that the facts that the proposed presidents would
continue to be called 'prime ministers' and that separate
ceremonial heads of state—the Dutch monarch and the Israeli
'president'—would be retained, would make the proposed sys-

tems fundamentally different from other presidential systems.[2]

Of course, Verney does not insist that all of his propositions represent *essential* criteria. They apply without exception to the two main prototypes, British parliamentarism and US presidentialism; but Verney admits that there is a continental European subtype of parliamentary government, and he sometimes uses qualifiers like 'usually' in stating his propositions. His juxtaposition of the British and American prototypes also has special value because of their importance as influential models exported to other countries, especially those in the former British Empire and in Latin America. It is worth noting that Great Britain has served not only as the principal model of parliamentarism but also, in the eighteenth and early nineteenth centuries, as the opposite separation-of-powers model—as seen in the writings of Montesquieu, Madison, and Bolívar (Chapters 2, 3, and 11).

CLASSIFICATIONS

How well do the three definitional criteria identified above serve to classify democracies in the real world as either parliamentary or presidential? The answer, suggested by Figure 1, is: very well. Since we have three dichotomous criteria, their joint application yields eight possible combinations. However, Figure 1 shows that the vast majority of contemporary and historical cases of democracy fit either the pure parliamentary or the pure presidential type.

The eightfold typology also works well in classifying some of the intermediate cases without difficulty or ambiguity— including Switzerland and Uruguay, which are extremely awkward to classify without using the distinction between one-person and collegial executives. The Swiss Federal Council is a seven-member co-equal executive elected by the legislature for

---

[2] These examples also make clear that presidential and parliamentary systems cannot be defined in terms of the mere presence or absence of a 'president' in a given country. The Dutch proposal would create a presidential system without creating any official called 'president'. Conversely, many systems have 'presidents' without being presidential: all of the non-monarchical or republican parliamentary systems, which have a president as their head of state.

	Collegial executive		One-person executive	
	Dependent on legislative confidence	Not dependent on legislative confidence	Dependent on legislative confidence	Not dependent on legislative confidence
Executive selected by legislature	*Parliamentary:* Most West European democracies Australia Canada India Israel Jamaica Japan Malaysia New Zealand Nigeria (1960–6)	Switzerland	No empirical examples (A)	Lebanon
Executive selected by voters	No empirical examples (B)	Cyprus (1960–3) Uruguay (1952–67)	No empirical examples (C)	*Presidential:* Most Latin American democracies Cyprus France (5th Rep.) Philippines South Korea United States Nigeria (1979–83)

FIG. 1 A typology of parliamentary, presidential, and 'mixed' forms of democracy, and some empirical examples

a fixed term of office. The Uruguayan *colegiado*, which operated from 1952 to 1967, was a Swiss-inspired nine-member body, also serving for a fixed term but popularly elected. For the Swiss founding fathers who wrote the 1848 constitution, the US constitution served as the principal model, but they deliberately rejected not only the popular, albeit indirect, election of the executive, but also the one-person executive, which they feared would have too much of a 'monarchical or dictatorial tendency' (Chapter 23). In a 1911 editorial in his newspaper *El Día*, the spiritual father of Uruguay's *colegiado*, José Batlle y Ordóñez, similarly argued in favour of a collegial executive on the ground that modern democratic principles require the sharing of power, including the sharing of executive power (Chapter 24). Cyprus was ruled by a directly elected duumvirate (a Greek Cypriot president and a Turkish Cypriot vice-president with virtually equal powers) during its first few years of independence, and therefore fits the same type as Uruguay in the *colegiado* phase. The Venezuelan executive triumvirate against which Bolívar argued in his famous 1819 Angostura Address (see Chapter 11) is another example.

The cell in the top right-hand corner of the Figure also has only a single occupant—Lebanon, a rather difficult case to which I shall return below. However, as Dahl's account of the American Constitutional Convention shows, the United States came close to adopting this form of government: the Convention voted several times in favour of the president's election by the legislature before finally settling on the electoral college solution (Chapter 5).

Three of the types are completely empty cells—which is not surprising because the logic of legislative confidence militates against them. Type (A) would be a strong form of *Kanzlerdemokratie*: a parliamentary system except that the prime minister's relationship to the cabinet resembles that of a president to his or her cabinet. On paper, the constitution of the Federal Republic of Germany appears to call for such a system, but since the chancellor needs the Bundestag's confidence, the negotiation of a collegial coalition cabinet takes place prior to the formal election of the chancellor by the Bundestag. Types (B) and (C) are problematic because a legislative vote of no confidence in a popularly elected executive would be seen as defiance of the popular will and of democratic legitimacy. The only democratically acceptable form of types (B) and (C) would be one in which a legislative vote of no confidence in the executive was matched by the executive's right to dissolve the legislature, and where either action would trigger new elections of both legislature and executive. The (C) form of such a system has indeed been suggested for the United States by the Committee on the Constitutional System (Chapter 9).

So far the eightfold typology has appeared to serve almost perfectly as an exhaustive classification with mutually exclusive categories. However, there are two sets of partly overlapping empirical cases that are difficult to classify. One set consists of systems that have both a popularly elected president and a parliamentary prime minister. In the other, different procedures and institutions may be used at different times. Maurice Duverger discusses the former, which he calls 'semi-presidential' governments, at length in Chapter 18. Some of these can be classified in the eightfold typology after all by asking the question: who is the *real* head of government—president or prime minister? For instance, Duverger argues that because the Austrian, Icelandic, and Irish presidents are weak in spite of being popularly elected, these democracies are, in practice, parliamentary. Similarly, he argues that France with its 'all-powerful presidency' is mainly presidential. Duverger wrote this analysis in 1980, before France had experienced the 1986–8 period of 'cohabitation' when President François Mitterrand lost his majority in the National Assembly and was forced to appoint his major political adversary, Jacques Chirac, to the premiership. Chirac became the head of government, Mitterrand's power was reduced to merely a special role in foreign policy, and thus French democracy, at least temporarily, shifted into a mainly parliamentary pattern.

Hence French semi-presidentialism does not mean either a synthesis of the parliamentary and presidential types or an intermediate category more or less halfway between them. Rather, it entails an *alternation* of parliamentary and presidential phases, depending on whether or not the president's party has a majority in the legislature. This has become the most widely accepted concept of semi-presidential democracy, and presidential–parliamentary alternation is now often regarded as a special advantage of this form of government, for instance, by the Council for the Consolidation of Democracy which recommended semi-presidentialism for Argentina (Chapter 21).

It is interesting to note that there is no hint of this meaning of semi-presidentialism in Charles de Gaulle's famous 1946 Bayeux Manifesto, in which he described the main features of what would later become the 1958 constitution of the Fifth Republic (see Chapter 17); nor, of course, did he recognize the importance of popular election for a powerful presidency until 1962 when he forced through a constitutional amendment to this effect. However, the logic that the combination of a popularly elected, powerful president with a cabinet subject to legislative confidence means presidential–parliamentary alternation was clearly recognized by Woodrow Wilson in his 1879 proposal for 'cabinet government' in the United States; the system he favoured would now be called semi-presidentialism, although even in a parliamentary phase the president's veto would ensure that he or she would retain considerable influence (Chapter 19). The logic of alternation is also explicitly recognized in A. Jeyaratnam Wilson's analysis of the semi-presidential 1978 constitution of Sri Lanka which was patterned after the French model (Chapter 20).

Of course, it is theoretically possible to have a non-alternating, genuinely mixed semi-presidentialism in which president and prime minister (and his or her cabinet) have more or less equal decision-making powers. According to Duverger, the German Weimar Republic, Finland, and Portugal fit this description. Other observers have regarded the last two as mainly parliamentary, similar to France in its parliamentary 'cohabitation' phase with the premier as head of government and the president's power limited to a special role in foreign affairs. For instance, in G. Bingham Powell's analysis (Chapter 33) Finland is grouped with the other west European parliamentary systems. Since 1982, after the departure of durable and prestigious President Urho Kekkonen in Finland and after a constitutional amendment restricting the president's power in Portugal, it seems to me that these two countries have indeed been mainly parliamentary, but prior to 1982 this question is debatable, and Duverger's judgement may well be correct.

Lebanon is another example of a political system that seems to fit two different categories in Figure 1 *simultaneously*. Lebanese democracy has, of course, not functioned normally since the outbreak of civil war in 1975, but its constitution provides for both a president elected by parliament for a fixed term and a prime minister subject to parliamentary confidence. Until 1990, the traditionally Christian president was clearly more powerful than the traditionally Moslem prime minister, and Lebanon therefore appears in the upper right-hand cell of Figure 1. However, the formal adoption of the Taif Accord in 1990 equalized the president's and prime minister's powers (as part of an attempt to place the Moslems on an equal political footing with the Christians)—placing Lebanon in both the top left-hand and the top right-hand cells.

The second set of hard-to-classify empirical cases consists of presidential systems in which the legislature has a role in the election of the president if the popular (or electoral college) vote fails to yield a majority winner. I do not include in this set countries like the United States and pre-1973 Chile, because there is almost always a majority winner in the United States, and Chile had a strong tradition of automatic legislative ratification of the plurality winner. However, the Bolivian legislature awarded the presidency to the runner-up instead of the plurality winner in 1985 and to the third-place finisher in 1989. Hence Bolivia seems to fit both right-hand cells of Figure 1—but, like the similar two-cell fit of most semi-presidential systems, sequentially rather than simultaneously.

Verney's final conclusion in Chapter 1 is that democracies have a strong tendency to be either parliamentary or presidential. If we interpret his words liberally, to include the phenomenon of parliamentary and presidential *phases* in the same country, this conclusion seems to be borne out by the above analysis. We have found very few examples of democracies that are simultaneously parliamentary and presidential or that, either simultaneously or at any one time, fit categories of Figure 1 other than the pure or mainly parliamentary and presidential types.

ADVANTAGES AND DISADVANTAGES

While questions of definition and classification are important—and, as we have seen, complicated—the more important question concerns the *consequences* of parliamentary and presidential systems: their advantages and disadvantages. We find a large number of such consequences discussed in the literature (the long lists drawn up by the International Forum of the Israel-Diaspora Institute in Chapter 28 provide good examples) but the debate has focused on three principal advantages and three principal disadvantages of each type of government. Presidentialism is said to have the advantages of executive stability, greater democracy, and more limited government, but the disadvantages of executive–legislative deadlock, temporal rigidity, and less inclusive, 'winner-take-all' government. Parliamentarism is said to have the opposite consequences: the advantages of presidentialism are its disadvantages and vice versa. I shall review the arguments concerning each of these points, adding the necessary qualifications and, in some cases, counter-arguments, as well as a discussion of the remedies that have been attempted or proposed to correct or alleviate some of the disadvantages.

Advantages of Presidentialism

1. The first advantage of presidential government, executive stability, is based on the president's fixed term of office; it contrasts with the executive instability that may result in a parliamentary system from the frequent use of the legislature's power to upset cabinets by votes of no confidence or, without any formal no-confidence motions being adopted, as a result of the cabinet's loss of majority support in the legislature. These were major problems in the Weimar Republic, in the French Third and Fourth Republics, and more recently, as A. Jeyaratnam Wilson recounts, in the parliamentary system of Sri Lanka that preceded its semi-presidential constitution (Chapter 20). There is no doubt that the cabinet's dependence on the legislature's confidence makes potential cabinet instability an inherent and inevitable feature of parliamentary systems.

A remedy that is frequently advocated is the so-called 'constructive vote of no confidence': the rule, found in the German and Spanish constitutions, that a prime minister can only be removed if, at the same time, a new prime minister is elected. This stipulation was prompted by the problem of negative majorities in the Weimar Republic, that is, majorities of the right and the left that combined forces against the political centre but that were ideologically too far apart to be able together to form an alternative coalition cabinet. However, the constructive vote of no confidence means that a cabinet may remain in power but, because it is opposed by a majority in the legislature, be unable to get any of its proposed legislation adopted. This ushers in the problem of executive–legislative deadlock—the very problem that besets presidential government but that is supposed *not* to occur in parliamentary systems. Hence, while the constructive vote of no confidence may be able to alleviate cabinet instability, it is far from a complete solution.

On the other hand, how serious is the problem of cabinet instability in parliamentary systems really? Two counter-arguments must be considered. One is that cabinet instability becomes a problem only when it assumes extreme forms, such as in the French Fourth Republic where the average cabinet life was only (depending on how cabinet duration is measured) seven to ten months. Such frequent changes may indeed have deleterious effects on the governing effectiveness of cabinets. But the vast majority of parliamentary systems have considerably more durable cabinets even when these cabinets tend to be multi-party coalitions. And when cabinets last for at least two or three years, the difference from guaranteed presidential terms of, say, four to five years becomes insignificant. The other counter-argument is that the executive 'instability' of parliamentary systems may give these systems the flexibility to change governments quickly when changed circumstances or serious executive failures call for new leadership, whereas the 'stability' of presidential executives may spell dangerous rigidity. I shall return to this point below.

2. The second major advantage of presidential government is that its popular election of the chief executive can be regarded as more democratic than the indirect 'election'—formal or informal—of the executive in parliamentary systems.

Democracy does not require the popular election of all public officials, of course, but the argument that heads of governments, who are the most important and powerful office-holders in democracies, should be directly elected by the people has great validity. It is one of Vasant Sathe's main arguments for a directly elected president, who would then also be much more than a ceremonial head of state, in India (Chapter 26), and even Juan J. Linz, one of the most outspoken critics of presidentialism, acknowledges the democratic value of popular election of the chief executive (Chapter 14).

In practice, however, many parliamentary systems offer the functional equivalent of popular election of the prime minister; this is especially true in two-party systems where the voters' choice of the governing party also signifies their choice of that party's leader to be the prime minister. It is less frequently true in multi-party systems, where the prime minister may emerge from complex post-election bargaining among the parties. Moreover, in multi-party systems, changes in governing coalitions and changes of prime minister may take place between elections without any popular involvement; dissatisfaction with this eventuality has in some multi-party parliamentary systems, notably Germany and The Netherlands, led to the adoption of an informal norm that any major change in the composition of the cabinet must be preceded or ratified by new elections.

Perhaps an even more important 'democratic' argument is that legislatures in parliamentary systems have two incompatible functions: making laws and supporting a cabinet in office. Since voting against the cabinet's legislative proposals may well entail the upheaval of a cabinet crisis, the cabinet can often 'blackmail' the legislature into accepting its wishes. The great paradox of legislative confidence is that, in Arthur M. Schlesinger's words, 'while the parliamentary system formally assumes legislative supremacy, in fact it assures the almost unassailable dominance of the executive over the legislature' (Chapter 10). This is particularly true in two-party parliamentary systems with one-party majority cabinets—Schlesinger's pronouncement is mainly based on the British case—but it also applies to some extent in multi-party systems with less dominant coalition cabinets, such as The Netherlands. The concept of cabinet 'blackmail' is used prominently by J. P. A. Gruijters, one of the founders in 1966 of a new Dutch political party which advocated a shift from parliamentary to presidential government (Chapter 27). Only in presidential systems can legislatures perform the main task for which they are democratically elected, namely, to legislate—provided, of course, that the president is granted only limited rule-making powers.

There are also two 'democratic' counter-arguments. One is that separation of powers also means division of responsibility, and hence diffuse and unclear responsibilities. For two major critics of presidentialism, Bagehot and Wilson, this is a crucial weakness: when the voters cannot know to whom—president or legislature—credit or blame for public policies should go, democratic accountability is lost (see Chapters 6 and 7). Of course, this problem can also occur in multi-party parliamentary systems where *party* accountability may be weak. Secondly, the concentration of executive power in the hands of one individual may be regarded as inherently undemocratic. This view was so strongly held by the framers of the 1848 Swiss constitution that a presidential executive was not even seriously considered (Chapter 23). And Batlle argues at great length that this feature of presidential systems must be seen as a pre-democratic atavism that survives in the early phases of democracy but that should disappear as systems progress towards full democracy (Chapter 24).

3. The third major advantage of presidential government is said to be that separation of powers means limited government—an indispensable protection of individual liberty against government 'tyranny'. This is Montesquieu's principal line of reasoning (Chapter 2). For James Madison it is an axiom that does not require justification, and his only concern in the *Federalist Papers* is to show that the proposed US constitution does not deviate from it (Chapter 3). A modern example of this argument is Schlesinger's contention that only in a separation-of-powers system could the Watergate scandal have been brought to light (Chapter 10). Most modern supporters of parliamentary government strongly disagree with the notion that parliamentary government entails any great danger to individual liberty. Independent courts, an alert and vocal parliamentary opposition, and the mutual suspicions within

multi-party coalition cabinets all provide protection against government abuses of individual rights. It may also be argued that in presidential systems the advantage of separation of powers is partly offset by the concentration of executive power; indeed, in a parliamentary system with a collegial executive, a scandal like Watergate might never have occurred in the first place.

Disadvantages of Presidentialism

Let us now take a look at the other side of the coin: the three major consequences of presidentialism and parliamentarism that are disadvantages of the former and advantages of the latter. The first of these—executive–legislative deadlock in presidential systems—has received the greatest attention in the literature and has been the main ground on which presidentialism has been criticized. It has also inspired the greatest number of attempts to solve or at least alleviate it, remedies that raise a great many further questions. The other two problems of presidentialism—its rigidity and its winner-take-all character—have played less prominent roles in the debate, probably both because they are regarded, rightly or wrongly, as less serious and because they are less complicated.

1. The problem of executive–legislative conflict, which may turn into 'deadlock' and 'paralysis', is the inevitable result of the co-existence of the two independent organs that presidential government creates and that may be in disagreement. When disagreement between them occurs, there is no institutional method of resolving it—unlike the factor of legislative confidence that keeps the legislature and executive in tune with each other in parliamentary systems. Montesquieu recognized this problem but did not believe it to be too serious: because the independent organs of government 'are constrained to move by the necessary motion of things, they will be forced to move in concert' (Chapter 2). Later writers have taken a less sanguine view. Bagehot argues that their mutual independence spells a mutual antagonism that weakens both of them (Chapter 6). For the Committee on the Constitutional System, deadlock is the main problem of presidential government in the United States that requires fundamental institutional reform (Chapter 9), and Scott Mainwaring argues that it has also been the greatest

problem of presidentialism in Latin American democracies (Chapter 13).

One solution is to keep the two powers separated but to unbalance them; in particular, to increase presidential power, compared with and at the expense of the legislature's power, in order to make the president into the spearhead of a more active and effective governmental system. But this course of action is often seen not as a real solution but as exemplifying and possibly exacerbating the problem. For instance, Harry Kantor shows that Latin American democrats have been much more concerned about presidents having too much than too little power (Chapter 12). The difference between Kantor's and Mainwaring's views can be partly explained in terms of the fact that Mainwaring focuses on presidentialism in those countries of Latin America that are unambiguously democratic. But they may both be right: presidentialism may suffer from both dead-lock and too much presidential power in the same system. Harold J. Laski argues that presidential systems tend to swing between 'normal' situations of deadlock and inactivity and 'crisis' situations marked by surges of presidential power and activism (Chapter 8). Similarly, Linz sees the problem of dead-lock as arising from the 'dual democratic legitimacy' of two popularly elected independent organs, but he also stresses the president's special 'plebiscitarian legitimacy', based on his or her election by the whole people and often used to justify pre-sidential claims of predominance over the legislature (Chapter 14). It is tempting for presidents to turn the undeniable fact that they represent the *whole* people—in contrast to individual legislators although obviously not to the legislature as a body—into the claim that they *alone* represent the people. In Chapter 18, Duverger cites a remarkable statement by de Gaulle to this effect.

If strong presidential power is seen as a problem rather than a solution, the solutions that are offered all entail limitations on presidential power. In Chapter 12, Kantor reviews the many attempts by Latin American countries to curb their presidents. One method is term limits: rules stipulating no re-election, no immediate re-election, or only one re-election. While such rules, all other factors being equal, are bound to limit presidential power to some extent, they may also work too well, making the president an ineffective 'lame duck' from the very beginning of his or her only or last term in office and thereby re-introducing the problem of deadlock. They also aggravate the second major disadvantage of presidential government—temporal rigidity (discussed below). And they detract from one of the advantages of presidentialism discussed above—the democratic quality of direct election—by denying the voters the right to choose whomever they want to choose and by removing the incentive for democratic responsiveness provided by an elected official's ambition to be re-elected.

The second solution Kantor mentions is the adoption of a collegial or plural executive, exemplified by Uruguay. As we have already seen, this entails a major change to a system, after which it is no longer fully presidential. Most of the other solutions reviewed by Kantor, and by Carlos Santiago Nino (Chapter 15), also appear to move away from pure presidentialism in the direction of parliamentary government, such as subjecting cabinet members to legislative confidence and requiring collective decision-making by the president with his or her cabinet. However, as long as the president remains a one-person executive and the ministers remain his or her subordinates, and/or as long as the president retains the power to appoint and dismiss his or her ministers, such measures are unlikely to have much effect. Full parliamentarism has been rare—arguably, non-existent—in Latin America. For instance, Kantor doubts that nineteenth-century Brazil is a valid example—a judgement that is supported by the analysis of Bolívar Lamounier in Chapter 16—and the experts disagree on how parliamentary Chile really was in 1891–1925.

Since the strengthening of presidential power creates more problems than it solves, the more modest solutions proposed by the Committee on the Constitutional System may offer better prospects (Chapter 9). Its basic approach is to try to minimize the likelihood of 'divided government'—that is, the presidency controlled by one party and Congress by the other—by holding simultaneous presidential and congressional elections (eliminating mid-term congressional elections) and by encouraging straight-ticket voting as much as possible. Another suggestion aimed at improving executive–legislative harmony is to allow members of Congress to serve in the cabinet without having to resign their legislative offices.

2. The second major disadvantage of presidential government is temporal rigidity. Linz writes that the president's fixed term in office 'breaks the political process into discontinuous, rigidly demarcated periods, leaving no room for the continuous readjustments that events may demand' (Chapter 14). Similarly, Bagehot states that presidentialism lacks an 'elastic' element: 'everything is rigid, specified, dated', and the 'revolutionary reserve' that governments need is totally absent (Chapter 6). The problem is exacerbated by the frequent provision for an automatically succeeding vice-president in the eventuality of the president's death or incapacity; such an automatic successor is selected long in advance and is therefore not necessarily the most suitable person in the new circumstances in which the succession takes place—nor even for the circumstances at the time of selection, since all kinds of political reasons other than basic presidential qualifications tend to influence the choice of vice-presidents.

The main methods advanced to alleviate the rigidity created by fixed presidential and legislative terms in office are the presidential power to dissolve the legislature, as in France, or both such a presidential power and a complementary power by the legislature to dismiss the president, as proposed by the Committee on the Constitutional System (Chapter 9). Both of these methods can also be seen as attempts to alleviate executive-legislative deadlock. In the French case, it entails the reinforcement of presidential power at the expense of the legislature's, but the proposal by the Committee on the Constitutional System is completely neutral: action by either the president or Congress would simply trigger new elections for both. The special problem of succession in presidential systems may also be alleviated by a French constitutional rule: the Senate's presiding officer serves as acting president until a new president is popularly elected. But the brief interregnum that it creates may have drawbacks of its own.

3. The third major disadvantage of presidential government is that it operates on the basis of the winner-take-all rule which, to cite Linz once more, 'tends to make democratic politics a zero-sum game, with all the potential for conflict such games portend' (Chapter 14). In a presidential election, only one

candidate and one party can win; everybody else loses. Moreover, the concentration of power in the president's hands gives
him or her very little incentive to form coalitions or other power-
sharing arrangements or to take part in give-and-take negotiations with the opposition that may be needed to deal with
divisive problems. Especially in an already divided and polarized nation, winner-take-all is highly likely to create even more
division and polarization. Politics becomes exclusive instead of
inclusive.

A slight improvement is to require an absolute majority for
election, for instance by instituting a run-off election when
no candidate wins a majority in the first round, or by using a
preferential ballot that permits the transfer of votes from the
weaker to the stronger candidates until one candidate has a
majority of the votes (as in the Sri Lankan alternative voting
system described by Donald L. Horowitz in Chapter 29). Such
rules ensure that the president will have the democratic legitimacy provided by majority election, and they also give the
major candidates an incentive to appeal to minorities. On the
other hand, winner-take-all is merely changed to *majority*-
winner-take-all, and polarization remains a potential danger,
especially in more or less evenly divided societies.

Stronger medicine is provided by the Nigerian presidential
election rules, also discussed by Horowitz: a plurality of the total
vote but also a minimum of 25 per cent support in two-thirds
of the states. The second requirement does give a presidential
candidate good reasons to conduct a broadly based campaign—
and, one hopes, to govern in a similarly inclusive manner after
having been elected. But there are drawbacks, too: the victorious candidate may have only weak plurality backing, or no
candidate may succeed in meeting the dual requirements of
plurality and broad distribution of support. And, most importantly, the person who is elected president is necessarily a
member of one particular group. One person cannot be a coalition; power-sharing coalitions require collegial executives. This
brings us back to the solutions suggested by the Uruguayan and
Swiss plural executives. It is worth noting in this context that
the collegial nature of the Swiss seven-member executive has
served the purpose of broadly representing not only all of the
major Swiss parties but also Switzerland's diverse religious,

linguistic, and regional groups, and that Uruguay's *colegiado* had to include both majority and minority party representatives.

Semi-presidentialism

How does semi-presidential government fare when we compare it with presidential and parliamentary government on the above six points? Its advocates claim that it combines many of the advantages of each of the pure alternatives. In particular, it is claimed that the alternation between presidential and parliamentary phases solves the problem of executive–legislative deadlock which is presidentialism's most serious disadvantage. The basic rationale is that presidentialism works well when the president has majority backing in the legislature: the two are likely to be in harmony, but the legislature is independent and does not need to support the president uncritically. The problem of deadlock tends to occur when the president lacks legislative majority support; but it is precisely at this point that the shift to parliamentarism occurs. For Argentina's Council for the Consolidation of Democracy, this alternative was of crucial importance, and the Council recommended that it be explicitly stipulated in the constitution, instead of merely implied, as in the French constitution and in Woodrow Wilson's proposal (see Chapters 19 and 21).

The admirers of semi-presidentialism also claim that it combines the advantages of direct democratic election and stable tenure associated with a presidential executive and the flexibility of a parliamentary cabinet and prime minister. Moreover, president, prime minister, and cabinet together offer much better opportunities than pure presidential systems for building power-sharing coalitions. Jean Blondel argues persuasively that semi-presidential government belongs to a general type of governmental system that he calls 'dual leadership', including both democratic and non-democratic forms, all of which have the above advantages to some extent, and which appear to be on the march since the 1970s. Blondel further points to the advantage that a president can act as an above-the-parties arbiter if he or she can delegate more controversial political tasks to the prime minister (Chapter 22).

The avoidance of deadlock and the president's potential arbitral role are particularly strong arguments, but critics note that all of the advantages of parliamentarism and presidentialism cannot logically be claimed *simultaneously* when the two forms do not operate simultaneously but in *phases*. For instance, in its presidential phase, semi-presidentialism has much less potential for coalition-building than parliamentarism, and in its parliamentary phase the head of government lacks the advantage of being directly elected. Nevertheless, semi-presidentialism does have undeniable merits, and it has great appeal—especially in presidential democracies in which dissatisfaction with presidentialism has been growing. It has been under active consideration in Argentina, Brazil, and Colombia, and has considerable support in many other Latin American countries (see Chapters 15, 16 and 21).

OTHER EXPLANATIONS

In the above lengthy discussion of the consequences of parliamentary and presidential government, the impact of additional causal variables—especially the party system and the electoral system—has been mentioned frequently. The most important point made by many of our authors in this respect is that it is not presidentialism itself, but the *combination* of presidentialism with a particular party-system configuration, that is responsible for the big problem of executive–legislative deadlock. The crucial point is whether the president can find sufficient support in the legislature, which is unlikely to be the case in a multi-party system, as Mainwaring argues (Chapter 13), or in a two-party system when there is 'divided government', as pointed out forcefully by the Committee on the Constitutional System (Chapter 9). The Committee also calls attention to the uncohesiveness of the American parties, which has the effect of denying the president sufficient political support even when the president's own party forms the congressional majority. Obviously, the most serious problem occurs in a presidential and two-party system with two cohesive parties when the president is faced with a cohesive one-party opposition in the legislature—not a problem in the United States, but a major worry in Argentina, as the report by the Council for the Consolidation of Democracy points out (Chapter 21).

The chapters in Part V of this volume represent attempts to examine such additional explanatory variables—either in combination with or as alternatives to the variable of parliamentary versus presidential government—as systematically as possible and on the basis of worldwide evidence. Several interesting and often compelling conclusions emerge. In Chapter 29, Horowitz points out that, in order to avoid winner-take-all, it is not sufficient to adopt a parliamentary form of government; elections by proportional representation, a multi-party system, and coalition cabinets are also necessary. In the following two chapters, Seymour Martin Lipset and Juan J. Linz basically endorse this conclusion. Together with Mainwaring's finding, this suggests that the parliamentary–multi-party and presidential–plurality combinations should be regarded as optimal.

However, Lipset's main intention is to raise basic doubts about even the *partial* explanatory power of the comparison between parliamentarism and presidentialism. Instead, he suggests the alternative explanatory frameworks of cultural difference and levels of economic development: democracies, whether parliamentary or presidential, that have worked well are to be found mainly in the more developed and more Protestant parts of the world (Chapter 30). These cultural–regional and economic-development patterns are indeed striking, but a number of qualifications are in order.

First, there are several clear exceptions: the non-Protestant countries of southern Europe in which democracy appears to have been firmly established in the 1970s (in Italy, considerably earlier); the Latin American countries with a long and uninterrupted record of democracy, such as Costa Rica since about 1950 and Colombia and Venezuela since about 1960; and India, which is the world's largest democracy but also among the world's poor countries. These exceptions show that an 'unfavourable' cultural background and level of economic development are not absolute obstacles to democracy; indeed, for countries negatively affected by particular background conditions, the question of whether parliamentarism or presidentialism would serve them better is especially important.

Second, as far as Lipset's link between culture and successful democracy is concerned, Powell's analysis in Chapter 33 (especially his Table 2) shows that there is also a strong relationship between cultural–regional groupings and forms of government. This means that, instead of explaining, for instance, Latin America's relatively poor democratic record directly in terms of its culture, it is at least equally plausible that presidentialism, or presidentialism together with multi-partism, is the crucial intervening variable and the true explanation for Latin America's problems with democracy. Because culture and forms of government are so closely related, it is very difficult to disentangle these potential causal factors. Third, the level of economic development does *not* have a similarly close link with parliamentary versus presidential government, which means that it is possible to control for the influence of this variable.

Fred W. Riggs's method for controlling for the level of economic development is to focus on the success rates of democracy among Third World countries, all of which fit the same category of underdevelopment (Chapter 32). He finds startling differences among the seventy-six Third World countries that adopted democratic constitutions: of the thirty-three presidential regimes, not one survived without serious interruption, whereas two-thirds of the forty-three parliamentary regimes managed to do so. Riggs's analysis covers the period from 1945 to 1985. A much earlier study by Philippine social scientist Ledivina V. Cariño (listed in Section V of the 'Guide to Further Reading' at the end of this volume) covers only the years from 1945 to 1963 and uses a slightly different criterion of democratic success; coups and revolutions are counted as democratic failures regardless of whether or not they actually overthrow the democratic system. But Cariño's overall conclusion parallels Riggs's: among the fifty-one Third World democracies, the parliamentary systems were significantly more successful than the presidential.

Powell's study is the most thorough multivariate analysis of the performance of parliamentary and presidential systems that has been done so far (Chapter 33). He analyses twenty-seven basically successful, large democracies (that is, democracies with a long life-span and with populations over 1 million). His indicators of democratic performance are executive durability, majority control, voting turnout, and control of violence. In addition to the level of economic development, he controls for the influence of the 'environmental advantages' of ethnic homogeneity and population size as well as for the type of electoral system.

The first two of Powell's indicators of performance—executive durability and majority control—are among the relative advantages of parliamentarism and presidentialism discussed earlier, and his findings confirm the tendencies that have already been identified: presidential government is significantly related to greater executive stability but also to less frequent majority control, that is, more frequent 'divided government'. The other two indicators are more basic measures of the successful operation of democracy. Voting turnout can be regarded as a measure of the quality of democracy, and parliamentarism performs significantly better in this respect—even when the superior performance of PR election laws, which also tend to promote electoral participation, is controlled for. Violence is explained much better in terms of environmental than of constitutional variables, but Powell argues that there remains a tendency for parliamentary systems, especially in combination with PR, to perform better in maintaining public order than presidential systems.

The systematic empirical evidence presented by Thomas A. Baylis concerns one of the differences between parliamentary and presidential government: he contrasts collegial with one-person or, to use his own term, 'monocratic' executive leadership (Chapter 34). Although he includes a few communist countries in his analysis, his data on political and economic performance are for the advanced industrialized democracies only—thus, like Riggs and Powell, controlling for level of economic development. These democracies are ranked on a five-point scale of collegiality: the two presidential systems (the United States and France) are at the bottom of the scale, Switzerland at the top, and the parliamentary systems in three decreasing groups of collegiality in between.

Baylis's indicators of political performance are very similar to Powell's. Some of his results are inconclusive, but where clear differences appear, especially with regard to measures of violence, the collegial regimes perform considerably better. His indicators of economic performance are the most important measures of the success of macroeconomic management, such as economic growth, inflation, unemployment, and strike activity. Here the differences are more pronounced and they again tend to show a better performance by the collegial than by the monocratic regimes.

CAUSES AND CHOICES

Can contemporary constitutional engineers choose a parliamentary, presidential, or semi-presidential form of government on the basis of the analysis of their relative merits in the literature highlighted in this volume? One problem is that all of the alternatives have their advantages and disadvantages, and that no obvious winner has emerged from the debate among their respective proponents. The empirical evidence favours the parliamentary model, at least to some extent, but this is only limited evidence that is unlikely to convince strong supporters of presidential government. Another problem is that democratic engineers face severe constraints on their freedom of choice, such as established traditions and basic institutional conservatism. These problems raise the question of how decisions to adopt parliamentary or presidential forms of government have been made in the past. What do we know about their causes and origins?

As already discussed above, culture has been one strong influence: parliamentarism and presidentialism occur in sharply delineated cultural–regional patterns (see especially Powell's analysis in Chapter 33). And, in many cases, these patterns originally developed because of the strength of particular models. The clearest examples are the democracies that once belonged to the British Empire; in theory, models other than the British might have been followed, but for both the colonial masters and the native constitutional engineers none of the potential competitors was as well known or as strongly admired. For the Latin American democracies in the early nineteenth century, the choice was even more limited, the presidential model being practically the only model available at the time. For Bolívar, Montesquieu's arguments and the American and British examples all pointed in the same direction; in fact, at the time of the Angostura Address, the British and American examples were really only slightly different instances of the same model (Chapter 11).

For many of the west European countries, which became democratic gradually and where democratization entailed the gradual erosion of the power of hereditary monarchs, the origin of parliamentary government can be explained in terms of Verney's first proposition which states the two alternative routes from monarchy to democracy: either the monarch is replaced by a democratically elected 'monarch', which means a presidential system, or the monarch loses most of his or her power and the cabinet becomes the parliament's instead of the monarch's agent, which means a parliamentary system (Chapter 1). Wherever the monarch was retained as a constitutional monarch, the second alternative was the most likely outcome. This explanation also applies to Brazil's nineteenth-century parliamentary (but, as Lamounier emphasizes in Chapter 16, not very democratic) system and to the adoption of a pure parliamentary system by Spain in the 1970s.

In the last couple of decades, these kinds of constraining influences on constitutional engineers appear to have weakened to some extent, and the full array of available models now appears to be considered more seriously, more dispassionately, and with less bias and prejudgement. For instance, French semi-presidentialism has become an important model not only in formerly French-ruled countries or for a close neighbour like Portugal, but also for distant countries like Sri Lanka and Argentina (Chapters 20 and 21). Nigeria acted against the strength of its British tradition when it adopted an American-style presidential constitution (Chapter 25); and the proposal for presidential government in The Netherlands shows that the presence of a constitutional monarch is no longer an insuperable obstacle to presidential government (Chapter 27). Institutional conservatism remains strong, however, and the actual shifts have typically involved 'halfway' changes to and from semi-presidentialism rather than complete shifts from parliamentary to presidential government and vice versa: shifts from parliamentarism to semi-presidentialism in France itself in 1958 and in Sri Lanka in 1978, and the other way around in Finland and Portugal in 1982. The complete shift in Nigeria in 1977 is the major exception. The reason why semi-presidentialism is a more serious option than parliamentarism in Latin America is that it has the appeal of being the less drastic reform.

In the light of the continuing debate in the 1990s, shifts away from presidential government seem slightly more likely than shifts away from parliamentarism. There is a great deal of dissatisfaction with presidentialism in just about all of the presidentially ruled countries, including the Latin American democracies, the Philippines, South Korea, and, as the work of the Committee on the Constitutional System makes clear, the United States. The corresponding sentiment can be found in parliamentary systems, as the proposals for presidential government in Israel and Italy indicate, but it tends to be weaker and occurs less frequently; the issue is no longer on the Dutch constitutional agenda. The only prediction that can be made with full assurance—based on the widespread dissatisfaction with existing forms of government, the need to draft constitutions in new democracies, the strength of established institutions and traditions, and the inconclusiveness of the debate between parliamentarists and presidentialists so far—is that this debate is bound to continue. Given the fundamental importance of the issues that are at stake, the debate deserves to be called a 'great debate' and it deserves the continued attention and involvement of democratic reformers.

PART I

BRITISH PARLIAMENTARISM
VERSUS AMERICAN
PRESIDENTIALISM

1

PARLIAMENTARY GOVERNMENT AND PRESIDENTIAL GOVERNMENT

DOUGLAS V. VERNEY

Parliamentarism is the most widely adopted system of government, and it seems appropriate to refer to British parliamentary experience in particular because it is the British system which has provided an example for a great many other countries. Nowadays when it is fashionable to speak of political systems and theories as 'not for export' it is worth bearing in mind the success with which a system adopted piecemeal to suit British constitutional developments has proved feasible in different situations abroad. This is not to imply that the British parliamentary system should be taken as the model and that others are, as it were, deviations from the norm, although generations of Englishmen have been tempted to make this assumption. . . .

Indeed an examination of parliamentarism in various countries indicates that there are two main types of parliamentary procedure, the British and the continental. . . .

This analysis of parliamentarism is concerned less with distinguishing the various forms of parliamentarism than with establishing the highest common factors in different parliamentary systems. . . . It may surprise those who have tended to regard British government as the model as well as the Mother of Parliaments to know that the United Kingdom could abolish the monarchy, adopt a single code of constitutional laws on the pattern of the French or American constitutions, transform the House of Lords into a senate (or even do away with it), introduce a multi-party system based on proportional representation, institute a number of parliamentary committees to deal with specific topics such as finance and foreign affairs, and still possess a parliamentary system.

There would seem to be a number of basic principles applicable to both of the chief varieties of parliamentary government. . . .

1

THE ASSEMBLY BECOMES A PARLIAMENT

Where parliamentary government has evolved rather than been the product of revolution there have often been three phases, though the transition from one to the other has not always been perceptible at the time. First there has been government by a monarch who has been responsible for the whole political system. Then there has arisen an assembly of members who have challenged the hegemony of the king. Finally the assembly has taken over responsibility for government, acting as a parliament, the monarch being deprived of most of his traditional powers.

This has certainly been the pattern in Britain. As late as the seventeenth century King James I could still preach the doctrine of the Divine Right of Kings. . . .

However, by establishing their power over the purse, assemblies were ultimately able to claim their own area of jurisdiction. Henceforth the monarch's role was increasingly that of an executive dependent ultimately on the goodwill of the legislature. Constitutional development entered a second phase in which the term 'legislative power' was given to assemblies to distinguish them from the 'executive power' of the king. . . .

But even as the theory of the separation of powers was coming into vogue the transition to the third and present phase was under way in Britain. In the eighteenth century the king was already losing his executive power to ministers who came to regard the assembly, not the monarch, as the sovereign to whom they were really responsible. Ministers were increasingly chosen from among members of the assembly and resigned when the assembly withdrew its confidence from them. . . .

In parliamentary monarchies such as Britain, Belgium and Sweden, the monarch has ceased in practice (though not in form) to exercise even the executive power. Government has passed to 'his' ministers who are responsible to the legislature. Parliamentary government implies a certain fusion of the executive and legislative functions, the body which has been merely an assembly of representatives being transformed into a parliament. . . .

It is true that for the most part the use of the term 'parliament' at one time to include the government and at others to exclude it seems to cause little difficulty, provided some knowledge of the parliamentary system is assumed. In a comparative study of political systems, however, such ambiguity presents certain problems if like is to be compared with like. It therefore becomes necessary to insist on a more precise usage. 'Parliament' will at all times signify a body which includes the government. When it is necessary to refer to the legislature excluding members of the government the term 'assembly' will be used. . . .

The first characteristic of parliamentarism may now be summarized. It is a political system where the executive, once separate, has been challenged by the assembly which is then transformed into a parliament comprising both government and assembly.

2
THE EXECUTIVE IS DIVIDED INTO TWO PARTS

One important consequence of the transformation of the assembly into a parliament is that the executive is now split in two, a prime minister or chancellor becoming head of the government and the monarch or president acting as head of state. Usually the monarch occupies his throne by hereditary title (though elected monarchies, e.g. in Malaya, are not unknown), while a president is elected by parliament. . . .

3

THE HEAD OF STATE APPOINTS THE HEAD
OF GOVERNMENT

The value of a divided executive in constitutional monarchies
is fairly obvious. For one thing, the proper business of state can
be carried on by a government responsible to the legislature
while the mystique of monarchy is preserved. There seems no
apparent reason, at first glance, for dividing it in republics.
Admittedly it is useful to have someone above the day-to-day
political warfare to receive ambassadors and to decorate ceremonial occasions, but this hardly seems to justify the expense
of such an office. After all, the president of the United States,
who as head of the American government bears the greatest
responsibilities of any statesman in the world, manages to com-
bine with his high and lonely eminence the even higher office
of head of state.

However, it is in the very nature of the parliamentary system
that there shall be two distinct offices, and that the head of the
government shall be appointed by the head of state. Were the
electorate itself to perform this task, directly or through a special
college of electors as in the United States or Finland, the
system would become, in this respect at least, presidential in
character. . . .

4

THE HEAD OF THE GOVERNMENT APPOINTS
THE MINISTRY

An interesting feature of parliamentarism is the distinction
made between the prime minister and other ministers. The
former is appointed by the head of state; the latter are nominated by the prime minister after his appointment. Usually
the selection of various ministers allows a certain amount
of personal choice to a head of government, which cannot
usually be said of the appointment of a prime minister by the
head of state. Ministers are formally appointed by the head of
state, who may often no doubt exert an informal influence upon

appointments—but so may the state of party alignments and factions in the assembly. . . .

5
THE MINISTRY (OR GOVERNMENT) IS A COLLECTIVE BODY

The transfer from the monarchical executive to a council of ministers has meant that a single person has been replaced by a collective body. Whereas under *anciens régimes* it was the king's pleasure (*le Roi le veult*), under parliamentarism the prime minister is merely first among equals (*primus inter pares*), though no doubt some prime ministers are more forceful than others. . . .

6
MINISTERS ARE USUALLY MEMBERS OF PARLIAMENT

Members of the government have a double role to play in the parliamentary system. They are not only ministers but are at the same time members of parliament, elected (unless they are members of the British House of Lords) like the members of the assembly and equally dependent upon the goodwill of their constituents. . . .

Since, according to the usage adopted in this chapter, parliament comprises both government and assembly, a member of the government is *ipso facto* a member of parliament, but by definition he cannot be a member of the assembly. In fully parliamentary countries such as the United Kingdom where ministers are members of parliament it is difficult to make the distinction between government, parliament and assembly clear. Indeed the attempt to make one seems artificial.

However, not all parliamentary countries have accepted the necessity for ministers to be members of one of the houses of parliament. In Sweden up to a third of the ministry of fifteen members have on occasion in recent years not been members of parliament. In The Netherlands, Norway and Luxembourg ministers are actually forbidden to be members of parliament after their appointment. Here there is a relic of the old doctrine of the separation of powers when ministers were responsible to the monarch. . . .

Generally speaking, nevertheless, it is usual for most if not all ministers to be members of parliament. Where they are not, the system may still be said to be of the parliamentary type if they can take part in parliamentary debates and are truly responsible to the assembly for the conduct of the executive. In Norway, Sweden, The Netherlands and Luxembourg, all parliamentary monarchies, these conditions are fulfilled. In the French Fifth Republic, where the government is not responsible to parliament for the conduct of the president, they are not.

7

THE GOVERNMENT IS POLITICALLY
RESPONSIBLE TO THE ASSEMBLY

In parliamentary systems the government is responsible to the assembly which may, if it thinks that the government is acting unwisely or unconstitutionally, refuse to give it support. By a formal vote of censure or by simply not assenting to an important government proposal the assembly can force the government to resign and cause the head of state to appoint a new government. . . .

8

THE HEAD OF GOVERNMENT MAY ADVISE THE
HEAD OF STATE TO DISSOLVE PARLIAMENT

In the pre-parliamentary monarchies of Europe the monarch could, if dissatisfied with his assembly, dissolve one or more houses in the hope of securing a more amenable selection of representatives after a new election. Today, when the executive is divided, it is still the head of state who dissolves parliament, but he does so on the request, and only on the request, of the head of government. . . .

Certain states generally regarded as parliamentary severely restrict the right of the executive to dissolve the assembly. In

Norway the Storting dissolves itself, the head of state being allowed to dissolve only special sessions, but this is a departure from parliamentarism inspired by the convention theory of the French Revolution. . . .

9
PARLIAMENT AS A WHOLE IS SUPREME OVER ITS CONSTITUENT PARTS, GOVERNMENT AND ASSEMBLY, NEITHER OF WHICH MAY DOMINATE THE OTHER

The notion of the supremacy of parliament as a whole over its parts is a distinctive characteristic of parliamentary systems. This may seem a glimpse of the obvious to those accustomed to parliamentary government, but it is in fact an important principle, all too often forgotten, that neither of the constituent elements of parliament may completely dominate the other. The government depends upon the support of the assembly if it is to continue in office, but the assembly is not supreme because the government can, if it chooses, dissolve parliament and appeal to the electorate at the polls. Many parliamentary systems have failed because one or other of them has claimed supremacy, and parliament as a whole has not been supreme over both government and assembly.

In practice the nature of parliamentary supremacy varies from country to country. In the United Kingdom and Scandinavia the emphasis is on the government's role in parliament and in Britain the system is actually called 'cabinet government'. In others, notably the French Third and Fourth Republics, the dominant role in parliament was played by the assembly. . . .

10
THE GOVERNMENT AS A WHOLE IS ONLY INDIRECTLY RESPONSIBLE TO THE ELECTORATE

A parliamentary government, though directly responsible to the assembly, is only indirectly responsible to the electorate. The government as a whole is not directly elected by the voters but is appointed indirectly from amongst the representatives whom they elect to the assembly. The earlier direct relationship of monarch and people whereby persons could petition their sovereign disappeared as parliamentarism was introduced. Today the route to the government lies through elected representatives though in Britain, for example, one may still formally petition the monarch. It is true that members of the government, like other members of parliament, must (unless they are peers) stand before their constituents for election. However, they do so not as members of the government but as candidates for the assembly in the ordinary way. The responsibility for transforming them, once elected, into ministers rests with the prime minister alone (and of course with the monarch in the case of the prime minister). . . .

11
PARLIAMENT IS THE FOCUS OF POWER IN THE POLITICAL SYSTEM

The fusion of the executive and legislative powers in parliament is responsible for the overriding ascendancy of parliament in the political order. It is the stage on which the drama of politics is played out; it is the forum of the nation's ideas; and it is the school where future political leaders are trained. For parliamentarism to succeed, the government must not fret at the constant challenge which the Assembly offers to its programme, nor wince at the criticism made of its administration. The Assembly in turn must resist the temptation to usurp the functions of Government. Here is a delicate balance of powers which check each other without the benefit of separate institutions. . . .

* * *

Presidential government is often associated with the theory of the separation of powers which was popular in the eighteenth century when the American constitution was framed. Two writers in particular drew attention to this notion. John Locke, writing at the end of the seventeenth century, suggested that the long conflict between the British monarch and the houses of parliament would best be resolved by the separation of the king as executive from the two houses as legislature, each body having its own sphere. In the mid-eighteenth century a French observer of the British political scene, Montesquieu, pronounced himself in favour of the British system of government as one which embodied, in contrast to the despotism of the Bourbons, the separation of the executive, legislative, and judicial powers. Historically the theory as expounded by Locke and more especially Montesquieu is important for an understanding of the climate of opinion in which the American constitution was framed.

However, it is one thing to study this celebrated theory for historical purposes but quite another to trace its contemporary significance for an understanding of presidential government. It was, after all, based on the assumption that a monarch would act as executive and an assembly as legislature. The theory was considered to be an improvement on the absolute monarchies of the continent, which it undoubtedly was, and was praised with them in mind. There was as yet no experience of parliamentarism. Today such constitutional monarchies as still survive are based on the parliamentary principle.

Another offspring and successor of the theory is presidential government, but the substitution of an elected president for a hereditary monarch has, as we have seen, created a system hardly comparable with pre-parliamentary limited monarchies. If presidential government is regarded simply as a direct form or expression of the eighteenth-century doctrine of the separation of powers then (as indeed many people have thought) the Americans may, by adopting their rigid constitution, have artificially prevented their political system from developing into parliamentarism. But if, as it is argued here, the system is a successor to that doctrine then it is not like limited monarchy, the precursor of parliamentary government, but one of its two offsprings, the other being parliamentarism. . . .

It seemed appropriate to begin an analysis of parliamentary government by reference to British political institutions. It is equally valuable to study presidentialism by first examining the American political system. The United States was the first important country to break with the European monarchical tradition and to shake off colonial rule. The break occurred in the eighteenth century when Britain was still a limited monarchy and the theory of the separation of powers was in vogue. The American constitution bears witness to these influences and to the colonial government of governor and legislature, an elected president replacing the king or governor as the executive power. A number of countries—all twenty American republics, Liberia, the Philippines, South Korea and South Vietnam—have followed the example of the United States, though rarely with comparable success. The American political system is therefore the model and prototype of presidential government. Yet the United States, like the United Kingdom, could abolish or transform many of its institutions and remain based on the same theory of government. For example, the framers of the 1787 constitution could have proposed an elective monarch instead of a president, a house of lords rather than a senate, and a unitary political system instead of a federal union of states without destroying the presidential principle—though the name 'presidential' would hardly be suitable for a system where the executive was an elective monarch. Presidential, like parliamentary, theory has certain basic characteristics irrespective of any particular political system.

The nature of presidential theory can best be understood by re-stating the eleven propositions [concerning parliamentary government—Ed.] as they apply to presidential government.

1

THE ASSEMBLY REMAINS AN ASSEMBLY ONLY

Parliamentary theory implies that the second phase of constitutional development, in which the assembly and judiciary claim their own areas of jurisdiction alongside the executive, shall give way to a third in which assembly and government are fused in a parliament. Presidential theory on the other hand requires the assembly to remain separate as in the second phase. The American Revolution led to a transfer from colonial rule to the second stage of separate jurisdiction, and there have been some observers who have thought that the rigid constitution has prevented the 'natural' development of the American political system towards parliamentarism. This is not so. By abolishing

the monarchy and substituting a president for the king and
his government, the Americans showed themselves to be truly
revolutionary in outlook. The presidential system as established
in the USA made parliamentarism both unnecessary and
impracticable in that country. The assembly (Congress in the
United States) remains an assembly.

2
THE EXECUTIVE IS NOT DIVIDED BUT IS A
PRESIDENT ELECTED BY THE PEOPLE FOR
A DEFINITE TERM AT THE TIME OF
ASSEMBLY ELECTIONS

The retention of a separate executive in the United States was
made feasible because the executive remained undivided. It was
not, of course, the same institution as the pre-parliamentary
monarchical executive. Such a monarch governed by virtue of
an ancient tradition into which he was born, and with all the
strength and potential weaknesses that this implied. The presidential executive is elected by the people. In an era when
governments have had to rely not on some mystique but on
popular support the Americans have found a solution which has
enabled their separate single executive to withstand criticism.
The suggestions that the United States should adopt parliamentarism have proved abortive largely because it cannot be said of
the presidency, as it could of hereditary monarchy, that the
institution lacked democratic roots. . . .

The president is elected for a definite term of office. This
prevents the assembly from forcing his resignation (except by
impeachment for a serious misdemeanour) and at the same time
requires the president to stand for re-election if he wishes to continue in office. It seems desirable that the chief executive's
tenure should be limited to a certain number of terms. . . .

Equally important for the proper operation of the presidential
system is the election of the president at the time of the assembly
elections. This associates the two branches of government,
encourages party unity, and clarifies the issues. Admittedly in
the United States simultaneous elections do not prevent the
return of a Republican President and a Democratic Congress,

but the tensions would be even greater if the president was elected for a seven-year term as in France. . . .

3
THE HEAD OF THE GOVERNMENT IS HEAD OF STATE

Whereas in pre-parliamentary monarchies the head of state was also the head of the government, in the presidential system it is the head of the government who becomes at the same time head of state. This is an important distinction because it draws attention to the limited pomp and circumstance surrounding the presidential office. The president is of little consequence until he is elected as political head by the electorate and he ceases to have any powers once his term of office has expired. The ceremonial aspect of his position is but a reflection of his political prestige. . . .

4
THE PRESIDENT APPOINTS HEADS OF DEPARTMENTS WHO ARE HIS SUBORDINATES

In parliamentarism the prime minister appoints his colleagues who together with him form the government. In presidential systems the president appoints secretaries (sometimes called ministers) who are heads of his executive departments. Formally, owing to the rule whereby appointments are subject to the confirmation of the assembly or one of its organs (in the United States the Senate, in the Philippines the Commission on Appointments) his choice may be restricted to persons of whom that body approves. In practice the president has a very wide choice. . . .

5
THE PRESIDENT IS SOLE EXECUTIVE

In contrast to parliamentary government, which is collective, the prime minister being first among equals, presidential government tends to be individual. Admittedly the term 'cabinet' is used in the United States to describe the meetings of the president with his secretaries, but it is not a cabinet or ministry in the parliamentary sense. . . .

6

MEMBERS OF THE ASSEMBLY ARE NOT ELIGIBLE FOR OFFICE IN THE ADMINISTRATION AND VICE VERSA

Instead of the parliamentary convention or law whereby the same persons may be part of both the executive and legislative branches of government, it is customary in presidential states for the personnel to be separate. Neither the President nor his aides may sit in the US Congress. Few of the other American republics have copied the complete separation practised in the United States. While ministers may not be members of the assembly (except in Cuba and Peru) they are usually entitled to attend and take part in debates. . . .

7

THE EXECUTIVE IS RESPONSIBLE TO THE CONSTITUTION

The president is not, like parliamentary governments, responsible to the assembly. Instead he is, like pre-parliamentary monarchs, responsible to the constitution. But whereas in the *anciens régimes* this was but a vague notion, in presidential systems it is usually laid down with some precision in a constitutional document. . . .

It is usually the assembly which holds the president ultimately responsible to the constitution by the impeachment process. This does not imply that he is responsible to that body in the parliamentary sense of depending on its confidence in any political capacity. Impeachment enforces *juridical* compliance with the (constitutional) letter of the law and is quite different from the exercise of political control over the president's ordinary conduct of his office. Political responsibility implies a day-to-day relationship between government and assembly; impeachment is the grave and ultimate penalty (only one American President, Andrew Johnson, was impeached, unsuccessfully) necessary where ordinarily the executive and assembly are not mutually dependent. . . .

8
THE PRESIDENT CANNOT DISSOLVE OR COERCE THE ASSEMBLY

The assembly, as we have just seen, cannot dismiss the president. Likewise, the president may not dissolve the assembly. Neither, therefore, is in a position to coerce the other, and it is not surprising that this system is, *par excellence*, one of checks and balances. In countless ways almost incomprehensible to those accustomed to parliamentarism the presidential system exhibits this mutual independence of the executive and legislative branches of government. . . .

9
THE ASSEMBLY IS ULTIMATELY SUPREME OVER THE OTHER BRANCHES OF GOVERNMENT AND THERE IS NO FUSION OF THE EXECUTIVE AND LEGISLATIVE BRANCHES AS IN A PARLIAMENT

It was remarked of parliamentary systems that neither the government nor the assembly is supreme because both are subordinate parts of the parliamentary institution. In presidential systems such fusion of the executive and legislative powers is replaced by separation, each having its own sphere. As we have just observed, constitutionally the executive cannot interfere in the proceedings of the assembly, still less dissolve it, and the assembly for its part cannot invade the province of the executive. . . .

Since there is no parliament there can be no parliamentary supremacy. Where, then, does supreme power lie in the event of a serious controversy? It has been demonstrated that the assembly cannot force the resignation of the president any more than he can dissolve the assembly. Moreover, both branches of government may find that their actions are declared unconstitutional by yet a third power, the judiciary. In a sense the constitution is supreme. The short answer is that it is intended in presidential government that the different branches shall check and balance one another and that none shall predominate.

Yet in a very real sense it is the assembly which is ultimately supreme. The president may have considerable authority allocated to him in the constitution but he may be powerless unless the assembly grants him the necessary appropriations. If he acts unconstitutionally the assembly may impeach him. In the event of a serious conflict even the judiciary must bow to the will of the assembly because this body has the right to amend the constitution. The American constitution is not, as is sometimes asserted, simply 'what the judges say it is'.

It may be suggested that the position does not appear to be altogether different from that in parliamentary states where ultimately the legislature may amend the constitution. This is not so. In parliamentary states the constitution has to be amended by both government and assembly acting as parliament, whereas in presidential systems the assembly may amend the constitution without regard to the president. For example, the American Congress has limited the presidential tenure of office to two terms. . . .

10

THE EXECUTIVE IS DIRECTLY RESPONSIBLE TO THE ELECTORATE

Governments in parliamentary countries are appointed by the head of state; they are not elected. By contrast the presidential executive is dependent on a popular vote and the president alone (and vice-president if there is one), of all the persons in the political system, is elected by the whole body of electors. Whereas the pre-parliamentary monarchies could not in the end withstand the pressure of the people's representatives upon their control of government, a president can say to members of the assembly: 'You represent your constituency: I represent the whole people.' There is no reply to this argument, and it is perhaps not surprising that in many South American countries and in France at various times the president has been able to go one step further and to assert that he *alone* represented the people. . . .

11
THERE IS NO FOCUS OF POWER IN THE POLITICAL SYSTEM

The political activities of parliamentary systems have their focal point in parliament. Heads of state, governments, elected representatives, political parties, interest groups, and electorates all acknowledge its supremacy.

It is tempting to assume that there must be a similar focal point in presidential systems. This is not so. Instead of concentration there is division; instead of unity, fragmentation. In the design of Washington DC the President's home, the White House, is at the opposite end of Pennsylvania Avenue to the Capitol, where Congress meets. Geographical dispersion symbolizes their political separation. . . .

Those who admire efficient government may be inclined towards the cabinet government form of parliamentarism. Those who prefer more limited government may turn towards presidentialism. It should not be assumed, however, that the presidential form, because it is divided, is necessarily one of weak government. Admittedly, where presidential leadership is lacking the system may even appear to be on the verge of breaking down. But where there is a vigorous executive he may in fact dominate the assembly, as several American Presidents (notably Franklin D. Roosevelt) have succeeded in doing.

Miraculously, in the United States this domination has never gone too far. In much of Central and South America, where there is the form of presidential government but not the substance, the presidential system has been distorted by dictatorship.

It is difficult to explain the failure of presidential government in so many parts of South America and it is perilous to confine such explanation to purely political factors. Historically and culturally South and Central America are utterly different from the United States. However, there are a number of particular political features of these countries' systems which deserve note, not least of which is the multi-party system which characterizes several of them. Where a president is elected by what is in effect a minority vote instead of by the clear majority customary in the United States he lacks that sense of being the people's representative which is so marked a feature of the American presidency. At the very least it adds a complicating factor to the relations of president, assembly, and people, and in all probability contributes to political instability.

Where there is a multi-party system there is the temptation to add to the president's status and independence by giving him a longer term of office than the assembly. Not surprisingly the French Fifth Republic's constitution gives the president a term of seven years compared to the assembly's [five]. Such a long term, while of small moment in a parliamentary system, may make a president in a non-parliamentary system a powerful figure.

Finally, it may be observed that few countries have been able to enjoy the clear distinction between president and assembly so characteristic of the United States. There has been an attempt to introduce something of the 'responsibility' common to parliamentary systems. Thus there is a separate 'government' in the new French constitution, and this 'government' (but not the president) is responsible to the assembly and may be dismissed by it. Yet the history of the Weimar Republic, to say nothing of Latin America, has shown that in practice (as if to confirm political theory) the president (i.e. the real government) may be unaffected by such a procedure and it then becomes an ineffective weapon in the hands of the assembly. If he *is* affected, then the system becomes parliamentary and the attempt to create a separate executive has failed.

For there should be either a separation as in the United States and *no* focus of the political system; or a fusion with parliament as the focus.

2

THE SPIRIT OF THE LAWS

MONTESQUIEU

In each state there are three sorts of powers: legislative power, executive power over the things depending on the right of nations, and executive power over the things depending on civil right.

By the first, the prince or the magistrate makes laws for a time or for always and corrects or abrogates those that have been made. By the second, he makes peace or war, sends or receives embassies, establishes security, and prevents invasions. By the third, he punishes crimes or judges disputes between individuals. The last will be called the power of judging, and the former simply the executive power of the state.

Political liberty in a citizen is that tranquillity of spirit which comes from the opinion each one has of his security, and in order for him to have this liberty the government must be such that one citizen cannot fear another citizen.

When legislative power is united with executive power in a single person or in a single body of the magistracy, there is no liberty, because one can fear that the same monarch or senate that makes tyrannical laws will execute them tyrannically.

Nor is there liberty if the power of judging is not separate from legislative power and from executive power. If it were joined to legislative power, the power over the life and liberty of the citizens would be arbitrary, for the judge would be the legislator. If it were joined to executive power, the judge could have the force of an oppressor.

All would be lost if the same man or the same body of principal

Charles Louis de Secondat, baron de Montesquieu, excerpted from *The Spirit of the Laws*, transl. and ed. by Anne M. Cohler, Basia Carolyn Miller, and Harold Samuel Stone, Cambridge Texts in the History of Political Thought (Cambridge: Cambridge University Press, 1989), part 2, bk. 11, ch. 6. Reprinted by permission of Cambridge University Press.

men, either of nobles, or of the people, exercised these three powers: that of making the laws, that of executing public resolutions, and that of judging the crimes or the disputes of individuals.

In most kingdoms in Europe, the government is moderate because the prince, who has the first two powers, leaves the exercise of the third to his subjects. Among the Turks, where the three powers are united in the person of the sultan, an atrocious despotism reigns. . . .

As, in a free state, every man, considered to have a free soul, should be governed by himself, the people as a body should have legislative power; but, as this is impossible in large states and is subject to many drawbacks in small ones, the people must have their representatives do all that they themselves cannot do. . . .

The representative body [should not] be chosen in order to make some resolution for action, a thing it would not do well, but in order to make laws or in order to see if those they have made have been well executed; these are things it can do very well and that only it can do well.

In a state there are always some people who are distinguished by birth, wealth, or honours; but if they were mixed among the people and if they had only one voice like the others, the common liberty would be their enslavement and they would have no interest in defending it, because most of the resolutions would be against them. Therefore, the part they have in legislation should be in proportion to the other advantages they have in the state, which will happen if they form a body that has the right to check the enterprises of the people, as the people have the right to check theirs.

Thus, legislative power will be entrusted both to the body of the nobles and to the body that will be chosen to represent the people, each of which will have assemblies and deliberations apart and have separate views and interests. . . .

The nobility should be hereditary. In the first place, it is so by its nature; and, besides, it must have a great interest in preserving its prerogatives, odious in themselves, and which, in a free state, must always be endangered.

But, . . . a hereditary power could be induced to follow its particular interests and forget those of the people; [hence] in the things about which [there is] a sovereign interest in corrupting, for instance, in the laws about levying silver coin, it must take part in legislation only through its faculty of vetoing and not through its faculty of enacting. . . .

The executive power should be in the hands of a monarch, because the part of the government that almost always needs immediate action is better administered by one than by many, whereas what depends on legislative power is often better ordered by many than by one.

If there were no monarch and the executive power were entrusted to a certain number of persons drawn from the legislative body, there would no longer be liberty, because the two powers would be united, the same persons sometimes belonging and always able to belong to both. . . .

If the executive power does not have the right to check the enterprises of the legislative body, the latter will be despotic, for it will wipe out all the other powers, since it will be able to give to itself all the power it can imagine.

But the legislative power must not have the reciprocal faculty of checking the executive power. For, as execution has the limits of its own nature, it is useless to restrict it; besides, executive power is always exercised on immediate things. . . .

But if, in a free state, legislative power should not have the right to check executive power, it has the right and should have the faculty to examine the manner in which the laws it has made have been executed; . . .

But, whether or not this examination is made, the legislative body should not have the power to judge the person, and consequently the conduct, of the one who executes. His person should be sacred because, as he is necessary to the state so that the legislative body does not become tyrannical, if he were accused or judged there would no longer be liberty.

In this case, the state would not be a monarchy but an unfree republic. But, as he who executes cannot execute badly without having as ministers wicked counsellors who hate the law although the laws favour them as men, these counsellors can be sought out and punished. . . .

Executive power, as we have said, should take part in legislation by its faculty of vetoing; otherwise it will soon be stripped of its prerogatives. But if legislative power takes part in execution, executive power will equally be lost.

If the monarch took part in legislation by the faculty of enacting, there would no longer be liberty. But as in spite of this, he must take part in legislation in order to defend himself, he must take part in it by the faculty of vetoing. . . .

Here, therefore, is the fundamental constitution of the government of which we are speaking. As its legislative body is composed of two parts, the one will be chained to the other by their reciprocal faculty of vetoing. The two will be bound by the executive power, which will itself be bound by the legislative power.

The form of these three powers should be rest or inaction. But as they are constrained to move by the necessary motion of things, they will be forced to move in concert.

3

THE FEDERALIST NOS. 47, 48

JAMES MADISON

The accumulation of all powers, legislative, executive, and judiciary, in the same hands, whether of one, a few, or many, and whether hereditary, self-appointed, or elective, may justly be pronounced the very definition of tyranny. . . .

The oracle who is always consulted and cited on this subject is the celebrated Montesquieu. If he be not the author of this invaluable precept in the science of politics, he has the merit at least of displaying and recommending it most effectually to the attention of mankind. Let us endeavour, in the first place, to ascertain his meaning on this point.

The British constitution was to Montesquieu what Homer has been to the didactic writers on epic poetry. As the latter have considered the work of the immortal bard as the perfect model from which the principles and rules of the epic art were to be drawn, and by which all similar works were to be judged, so this great political critic appears to have viewed the constitution of England as the standard, or, to use his own expression, as the mirror of political liberty; and to have delivered, in the form of elementary truths, the several characteristic principles of that particular system. That we may be sure, then, not to mistake his meaning in this case, let us recur to the source from which the maxim was drawn.

On the slightest view of the British constitution, we must perceive that the legislative, executive, and judiciary departments are by no means totally separate and distinct from each other. . . .

James Madison, excerpted from 'The Federalist No. 47' and 'The Federalist No. 48', in Alexander Hamilton, John Jay, and James Madison, *The Federalist: A Commentary on the Constitution of the United States*, intr. by Edward Mead Earle (New York: Random House, Modern Library College Editions, n.d.).

From these facts, by which Montesquieu was guided, it may clearly be inferred that, in saying 'There can be no liberty where the legislative and executive powers are united in the same person, or body of magistrates,' or, 'If the power of judging be not separated from the legislative and executive powers,' he did not mean that these departments ought to have no *partial agency* in, or no *control* over, the acts of each other. His meaning, as his own words import, and still more conclusively as illustrated by the example in his eye, can amount to no more than this, that where the *whole* power of one department is exercised by the same hands which possess the *whole* power of another department, the fundamental principles of a free constitution are subverted. . . .

It was shown in the last paper that the political apothegm there examined does not require that the legislative, executive, and judiciary departments should be wholly unconnected with each other. I shall undertake, in the next place, to show that unless these departments be so far connected and blended as to give to each a constitutional control over the others, the degree of separation which the maxim requires, as essential to a free government, can never in practice be duly maintained.

It is agreed on all sides, that the powers properly belonging to one of the departments ought not to be directly and completely administered by either of the other departments. It is equally evident, that none of them ought to possess, directly or indirectly, an overruling influence over the others, in the administration of their respective powers. It will not be denied, that power is of an encroaching nature, and that it ought to be effectually restrained from passing the limits assigned to it. After discriminating, therefore, in theory, the several classes of power, as they may in their nature be legislative, executive, or judiciary, the next and most difficult task is to provide some practical security for each, against the invasion of the others.

4

THE FEDERALIST NO. 70

ALEXANDER HAMILTON

Energy in the executive is a leading character in the definition of good government. It is essential to the protection of the community against foreign attacks; it is not less essential to the steady administration of the laws; to the protection of property against those irregular and high-handed combinations which sometimes interrupt the ordinary course of justice; to the security of liberty against the enterprises and assaults of ambition, of faction, and of anarchy. Every man the least conversant in Roman story, knows how often that republic was obliged to take refuge in the absolute power of a single man, under the formidable title of dictator, as well against the intrigues of ambitious individuals who aspired to the tyranny, and the seditions of whole classes of the community whose conduct threatened the existence of all government, as against the invasions of external enemies who menaced the conquest and destruction of Rome.

There can be no need, however, to multiply arguments or examples on this head. A feeble executive implies a feeble execution of the government. A feeble execution is but another phrase for a bad execution; and a government ill executed, whatever it may be in theory, must be, in practice, a bad government.

Taking it for granted, therefore, that all men of sense will agree in the necessity of an energetic executive, it will only remain to inquire, what are the ingredients which constitute this energy? How far can they be combined with those other ingredients which constitute safety in the republican sense? And how

Alexander Hamilton, excerpted from 'The Federalist No. 70', in Alexander Hamilton, John Jay, and James Madison, *The Federalist: A Commentary on the Constitution of the United States*, intr. by Edward Mead Earle (New York: Random House, Modern Library College Editions, n.d.).

far does this combination characterize the plan which has been reported by the convention?

The ingredients which constitute energy in the executive are, first, unity; secondly, duration; thirdly, an adequate provision for its support: fourthly, competent powers.

The ingredients which constitute safety in the republican sense are, first, a due dependence on the people; secondly, a due responsibility.

Those politicians and statesmen who have been the most celebrated for the soundness of their principles and for the justice of their views, have declared in favour of a single executive and a numerous legislature. They have, with great propriety, considered energy as the most necessary qualification of the former, and have regarded this as most applicable to power in a single hand; while they have, with equal propriety, considered the latter as best adapted to deliberation and wisdom, and best calculated to conciliate the confidence of the people and to secure their privileges and interests.

That unity is conducive to energy will not be disputed. Decision, activity, secrecy, and despatch will generally characterize the proceedings of one man in a much more eminent degree than the proceedings of any greater number; and in proportion as the number is increased, these qualities will be diminished.

This unity may be destroyed in two ways: either by vesting the power in two or more magistrates of equal dignity and authority; or by vesting it ostensibly in one man, subject, in whole or in part, to the control and co-operation of others, in the capacity of counsellors to him. . . .

Wherever two or more persons are engaged in any common enterprise or pursuit, there is always danger of difference of opinion. If it be a public trust or office, in which they are clothed with equal dignity and authority, there is peculiar danger of personal emulation and even animosity. From either, and especially from all these causes, the most bitter dissensions are apt to spring. Whenever these happen, they lessen the respectability, weaken the authority, and distract the plans and operations of those whom they divide. If they should unfortunately assail the supreme executive magistracy of a country, consisting of a plurality of persons, they might impede or frustrate the most important measures of the government, in the most critical emergencies of the state. And what is still worse, they might split the community into the most violent and irreconcilable factions, adhering differently to the different individuals who composed the magistracy. . . .

But one of the weightiest objections to a plurality in the executive, and which lies as much against the last as the first plan, is, that it tends to conceal faults and destroy responsibility. Responsibility is of two kinds—to censure and to punishment. The first is the more important of the two, especially in an elective office. Man, in public trust, will much oftener act in such a manner as to render him unworthy of being any longer trusted, than in such a manner as to make him obnoxious to legal punishment. But the multiplication of the executive adds to the difficulty of detection in either case. It often becomes impossible, amidst mutual accusations, to determine on whom the blame or the punishment of a pernicious measure, or series of pernicious measures, ought really to fall. It is shifted from one to another with so much dexterity, and under such plausible appearances, that the public opinion is left in suspense about the real author. The circumstances which may have led to any national miscarriage or misfortune are sometimes so complicated that, where there are a number of actors who may have had different degrees and kinds of agency, though we may clearly see upon the whole that there has been mismanagement, yet it may be impracticable to pronounce to whose account the evil which may have been incurred is truly chargeable.

5

AT THE CONVENTION: THE PAUCITY OF MODELS

ROBERT A. DAHL

To understand the presidency it is instructive to put ourselves briefly in the shoes of the men at the Convention. That some functions of leadership had to be performed in the political system for which they were designing a constitution, these men were both too practical and too versed in political experience to doubt. They knew they had to design the office of 'national executive', 'executive magistracy', 'magistrate', or 'executive', as they referred to it at various times.

Yet how were they to create an 'executive magistrate' who would perform whatever functions the other institutions could not properly execute and who at the same time would not be a political monstrosity? In 1787, the problem was far more baffling than it would be today, because the alternatives we are familiar with today were unknown. A popularly elected president was a novelty; the chief alternative solution, a prime minister chosen by the parliament, had not yet emerged in its modern form even in Britain.

Every problem was unsolved, every proposal debatable, every solution risky. How many executives should there be: one or several? How should the executive be chosen? For how long? What should the qualifications be for executive office? What constitutional powers and limits were required? Whatever was written into the constitution, what would be the real role of the executive in the new political system? The answers necessarily had to be highly speculative.

Robert A. Dahl, excerpted from *Democracy in the United States: Promise and Performance*, 2nd edn. (Chicago: Rand McNally, 1972), ch. 10 (footnotes omitted). Copyright 1967, 1972 Rand McNally and Company.

HOW MANY?

It is true that earlier republics furnished some experience, but republican executives had generally been collegial, consisting of several men, each of whom served as a check on the others. This was the famous solution of the Roman Republic. Although the plural executive is designed to solve one problem, it creates another. The plural executive may help to prevent any single man from gaining too much power; yet where one executive checks another, decisions may be paralysed. That system must, therefore, avoid great emergencies, particularly those requiring decisive action in international affairs and war; or else, as in the Roman Republic, it must have some provision for a temporary 'dictator' armed with emergency powers.

Because of these disadvantages, the plural executive is rarely used in polyarchies. Switzerland has employed it most successfully—but Switzerland is small, maintains a vigorous neutrality, remains free of alliances and international organizations, and avoids war. In 1951, one of the few polyarchies of Latin America, Uruguay, shifted from a presidential executive to a nine-member council. Uruguay, like Switzerland, is small and peaceful; even so, in 1966, Uruguay decided to restore the single executive. No other nation has chosen the collegial form, though the cabinet system bears a superficial resemblance to it.

The idea of a plural executive had little support at the Convention. Randolph of Virginia 'strenuously opposed a unity in the Executive magistracy. He regarded it as the foetus of monarchy. . . . He could not see why the great requisites for the Executive department, vigor, despatch & responsibility could not be found in three men, as well as in one man.' But Randolph won few converts. After all, the Articles of Confederation had followed the pattern of the ancient republics; the only executive provided for in the Articles was a committee, appointed by Congress, 'to sit in the recess of congress, to be denominated "A Committee of the States," and to consist of one delegate from each state'. Not even Randolph wanted to duplicate that feeble system in the new constitution. In their own constitutions, the states (except for Pennsylvania) had settled, nominally, for a single executive—though often he was so hedged around by a legislative council that the executive was in fact collegial. One famous republic, it is true, had in outward form a single executive: the Doge of Venice. That republic, the longest-lived republic in history, was after some seven or eight centuries approaching its final *coup de grâce* at the hands of Napoleon. But the Doge was virtually all figurehead and no power; executive authority was in fact lodged in numerous councils, commissions, and officials.

Whatever the reasons, the proposal for a single executive was agreed to in the early days of the Convention. It was almost the only question having to do with the presidency on which the Convention, having once made a decision, did not later change its mind.

HOW LONG?

In the absence of an appropriate model for a republican executive, the most visible alternative was the form that all members of the Convention knew best: a hereditary monarchy. Yet it was precisely because this solution was barred to them by their own beliefs and the attitudes of the country—'. . . there was not a one-thousandth part of our fellow citizens who were not against every approach toward monarchy', said Gerry—that there existed the vacuum they had to fill. To Alexander Hamilton—if we can rely on Madison's notes—a republic was inherently a second-best form of government because, unlike a monarchy, it could provide no good solution to the problem of the executive:

. . . As to the Executive [Madison reports Hamilton as saying on June 18], it seemed to be admitted that no good one could be established on Republican principles. Was not this giving up the merits of the question: for can there be a good Gov^t without a good Executive. The English model was the only good one on this subject. The Hereditary interest of the King was so interwoven with that of the Nation, and his personal emoluments so great, that he was placed above the danger of being corrupted from abroad—and at the same time was both sufficiently independent and sufficiently controuled, to answer the purpose of the institution at home. . . . What is the inference from all these observations? That we ought to go as far in order to attain stability and permanency, as republican principles will admit. Let one branch of the Legislature hold their places for life or at least during good behaviour. Let the Executive also be for life.

One week spot of Hamilton's argument was, as everyone knew, the simple matter of genes and the accidents of human personality. A great king may have a son less suited to kingship than his own fool. A king famed for his justice may beget a tyrant. To a king of intelligence, vision, courage, and resolution, the mysteries of genes and child-rearing may produce an heir, shortsighted, feckless, weak, and irresolute. Writing some years later, Jefferson reflected on the monarchs of Europe:

While in Europe, I often amused myself with contemplating the characters of the then reigning sovereigns. . . . Louis XVI was a fool, of my own knowledge. . . . The King of Spain was a fool, and of Naples the same. They passed their lives in hunting, and despatched two couriers a week, one thousand miles, to let each other know what game they had killed the preceding days. The King of Sardinia was a fool. All these were Bourbons. The queen of Portugal, a Braganza, was an idiot by nature. And so was the King of Denmark. Their sons, as regents, exercised the powers of government. The King of Prussia, successor to the great Frederick, was a mere hog in body as well as in mind. Gustavus of Sweden, and Joseph of Austria, were really crazy, and George of England, you know, was in a straight waistcoat. There remained, then, none but old Catherine, who had been too lately picked up to have lost her common sense. . . . These animals had become without mind and powerless; and so will every hereditary monarch be after a few generations. . . . And so endeth the book of Kings, from all of whom the Lord deliver us.

The Americans had thrown off one hereditary monarch; it was obvious to all—including Hamilton—that they would not tolerate another.

An executive for life might solve some of these problems; but such a system would create others. To give a man a lifetime in which to accumulate power is dangerous. A lifetime tenure might even be enough to establish a dynasty. Sickness, senility, degeneration, insanity have turned good leaders into evil ones; yet an executive appointed for life might not yield power gladly and might have too much power to be dispossessed without violence. The Roman emperors were the obvious model: they had held office for life. Yet while some of them, like Hadrian, were undoubtedly great leaders and ruled during times of great prosperity and peace, many were brutal tyrants: Caligula, Nero, Commodus, Caracalla.

An executive chosen for life had no support at the Convention. Even Hamilton, when he got down to his specific proposals, called for an appointment not explicitly for life, but 'during good behavior'. When James McClurg (a delegate from Virginia whose role at the Convention was brief and unimportant) moved that the executive hold office 'during good behavior', the idea won little acclaim. That distinguished advocate of an aristocratic republic, Gouverneur Morris, briefly endorsed it but changed his mind a few days later. Madison tactfully suggested that 'respect for the mover entitled his proposition to a fair hearing & discussion'. Mason remarked:

. . . He considered an Executive during good behavior as a softer name only for an Executive for life. And that the next would be an easy step to hereditary Monarchy. If the motion should finally succeed, he might himself live to see such a Revolution. If he did not it was probable his children or grand children would. He trusted there were few men in that House who wished for it. No state he was sure had so far revolted from Republican principles as to have the least bias in its favor.

The proposal was turned down by a close vote—four states in favour, six against—which, according to Madison, grossly exaggerated the actual support the proposal had enjoyed at the Convention.

This vote [he wrote in a comment on his own notes] is not to be considered as any certain index of opinion, as a number in the affirmative probably had it chiefly in view to alarm those attached to a dependence of the Executive on the Legislature, & thereby facilitate some final arrangement of a contrary tendency. The avowed friends of an Executive, 'during good behaviour' were not more than three or four, nor is it certain they would finally have adhered to such a tenure.

Yet, while this proposal was disposed of fairly easily, the Convention twisted and turned like a man tormented in his sleep by a bad dream as it tried to decide just what term would be proper. On 24 July, the Convention had a particularly trying day: Luther Martin proposed a term of eleven years; Gerry suggested fifteen; King, twenty years—'the medium life of princes'; Davie, eight years. After that day's work, the Convention adjourned without having decided anything at all.

The log of votes in the Convention on the length of term of the president reveals the uncertainty of the delegates:

1 June: Seven-year term, *passed*, 5 states to 4.
2 June: Ineligible for re-election after seven years, *passed*, 7–2.
19 July: Seven-year term, *defeated*, 5–3.
  Six-year term, *passed*, 9–1.
  Ineligibility for a second term, *defeated*, 8–2.
26 July: Seven-year term, with ineligibility for re-election, *passed*, 7–3.
6 Sept.: Seven-year term, *defeated*, 8–3.
  Six-year term, *defeated*, 9–2.
  Four-year term, *passed*, 10–1.

HOW CHOSEN?

But having settled on a four-year term, how was the executive to be chosen? On this question the Convention could never quite make up its mind. Almost to the end, it would move towards a solution and then, on second thought, reverse itself in favour of some different alternative. On no question was experience so uncertain a guide. If ultimately the Convention invented the popularly elected presidency, it would be excessively charitable to say that the men in Philadelphia foresaw what they were doing.

The most obvious solution in 1787 was the election of the executive by the legislature. This was the essence of the cabinet system that was evolving in Britain. Yet, in 1787, that evolution was far from complete; neither in Britain nor in this country did anyone quite realize how much the prime minister was ceasing to be the agent of the king and becoming instead the representative of a parliamentary majority. When one spoke of the British executive in 1787 one still meant the king, not the prime minister.

In the American states, too, under new or revised state constitutions, the governor was generally chosen by the legislature. Yet the experience of the various states suggested some of the disadvantages of that solution: if the executive were elected by the legislature, what was to prevent him from becoming a mere creature of that body? To some of the men at the Convention, this was exactly what was needed. Thus Sherman of Connecticut 'was for the appointment by the Legislature, and for making him absolutely dependent on that body, as it was the will of that which was to be executed. An independence of the Executive on the supreme Legislature, was in his opinion the very essence of tyranny if there was any such thing.' Was Sherman thinking of his own state—one of the few in which the governor was popularly elected?

The main reason those who opposed election by the Congress gave for their opposition was a fear that the executive would be too weak. The chief spokesman for an aristocratic republic, Gouverneur Morris, joined with the spokesmen for the democratic republic, Madison and Wilson, in opposing election by the Congress. But to find an alternative was infinitely more difficult. If the executive were elected by the people, as Wilson proposed, would he not then be too dependent on the whims of popular majorities? And could the people possibly know enough to make a wise choice? Even to Mason, who usually favoured the more democratic solutions, it seemed 'as unnatural to refer the choice of a proper character for chief Magistrate to the people, as it would, to refer a trial of colours to a blind man. The extent of the Country renders it impossible that the people can have the requisite capacity to judge of the respective pretensions of the Candidates.'

Thus the argument went on. Every possible solution seemed fatally flawed. Should the president be chosen by the congress? By the senate only? By the people? By the state governors? By the state legislatures? By electors chosen by the people? As Madison wearily concluded in late July, 'there are objections agst every mode that has been, or perhaps can be proposed'.

The United States came within a hairsbreadth of adopting a kind of parliamentary system. The Virginia plan had proposed that the executive be chosen by the national legislature. On 17 July this mode was unanimously agreed to. It won another trial vote, 6–3, on 26 July. As late as 24 August the Convention voted against an attempt to substitute election by the people or by electors for choice by the legislature. Yet when a committee reported out on 4 September—two weeks before the end of the Convention—it suggested the 'electoral college' solution which was embodied in Article II of the constitution. No one altogether knows what happened in the interval; perhaps many delegates who had earlier voted for election by the legislature were so unsure of their grounds, so weary of the dispute, and so fearful of further haggling and possible deadlock that they eagerly accepted the compromise suggested by the committee. Whatever the reasons, all who struggle today with the task of inventing new political institutions may be comforted by this record of the Convention's torment:

2 June: Virginia plan (Randolph) proposes a national executive 'to be chosen by the National Legislature'. Discussed.
Wilson's proposal for presidential electors chosen by the people, *defeated*, 8–2.

9 June: Gerry's proposal that the executive be chosen 'by the executives of the states', *defeated*, 9–0.

17 July: Wilson's proposal for election by the people, *defeated*, 9–1. Luther Martin's proposal for choice by electors appointed by state legislatures, *defeated*, 8–2. Randolph's original proposal, 'to be chosen by the National Legislature', *passed unanimously*.

19 July: Ellsworth's proposal that the national executive be chosen by electors appointed by state legislatures, *passed*, 6–3 (Massachusetts divided).

24 July: Houston's proposal that 'the Executive be appointed by the National Legislature', *passed*, 7–4.

25 July: Ellsworth's proposal that 'the Executive be appointed by the Legislature', except for re-election 'in which case the choice shall be by Electors appointed by the Legislators in the States', *defeated*, 7–4.

26 July: A comprehensive resolution on the national executive proposing among other things that he be 'chosen by the National Legislature', *passed*, 6–3 (Virginia divided, with Washington and Madison against). This article, as approved, referred to Committee of Detail.

6 August: Constitution as reported by Committee of Detail reads 'he shall be elected by ballot by the legislature'.

24 August: Carroll's proposal to strike out 'by the legislature'

and insert 'by the people', *defeated*, 9–2. G. Morris's proposal that the President 'shall be chosen by electors', *failed*, 4–4 (Connecticut and Maryland, divided, Massachusetts absent).

4 September: Committee of Eleven, to which this and other sections had been referred, propose essentials of present constitution: 'Each State shall appoint in such manner as its Legislature may direct, a number of electors equal to the whole number of Senators and members of the House of Representatives to which the State may be entitled in the Legislature.'

6 September: This proposal *adopted*, 9–2.

17 September: Constitution signed; Convention adjourns.

6

THE ENGLISH CONSTITUTION: THE CABINET

WALTER BAGEHOT

This fusion of the legislative and executive functions may, to those who have not much considered it, seem but a dry and small matter to be the latent essence and effectual secret of the English constitution; but we can only judge of its real importance by looking at a few of its principal effects, and contrasting it very shortly with its great competitor, which seems likely, unless care be taken, to outstrip it in the progress of the world. That competitor is the presidential system. The characteristic of it is that the president is elected from the people by one process, and the house of representatives by another. The independence of the legislative and executive powers is the specific quality of the presidential government, just as their fusion and combination is the precise principle of cabinet government.

First, compare the two in quiet times. The essence of a civilized age is, that administration requires the continued aid of legislation. One principal and necessary kind of legislation is *taxation*. The expense of civilized government is continually varying. It must vary if the government does its duty. The miscellaneous estimates of the English government contain an inevitable medley of changing items. Education, prison discipline, art, science, civil contingencies of a hundred kinds, require more money one year and less another. The expense of defence—the naval and military estimates—vary still more as

Walter Bagehot, excerpted from *The English Constitution*, intr. by the First Earl of Balfour (London: Oxford University Press, first published in 1867; second edition, with an additional chapter, published in 1872; first published in 'The World's Classics' in 1928 and reprinted in 1929, 1933, 1936, 1942, 1944, 1949, 1952, 1955, 1958, and 1961), ch. 1.

the danger of attack seems more or less imminent, as the means of retarding such danger become more or less costly. If the persons who have to do the work are not the same as those who have to make the laws, there will be a controversy between the two sets of persons. The tax-imposers are sure to quarrel with the tax-requirers. The executive is crippled by not getting the laws it needs, and the legislature is spoiled by having to act without responsibility: the executive becomes unfit for its name since it cannot execute what it decides on; the legislature is demoralized by liberty, by taking decisions of which others (and not itself) will suffer the effects.

In America so much has this difficulty been felt that a semi-connection has grown up between the legislature and the executive. When the secretary of the treasury of the federal government wants a tax he consults upon it with the chairman of the financial committee of Congress. He cannot go down to Congress himself and propose what he wants; he can only write a letter and send it. But he tries to get a chairman of the finance committee who likes his tax; through that chairman he tries to persuade the committee to recommend such tax; by that committee he tries to induce the house to adopt that tax. But such a chain of communications is liable to continual interruptions; it may suffice for a single tax on a fortunate occasion, but will scarcely pass a complicated budget—we do not say in a war or a rebellion—we are now comparing the cabinet system and the presidential system in quiet times—but in times of financial difficulty. Two clever men never exactly agreed about a budget. . . . They are sure to quarrel, and the result is sure to satisfy neither. And when the taxes do not yield as they were expected to yield, who is responsible? Very likely the secretary of the treasury could not persuade the chairman—very likely the chairman could not persuade his committee—very likely the committee could not persuade the assembly. Whom, then, can you punish—whom can you abolish—when your taxes run short? There is nobody save the legislature, a vast miscellaneous body difficult to punish, and the very persons to inflict the punishment.

Nor is the financial part of administration the only one which requires in a civilized age the constant support and accompaniment of facilitating legislation. All administration does so. In England, on a vital occasion, the cabinet can compel legislation by the threat of resignation, and the threat of dissolution; but neither of these can be used in a presidential state. There the legislature cannot be dissolved by the executive government; and it does not heed a resignation, for it has not to find the successor. Accordingly, when a difference of opinion arises, the legislature is forced to fight the executive, and the executive is forced to fight the legislature; and so very likely they contend to the conclusion of their respective terms. . . .

Nor is this the worst. Cabinet government educates the nation; the presidential does not educate it, and may corrupt it. It has been said that England invented the phrase, 'Her Majesty's Opposition'; that it was the first government which made a criticism of administration as much a part of the polity as administration itself. This critical opposition is the consequence of cabinet government. The great scene of debate, the great engine of popular instruction and political controversy, is the legislative assembly. A speech there by an eminent statesman, a party movement by a great political combination, are the best means yet known for arousing, enlivening, and teaching a people. The cabinet system ensures such debates, for it makes them the means by which statesmen advertise themselves for future and confirm themselves in present governments. . . .

The nation feels that its judgement is important, and it strives to judge. It succeeds in deciding because the debates and the discussions give it the facts and the arguments. But under a presidential government a nation has, except at the electing moment, no influence; it has not the ballot-box before it; its virtue is gone, and it must wait till its instant of despotism again returns. It is not incited to form an opinion like a nation under a cabinet government; nor is it instructed like such a nation. There are doubtless debates in the legislature, but they are prologues without a play. There is nothing of a catastrophe about them; you cannot turn out the government. The prize of power is not in the gift of the legislature, and no one cares for the legislature. The executive, the great centre of power and place, sticks irremovable; you cannot change it in any event. The teaching apparatus which has educated our public mind, which prepares our resolutions, which shapes our opinions, does not exist. No presidential country needs to form daily, delicate opinions, or is helped in forming them. . . .

After saying that the division of the legislature and the executive in presidential governments weakens the legislative power, it may seem a contradiction to say that it also weakens the executive power. But it is not a contradiction. The division weakens the whole aggregate force of government—the entire imperial power; and therefore it weakens both its halves. The executive is weakened in a very plain way. In England a strong cabinet can obtain the concurrence of the legislature in all acts which facilitate its administration; it is itself, so to say, the legislature. But a president may be hampered by the parliament, and is likely to be hampered. The natural tendency of the members of every legislature is to make themselves conspicuous. They wish to gratify an ambition laudable or blameable; they wish to promote the measures they think best for the public welfare; they wish to make their *will* felt in great affairs. All these mixed motives urge them to oppose the executive. They are embodying the purposes of others if they aid; they are advancing their own opinions if they defeat: they are first if they vanquish; they are auxiliaries if they support. The weakness of the American executive used to be the great theme of all critics before the Confederate rebellion. Congress and committees of Congress of course impeded the executive when there was no coercive public sentiment to check and rule them.

But the presidential system not only gives the executive power an antagonist in the legislative power, and so makes it weaker; it also enfeebles it by impairing its intrinsic quality. A cabinet is elected by a legislature; and when that legislature is composed of fit persons, that mode of electing the executive is the very best. It is a case of secondary election, under the only conditions in which secondary election is preferable to primary. Generally speaking, in an electioneering country (I mean in a country full of political life, and used to the manipulation of popular institutions), the election of candidates to elect candidates is a farce. The electoral college of America is so. It was intended that the deputies when assembled should exercise a real discretion, and by independent choice select the president. But the primary electors take too much interest. They only elect a deputy to vote for Mr Lincoln or Mr Breckenridge, and the deputy only takes a ticket, and drops that ticket in an urn. He never chooses or thinks of choosing. He is but a messenger—a transmitter: the real decision is in those who chose him—who chose him because they knew what he would do.

It is true that the British House of Commons is subject to the same influences. Members are mostly, perhaps, elected because they will vote for a particular ministry, rather than for purely legislative reasons. But—and here is the capital distinction— the functions of the House of Commons are important and *continuous*. It does not, like the electoral college in the United States, separate when it has elected its ruler; it watches, legislates, seats and unseats ministries, from day to day. Accordingly it is a *real* electoral body. The parliament of 1857, which, more than any other parliament of late years, was a parliament elected to support a particular premier—which was chosen, as Americans might say, upon the 'Palmerston ticket'—before it had been in existence two years, dethroned Lord Palmerston. Though selected in the interest of a particular ministry, it in fact destroyed that ministry. . . .

All these differences are more important at critical periods, because government itself is more important. A formed public opinion, a respectable, able, and disciplined legislature, a well-chosen executive, a parliament and an administration not thwarting each other, but co-operating with each other, are of greater consequence when great affairs are in progress than when small affairs are in progress—when there is much to do than when there is little to do. But in addition to this, a parliamentary or cabinet constitution possesses an additional and special advantage in very dangerous times. It has what we may call a reserve of power fit for and needed by extreme exigencies.

The principle of popular government is that the supreme power, the determining efficacy in matters political, resides in the people—not necessarily or commonly in the whole people, in the numerical majority, but in a *chosen* people, a picked and selected people. It is so in England; it is so in all free countries. Under a cabinet constitution at a sudden emergency this people can choose a ruler for the occasion. It is quite possible and even likely that he would not be ruler *before* the occasion. The great qualities, the imperious will, the rapid energy, the eager nature fit for a great crisis are not required—are impediments—in common times. A Lord Liverpool is better in everyday politics than a Chatham—a Louis Philippe far better than a Napoleon. By the structure of the world we often want, at the sudden occurrence of a grave tempest, to change the helmsman—to replace the pilot of the calm by the pilot of the storm. . . .

But under a presidential government you can do nothing of the kind. The American government calls itself a government of the supreme people; but at a quick crisis, the time when a sovereign power is most needed, you cannot *find* the supreme people. You have got a congress elected for one fixed period, going out perhaps by fixed instalments, which cannot be accelerated or retarded—you have a president chosen for a fixed period, and immovable during that period: all the arrangements are for *stated* times. There is no *elastic* element, everything is rigid, specified, dated. Come what may, you can quicken nothing and can retard nothing. You have bespoken your government in advance, and whether it suits you or not, whether it works well or works ill, whether it is what you want or not, by law you must keep it. . . .

Even in quiet times, government by a president is, for the various reasons which have been stated, inferior to government by a cabinet; but the difficulty of quiet times is nothing as compared with the difficulty of unquiet times. The comparative deficiencies of the regular, common operation of a presidential government are far less than the comparative deficiencies in time of sudden trouble—the want of elasticity, the impossibility of a dictatorship, the total absence of a *revolutionary reserve*.

7

COMMITTEE OR CABINET GOVERNMENT?

WOODROW WILSON

It is only by making parties responsible for what they do and advise that they can be made safe and reliable servants. . . . Let, therefore, the leaders of parties be made responsible. Let there be set apart from the party in power certain representatives who, leading their party and representing its policy, may be made to suffer a punishment which shall be at once personal and vicarious when their party goes astray, or their policy either misleads or miscarries. This can be done by making the leaders of the dominant party in Congress the executive officers of the legislative will; by making them also members of the President's cabinet, and thus at once the executive chiefs of the departments of state and the leaders of their party on the floor of Congress; in a word, by having done with the standing committees, and constituting the cabinet advisers both of the President and of Congress. This would be cabinet government.

Cabinet government is government by means of an executive ministry chosen by the chief magistrate of the nation from the ranks of the legislative majority—a ministry sitting in the legislature and acting as its executive committee; directing its business and leading its debates; representing the same party and the same principles; 'bound together by a sense of responsibility and loyalty to the party to which it belongs', and subject to removal whenever it forfeits the confidence and loses the

Woodrow Wilson, excerpted from 'Committee or Cabinet Government', in Ray Stannard Baker and William E. Dodd (eds.), *College and State: Educational, Literary and Political Papers (1875–1913) by Woodrow Wilson* (New York and London: Harper and Brothers, 1925; New York: Kraus Reprint Co., 1970), i. 95–129. The essay was first published in the *Overland Monthly*, January 1884, series 2, vol. 3: pp. 17–33.

support of the body it represents. Its establishment in the United States would involve, of course, several considerable changes in our present system. It would necessitate, in the first place, one or two alterations in the constitution. The second clause of Section 6, Article I, of the constitution runs thus: 'No Senator or Representative shall, during the term for which he was elected, be appointed to any civil office under the authority of the United States which shall have been created, or the emoluments whereof shall have been increased, during such time; and no person holding any office under the United States shall be a member of either House during his continuance in office.' Let the latter part of this clause read: 'And no person holding any other than a cabinet office under the United States shall be a member of either House during his continuance in office', and the addition of four words will have removed the chief constitutional obstacle to the erection of cabinet government in this country. The way will have been cleared, in great part at least, for the development of a constitutional practice, which, founded upon the great charter we already possess, might grow into a governmental system at once strong, stable, and flexible. Those four words being added to the constitution, the President might be authorized and directed to choose for his cabinet the leaders of the ruling majority in Congress; that cabinet might, on condition of acknowledging its tenure of office dependent on the favour of the houses, be allowed to assume those privileges of initiative in legislation and leadership in debate which are now given, by an almost equal distribution, to the standing committees; and cabinet government would have been instituted. . . .

Cabinet government has in it everything to recommend it. Especially to Americans should it commend itself. It is, first of all, the simplest and most straightforward system of party government. It gives explicit authority to that party majority which in any event will exercise its implicit powers to the top of its bent; which will snatch control if control be not given it. It is a simple legalization of fact; for, as every one knows, we are not free to choose between party government and no-party government. Our choice must be between a party that rules by authority and a party that, where it has not a grant of the right to rule, will make itself supreme by stratagem. . . .

It cannot be too often repeated, that while Congress remains the supreme power of the state, it is idle to talk of steadying or cleansing our politics without in some way linking together the interests of the executive and the legislature. So long as these two great branches are isolated, they must be ineffective just to the extent of the isolation. Congress will always be master, and will always enforce its commands on the administration. The only wise plan, therefore, is to facilitate its direction of the government, and to make it at the same time responsible, in the persons of its leaders, for its acts of control, and for the manner in which its plans and commands are executed. The only hope of wrecking the present clumsy misrule of Congress lies in the establishment of responsible cabinet government. Let the interests of the legislature be indissolubly linked with the interests of the executive. Let those who have authority to direct the course of legislation be those who have a deep personal concern in building up the executive departments in effectiveness, in strengthening law, and in unifying policies; men whose personal reputation depends upon successful administration, whose public station originates in the triumph of principles, and whose dearest ambition it is to be able to vindicate their wisdom and maintain their integrity.

Committee government is too clumsy and too clandestine a system to last. Other methods of government must sooner or later be sought, and a different economy established. First or last, Congress must be organized in conformity with what is now the prevailing legislative practice of the world. English precedent and the world's fashion must be followed in the institution of cabinet government in the United States.

8

THE PRESIDENT AND CONGRESS

HAROLD J. LASKI

A distinction must be drawn between the 'crisis' situation and the 'normal' situation. In the first, the President's position is so overwhelming that it is, broadly, imperative for Congress to follow where he chooses to lead. Then, the nation requires action, and it looks to the President to define the kind of action that is required. It assumes the necessity, in crisis, for the conference upon him of wide powers; it is impatient of doubt about, or hostility to, their conference. It may, indeed, almost be said that it is too impatient; no one can analyse, for instance, the workings of the Espionage Act of 1917 without seeing that Congress then practically abdicated before the President. Much the same is true of the 'hundred days' of Franklin Roosevelt. It would have been literally impossible, in the face of public opinion, for Congress to have resisted the pressure to give the President what he chose to demand; there are, indeed, careful observers who believe that if, at that moment, he had demanded even so drastic a measure as the nationalization of the banks, Congress would have had to accept it. In a crisis, to put it shortly, public opinion compels the abrogation of the separation of powers. There is really only one will in effective operation, and that is the will of the President. He is as powerful, while the emergency has a psychological hold on the country, as the British prime minister at a moment of national emergency.

But in a 'normal' situation the position is very different. The American system, in its ultimate foundations, is built upon a belief in weak government. It must never be forgotten that the constitution is the child of the eighteenth century; that the

Harold J. Laski, excerpted from *The American Presidency: An Interpretation* (New York and London: Harper and Brothers, 1940), ch. 3 (footnotes omitted). Copyright 1940 Harper and Brothers. Reprinted by permission of Harper-Collins Publishers.

influence of Locke and Montesquieu is written deeply into its clauses. Those who made it were, out of actual and inferred experience, above all afraid of arbitrary power. They constructed a system of checks and balances as a bulwark against its emergence. They did so because they believed, with Madison, that 'the accumulation of powers in a single hand is the very definition of tyranny'. They did so because the effective citizen whom they were above all considering was the bourgeois man of adequate property who needed protection, on the one hand against an ambitious executive, and on the other against a legislature unduly under the influence of the propertyless mob. Naturally enough, in their day, the good state seemed to be the negative state. . . .

For once the need for a positive state began to be admitted— as it was reluctantly admitted in the presidency of Theodore Roosevelt—one outstanding principle was clear. It was the principle, long ago adumbrated by John Stuart Mill, that the formulation of legislative proposals is not a task for which a legislature is fitted. A legislature can criticize; it can ventilate grievance; its power to investigate through committees is invaluable; and, not least, as it fulfils these tasks it provides a process of public education which is pivotal to democratic government. But a legislature like Congress is at once too big and too incoherent of itself to devise an organic and unified approach to the problems of the time. It is not effectively organized to take a continuous initiative. Its members are not compelled to think by their position in terms of the problems of the whole nation. Each house of Congress has a separate prestige; their common prestige is, by their nature, inherently anti-presidential in character. To be something, Congress is forced to take a stand against the President; it cannot be anything if it merely follows his lead. And the weakness of the system is magnified by the fact that though it can seek its own elevation only by discrediting him, it cannot destroy him. He is there, whether it will or no, for his term; and his power to appeal against its decisions is but interstitial in character. The result of the system, normally, is therefore to dissipate strength rather than to integrate it. The President is usually less than he might be, because the stature of Congress is diminished the more fully he has his way; and Congress is never all that it might become, because it is so organized as to prevent the acceptance of clear sailing directions.

It is, of course, true that the ties of party provide a barrier against the consequences of this dissipation of strength. The President and his supporters have always a common interest in getting something done because their record measures the chance of later success at the polls. Yet that common interest is tempered by a number of hindrances. It is hindered by the fact that the committee system makes a number of little presidents, as it were, in the congressional sphere; there is a dual quasi-executive within the legislature, even though it does not enjoy executive power. It is hindered again by the fact that, as the President's term draws to its close, the temptation to withdraw from him what allegiance the party system enforces is maximized.

In 'normal' times, indeed, the relation between the President and Congress has a curious analogy with that between the French governments of the Third Republic and the Chamber of Deputies. No doubt, there is far greater executive stability in the American system; the constitution provides for that. But there is in both an incoherence and irresponsibility in the relations between executive and legislature which it is impossible not to remark; in both, also, factionalism tends greatly to destroy the prospect that any government may hope continuously to drive through an ample programme of social change. In both, also, embarkation upon that programme results in a withdrawal of business confidence; and a reforming government is presented with the alternatives of recovery or reform. In both, too, the individual legislator is prone to take every opportunity to mark his independence of the executive; and his support, only too often, has to be purchased by administrative favours. Both show, especially in the last generation, the striking phenomenon of 'normal' governments being succeeded, every so often, by 'crisis' governments, in which legislative irresponsibility compels the conference of wide powers upon the executive as a remedy for the irresponsibility. In both, also, a return to 'normality' produces a return to the earlier characteristics. Neither shows any propensity to embark upon those fundamental reforms which the incoherence and instability suggest as imperative.

9

A BICENTENNIAL ANALYSIS OF THE AMERICAN POLITICAL STRUCTURE

COMMITTEE ON THE CONSTITUTIONAL SYSTEM

SIGNS OF STRAIN

As the bicentennial draws near, the signs of strain in our governing processes are unmistakable.

Perhaps the most alarming evidence is the mounting national debt, fuelled anew each year by outsized and unsustainable deficits that defy the good intentions of legislators and Presidents.

Consistency in our foreign and national security policies is also frustrated by an institutional contest of wills between Presidents and shifting, cross-party coalitions within the Congress. Over forty treaties submitted to the Senate for ratification since the Second World War have either been rejected or have never come to a vote. Among those that have never come to a vote are SALT II, the 1974 and 1976 treaties on underground nuclear tests and explosions, maritime boundary treaties with Mexico and Canada, several UN and OAS human rights conventions, and a wide variety of bilateral trade, tax, and environmental treaties. Meanwhile presidential concern over 'leaks' and frustration with congressionally imposed restrictions have led Presidents and their staffs to launch important diplomatic, military, and covert activities in secret and without consulting Congress.

Further problems—particularly damaging in a nation dedicated to the principle of self-government—stem from malfunctions of the modern electoral system: the high cost of running for office, the corroding influence of campaign con-

Committee on the Constitutional System, excerpted from *A Bicentennial Analysis of the American Political Structure: Report and Recommendations of the Committee on the Constitutional System* (Washington, DC: Committee on the Constitutional System).

tributions from single-interest groups, the stupefying length of campaigns (for the presidency, usually several years from initiation to inauguration), and persistently low turnout rates (among the lowest in the world for nations with competitive elections).

CAUSES

Sensing the failures and weaknesses in governmental performance, people tend to blame particular politicians or the complexity of the modern world. But our public officials are no less competent, either individually or as a group, than they used to be. Nor do our problems, as complex as they are, defy rational solutions consistent with our basic constitutional liberties. The difficulty lies mainly in the diffuse structure of the executive-legislative process and in the decline of party loyalty and cohesion at all levels of the political system.

The separation of powers, as a principle of constitutional structure, has served us well in preventing tyranny and the abuse of high office, but it has done so by encouraging confrontation, indecision, and deadlock, and by diffusing accountability for the results.

Ideally our two-party system should counteract the centrifugal tendencies of the separation of powers, with each party's politicians committed to a common philosophy of government and to specific programme goals for which they stand accountable at the next election. In fact, throughout most of the nineteenth century and until after the end of the Second World War, the loyalty of most politicians to their party was deeply felt. They ran for office on a ticket selected by the party's leaders. Once in office, they recognized a common stake in the success of their party's governance and their joint accountability as candidates of the party at the next election.

In recent decades, however, political reforms and technological changes have worked together to weaken the parties and undermine their ability to draw the separated parts of the government into coherent action. Beginning in the late nineteenth century, Congress enacted a series of measures that redistributed functions previously performed by the parties.

Civil service systems stripped the parties of much of their patronage.

The rise of the welfare state took away many opportunities for service by which the parties had won and held the loyalty of their followers. The secret ballot replaced the 'tickets' which had previously been prepared by the parties and handed to the voters to cast into the ballot box. The Seventeenth Amendment (ratified in 1913), which required the direct election of Senators, dealt another blow to party cohesiveness. So did the direct primary, which came to dominate the nomination of presidential candidates, particularly after 1968.

Modern technology has enabled candidates to appeal to voters directly, through television, computer-assisted mailings, and telephone campaigns, and by quick visits in jet airplanes, all of which have lessened their dependence on party organizations and leaders. The key to these technologies is money, but candidates found they could raise it directly for themselves better than through the party organization. At the same time, interest groups found they could exercise more power over legislative votes by contributing directly to selected candidates rather than to a party.

The habits of voters also changed in this new environment. Party loyalty had been the rule for most of the nineteenth century, but by the last quarter of the twentieth century, one-third of all voters were registered as independents, and even among voters registering with parties, ticket-splitting became the norm.

Many of these changes resulted from laudable reforms and were, in any case, inevitable. No one wants to roll the clock back to the time when party bosses and local 'machines' dominated the political process.

Nevertheless, we need to recognize that the weakening of parties in the electoral arena has contributed to the disintegration of party cohesion among the officials we elect to public office. Members of Congress who owe their election less to their party than to their own endeavours and their own sources of funds have little incentive to co-operate with party leaders in the Congress, much less their party's incumbent in the White House. And the proliferation of congressional committees and subcommittees has increased the disarray. There are now so many that almost every member is the chairman or ranking minority member of at least one committee or subcommittee, with all the political influence, proliferating staffs, publicity, and fund-raising potential needed to remain in office.

EFFECTS

Because the separation of powers encourages conflict between the branches and because the parties are weak, the capacity of the federal government to fashion, enact, and administer coherent public policy has diminished and the ability of elected officials to avoid accountability for governmental failures has grown. More specifically, the problems include:

Brief Honeymoons

Only the first few months of each four-year presidential term provide an opportunity for decisive action on domestic problems. By the second year, congressional incumbents are engrossed in the mid-term election and defer difficult decisions that will offend any important interest group.

The mid-term election usually results in a setback for the President's party that weakens his leadership and increases the stalemate and deadlock in the Congress. After the mid-term election, the government comes close to immobility as the President and Congress focus their energies on the imminent presidential election.

Divided Government

We have had divided government (one party winning the White House and the other a majority in one or both houses of Congress) 60 per cent of the time since 1956 and 80 per cent of the time since 1968, compared to less than 25 per cent of the time from the adoption of the constitution until the Second World War.

This has led to inconsistency, incoherence and even stagnation in national policy. Affirmative policy decisions, as well as the *non*-decisions resulting from frequent deadlocks that block any action at all, are reached by shifting majorities built out of cross-party coalitions that change from one issue to the next.

Divided government in turn reflects the decline in party loyalty and the growing practice of ticket-splitting among the electorate. In 1900 only 4 per cent of all congressional districts were carried by one party's presidential candidate and the other party's candidate for member of the House. By 1984, because of the growth of ticket-splitting, this happened in 44 per cent of all congressional districts.

One of Woodrow Wilson's themes during the campaign of 1912—a time of divided government—was that only party government (with one party successfully bridging the separated powers by winning control of the presidency and both houses of Congress) could carry a coherent programme into effect. The voters in 1912 responded by choosing party government, and Wilson's New Freedom programme was successfully legislated.

Lack of Party Cohesion in Congress

Even in times of united government, disunity persists between the branches—and between and within the two houses of Congress—because many members of both the President's party and the opposition party reject the positions taken by their leaders. Legislators today have less reason to stick with their party's position and more reason to follow the urgings of non-party-political action committees, which provide more of their campaign funds than the party does. The summary rejection of President Reagan's budget in 1986, even by members of his own party in the Republican-controlled Senate, dramatically illustrates the lack of party cohesion in the current political environment. This lack of cohesion induces Presidents and their staffs, as noted above, to conceal important foreign policy initiatives even from the leaders of their own party in Congress.

Loss of Accountability

Divided government and party disunity also lead to diffused accountability. No elected official defends the sum of all the inconsistent policy decisions made by so many shifting cross-party coalitions, and each successfully shifts the blame to others.

Polls show the public is dissatisfied with the governmental institutions—especially Congress and the bureaucracy—that legislate and administer this hodge-podge of policies. But the public seldom holds a party accountable for these failures, and it hardly ever holds individual legislators responsible.

Since the Second World War, 90 per cent of each party's incumbent legislators who sought another term have been re-elected, even in years when their party lost the White House. In 1986 the figure was 97 per cent. Benjamin Franklin's famous maxim, 'We must all hang together, or assuredly we shall all hang separately,' no longer applies to the Members of Congress of either party.

Lack of a Mechanism for Replacing Failed or Deadlocked Government

Presently there is no way between our fixed election dates to resolve basic disagreements between the President and Congress by referring them to the electorate. The only way to remove a failed President is by a House impeachment and Senate trial for 'treason, bribery, or other high crimes and misdemeanors'. And between the fixed election dates there is no way to reorient a Congress in which one or both houses obstruct an important and popular presidential programme.

REMEDIES

In seeking to adjust the constitutional system to modern conditions, we must be careful to preserve its enduring virtues. We must continue to respect the Bill of Rights, protected by an independent judiciary, and we must continue to insist that elected offificials be able to monitor one another's performance and call one another to account.

Consistent with these principles, it should be possible to design improvements that would encourage party cohesion and lessen the deadlock between the executive and legislative branches without sacrificing essential checks and balances. The Committee on the Constitutional System offers the following proposals as sufficiently meritorious to warrant national consideration and debate. Some of these proposals call only for adopting new party rules or statutes, while others would require amendments to the constitution.

<h2 style="text-align:center">PROPOSALS WHICH COMMAND MAJORITY SUPPORT AMONG OUR MEMBERSHIP</h2>

Strengthening Parties as Agents of Cohesion and Accountability

1. *The party presidential nominating convention* The parties should amend their rules for the presidential nominating conventions so as to entitle all winners of the party nominations for the House and Senate, plus the holdover Senators, to seats as uncommitted voting delegates in the presidential nominating convention. This would give the congressional candidates of the party a significant voice in selecting the presidential candidate, increase the loyalties between them in the election campaign, improve cohesion between the President and the legislative incumbents of his party, and tend to make them jointly accountable to the voters in the next election.

2. *Optional straight-ticket balloting* Congress should enact a statute requiring all states to include a line or lever on federal election ballots enabling voters, if they so desire, to cast a straight-line party ballot for a party's candidates for all open federal offices.

A recent survey shows that nineteen states, including Illinois, New York, and Pennsylvania, already have such statutes and that ticket-splitting is less common in those states. This would encourage party loyalty at the voter level and among a party's federal candidates. To the extent that it reduced ticket-splitting, it would lessen the likelihood of divided federal government, while still leaving voters free to split their tickets if they chose.

3. *Public financing of congressional campaigns* Congress should amend the campaign financing laws to create a Congressional Broadcast Fund similar to the existing Presidential Campaign Fund. This fund would be available to each party under a formula similar to that used for the Presidential Campaign Fund, on condition that the party and its candidates expend no

other funds on campaign broadcasts. Half of each party's share would go to the nominees themselves. The other half would go to the party's Senate and House campaign committees, which could apportion the funds among candidates so as to maximize the party's chances of winning a legislative majority.

By requiring candidates to look to the party for a substantial part of their broadcast funds, this proposal would help to build party loyalty and cohesion. It would also provide a constitutional way of limiting expenditures on the largest single component of campaign financing costs.

Improving Collaboration Between the Executive and Legislative Branches

1. *Four-year terms for House members and eight-year terms for Senators, with federal elections every fourth year*   The present system of staggered elections has the effect of pulling the branches apart. Members of the House, who run every two years, feel a political need to demonstrate their independence from the White House, particularly in off-year elections. So do the one-third of the Senators who face an election within two years. Every other time an incumbent in either house runs for re-election, there is no presidential campaign.

The effect is to encourage legislators to distance themselves from the President and from presidential programmes that may involve a difficult, short-term adjustment on the way to a worthwhile, longer-term result.

The constitution could be amended so that the President and members of the House would serve concurrent, four-year terms, and one Senator from each state would be elected for an eight-year term at each presidential election. This would eliminate the present House and Senate elections in the middle of the presidential term. It would lengthen and co-ordinate the political horizons of all incumbents. Presidents and legislators could join to enact necessary measures with the promise of longer-run benefits, without having to worry about an imminent election before the benefits were realized.

With fewer elections, the aggregate cost of campaign financing should go down, and legislators would be less frequently or immediately in thrall to the interest groups on whom they depend for funds. The honeymoon for enacting a President's programme would be longer. With a four-year life for each Congress, the legislative process for the budget and other measures could be made more orderly and deliberate.

Alternatives: If the eight-year term for Senators were deemed too long, the Senate term could be shortened to four years, concurrent with the terms of the President and the House, which would also eliminate the mid-term election. Or, if the Senate would not accept a shortened term, we could keep the present six-year term. This would retain a limited mid-term election (for one-third of the Senate), permitting a partial referendum on government policy, at the cost of shortening the political horizon of one-third of the Senate.

2. *Permitting members of Congress to serve in the cabinet*   The Constitution now bars members of Congress from serving as heads of administrative departments or agencies or holding any other executive-branch position. This provision was intended to prevent the President from dominating Congress by offering executive positions to key legislators. But its principal effect has been to deprive the nation of administrators who would have the confidence of both the executive and legislative branches.

If the barrier were removed from the constitution, Presidents would have the option of appointing leading legislators to cabinet positions, and legislators would have the option of accepting such offers, without being required to give up their seats in Congress. Such ties between the branches might encourage closer collaboration and help to prevent stalemates. They would broaden both the range of talent available to a President in forming his administration and the base of political leadership in the executive branch.

Under such an amendment, of course, a President would not be obliged to appoint any members of Congress to his cabinet, nor would they be obliged to accept.

Woodrow Wilson strongly favoured this amendment, as a means to encourage closer collaboration between the branches. While modern legislators may have less time and incentive to join the cabinet than earlier generations, there is no longer any reason for a constitutional barrier to an experiment that has considerable promise and little risk.

ADDITIONAL PROPOSALS WORTH CONSIDERING

The changes recommended in the previous section command majority support among members of the Committee on the Constitutional System. A number of other ideas have found less than majority support to date, but some members believe they are important enough to deserve further discussion. . . .

Strengthening Party Cohesion and Party Accountability

1. *Encouraging presidential appearances before Congress*   Congress and the President should work out mutually agreeable voluntary arrangements for periodic presidential appearances before major congressional committees. These appearances would be used to present presidential positions and to answer congressional questions about presidential actions and proposals. Such arrangements would be consistent with the provision in Article II that the President 'shall from time to time give to the Congress information on the State of the Union'. They would also encourage greater cohesion between the President and the members of his party in Congress.

2. *Creating a shadow cabinet for the legislative opposition*   Legislators of the party losing the presidential election should organize a 'shadow cabinet'. The party's leaders in each house might alternate annually as leader and spokesman of the shadow cabinet, and the party's chairman or ranking member of the major committees in each house might alternate annually as shadow spokesmen in their particular fields, with their counterparts in the other house serving as deputy spokesmen. The shadow cabinet could co-ordinate party positions on legislative issues and act as party spokesmen before the public.

Reducing the Likelihood of Divided Government

For twenty of the last thirty-two years—and for fourteen out of the last eighteen—the White House and at least one house of Congress have been controlled by opposing parties. Some of the measures suggested above should reduce the likelihood of divided government, but they may be insufficient to eliminate it. If divided government is recognized as the pre-eminent cause of inter-branch conflict and policy stalemate and deadlock, two stronger approaches are worth considering.

1. *Mandatory straight tickets* The first approach is to make straight-ticket voting not merely easier, as suggested above, but compulsory. By constitutional amendment, each party's nominees for President, Vice-President, Senate and House could be placed on the ballot as a single slate, with the voter required to cast his or her vote for one of the party slates in its entirety.

The drawback to this idea is that Americans are strongly committed to voting for the person rather than the party. They would not be easily convinced to sacrifice this freedom in the interest of party loyalty and cohesion.

2. *Sequential elections* The second approach is for Congress to enact a statute providing for sequential elections in presidential years, with the voting for President and Vice-President to be conducted two to four weeks before the voting for members of Congress. Under such a proposal voters would already know, at the time they balloted for members of Congress, which party they have entrusted with the presidency. This would give the newly elected President an opportunity to persuade voters to elect a majority of the same party to Congress and thus give the party a better opportunity to carry out its programme.

The drawbacks here are that in the congressional election Americans might still vote for the person rather than the party. Also, there would probably be a considerable fall-off in the number of voters in the congressional election.

Calling New Elections in the Event of Deadlock or Governmental Failure

If it were possible for a President to call new elections, or for Congress to do so, we would have a mechanism for resolving deadlocks over fundamental policy issues. Indeed, the very existence of such a mechanism would be an inducement to avoid a deadlock that could trigger new elections. It would also make it possible to reconstitute a government that had palpably failed for any other reason.

There are formidable obstacles to incorporating such a device in our present system. Should the President alone, or Congress alone, or both the President and Congress, be empowered to call for new elections? How soon should they follow after the passage of the resolution calling for them? Are we prepared to vote in a month other than November? Should there be full new terms for the winners (perhaps adjusted to the regular January expiration dates), or should they fill just the unexpired terms?

These questions can probably be answered. The real questions are whether we need such a strong device for breaking deadlocks or for removing Presidents who have failed for reasons other than impeachable conduct, and whether it is likely that in a special election the electorate would break the deadlock or would simply re-elect all the incumbents.

Most constitutional democracies employ such a device, and it deserves serious consideration. It is not inconsistent with separated powers, and it might well operate to encourage co-operation between the branches in order to forestall the ordeal of special elections.

10

LEAVE THE CONSTITUTION ALONE

ARTHUR M. SCHLESINGER, JR

There is a revival of interest in fundamental constitutional change. I am not referring to special-interest amendments—proposals, for example, to permit school prayer or to forbid abortion or to require an annually balanced budget. I have in mind rather the rising feeling that we must take a hard fresh look at our government and determine whether its basic structure is adequate to the challenges of the future.

Those calling for such re-examination aren't just academic theoreticians. They include distinguished public servants, persons with long and honourable government experience, like Douglas Dillon and Lloyd Cutler. Without prejudging conclusions, they raise searching questions. In particular, they ask whether the separation of powers hasn't become a crippling disability. The separation, they suggest, leads to legislative stalemate, increases voter frustration and apathy, invites the meddling of single-interest groups and makes it impossible for any party or person to be held accountable for policy. The 'question transcending all immediate issues', Mr Dillon writes, 'is whether we can continue to afford the luxury of the separation of power in Washington' and whether we shouldn't consider 'a change to some form of parliamentary government that would eliminate or sharply reduce the present division of authority between the executive and legislative arms of government'.

These are certainly interesting questions. One wishes the new

Arthur M. Schlesinger, Jr, excerpted from 'Leave the Constitution Alone', in Donald L. Robinson (ed.), *Reforming American Government: The Bicentennial Papers of the Committee on the Constitutional System* (Boulder, Col., and London: Westview, 1985), ch. 7. The essay was originally published in *The Wall Street Journal* (1982), copyright © 1982 Arthur Schlesinger, Jr. Reprinted by permission of Westview Press.

bicentennial Committee on the Constitutional System all luck in exploring them. They aren't new questions. In the 1880s, for example, Senator George Pendleton and Professor Woodrow Wilson argued for movement toward a parliamentary system. After the Second World War Thomas K. Finletter in his closely reasoned book *Can Representative Government do the Job?*—still perhaps the best book on the subject—and Congressman Estes Kefauver proposed modifications of the constitution in the parliamentary direction.

A FUNCTION OF WEAKNESS

The parliamentary system is to be defined by a fusion rather than by a separation of powers. The executive is drawn from the legislative majority and can count on automatic enactment of its programme. No one doubts where responsibility lies for success or failure. But while the parliamentary system formally assumes legislative supremacy, in fact it assures the almost unassailable dominance of the executive over the legislature.

Parliament's superiority over Congress in delivering whatever the executive requests is a function of weakness, not of strength. The no-confidence vote is so drastic an alternative that in Britain, for example, it succeeds in forcing a new general election only two or three times a century.

Churchill made the point to Roosevelt in a wartime conversation. 'You, Mr President,' Churchill said, 'are concerned to what extent you can act without the approval of Congress. You don't worry about your cabinet. On the other hand, I never worry about parliament, but I continuously have to consult and have the support of my cabinet.'

Thus the prime minister appoints people to office without worrying about parliamentary confirmation, concludes treaties without worrying about parliamentary ratification, declares war without worrying about parliamentary authorization, withholds information without worrying about parliamentary subpoenas, is relatively safe from parliamentary investigation and in many respects has inherited the authority that once belonged to absolute monarchy. As Lloyd George told a select committee in 1931, 'Parliament has really no control over the executive; it is a pure fiction.' The situation has not improved in the half century since. Only the other day the *Economist* spoke of 'Whitehall's continuing contempt for Parliament'.

Congress is far more independent of the executive, far more responsive to a diversity of ideas, far better staffed, far more able to check, balance, challenge, and investigate the executive government. Take Watergate as an example. The best judgement is that such executive malfeasance would not have been exposed under the British system. 'Don't think a Watergate couldn't happen here,' writes Woodrow Wyatt, a former British MP. 'You just wouldn't hear about it.'

In a recent issue of the British magazine *Encounter*, Edward Pearce of the *London Daily Telegraph* agrees:

If only Mr Nixon had had the blessing of the British system. . . . Woodward and Bernstein would have been drowned in the usual channels, a D-Notice would have been erected over their evidence, and a properly briefed judge, a figure of outstanding integrity, would have found the essential parts of the tapes to be either not relevant or prejudicial to national security or both. The British system of protecting the authorities is almost part of the constitution.

While American constitutional reformers muse about the virtues of a fusion of powers, British reformers yearn for separation. They want to set parliament free. They want to increase executive accountability. They want a written bill of rights. They have finally achieved standing parliamentary committees and want to increase the professional staffs and extend the powers of investigation and oversight. They want the right to examine witnesses in committee during the consideration of pending legislation. They want a select committee to monitor the intelligence services. And the government, the *Economist* recently reported, 'is faced with an all-party parliamentary coup aimed at seizing from the treasury the appointment and functions of the comptroller and auditor general, and restoring to the House of Commons power over many aspects of government spending'. . . .

Before succumbing to romantic myths of the parliamentary advantage, Americans would be well advised to listen to those who must live with the realities of the parliamentary order. But fortunately, given the nature of the American political tradition, the parliamentary system is an unreal alternative. The thought that in this era of conspicuous and probably irreversible party decay we can make our parties more commanding and cohesive than they have ever been is surely fantasy. Centralized and rigidly disciplined parties, the abolition of primaries, the intolerance of mavericks, the absence of free voting—all such things are against the looser genius of American politics.

One must raise a deeper question: is the difficulty we encounter these days in meeting our problems really the consequence of defects in the structure of our government? After all, we have had the separation of powers from the beginning of the republic. This has not prevented competent Presidents from acting with decision and dispatch. The separation of powers did not notably disable Jefferson or Jackson or Lincoln or Wilson or the Roosevelts. The most powerful plea of this century for a strong national authority—Herbert Croly's *The Promise of American Life*—didn't see the separation of powers as an obstacle to effective government. Why are things presumed to be so much worse today?

It cannot be that, nuclear weapons apart, we face tougher problems than our forefathers. Tougher problems than slavery? the Civil War? the Great Depression? the Second World War? Let us take care to avoid the fallacy of self-pity that leads every generation to suppose that it is peculiarly persecuted by history.

The real difference is that the Presidents who operated the system successfully *knew what they thought should be done*—and were able to persuade Congress and the nation to give their remedies a try. . . .

When the country is not sure what ought to be done, it may be that delay, debate, and further consideration are not a bad idea. And if our leadership is sure what to do, it must in our democracy educate the rest—and that is not a bad idea either. An effective leader with a sensible policy, or even (as in the recent Reagan case) with a less than sensible policy, has the resources under the present constitution to get his way.

I believe that in the main our constitution has worked pretty well. It has ensured discussion when we have lacked consensus and has permitted action when a majority can be convinced that the action is right. It allowed Franklin Roosevelt, for example, to enact the New Deal but blocked him when he tried to pack the Supreme Court. The court bill couldn't have failed if we had had a parliamentary system in 1937. In short, when the executive has a persuasive remedy, you don't need basic constitutional change. When the executive remedy is not persuasive, you don't want constitutional change.

My concern is that this agitation about constitutional reform is a form of escapism. Constitution-tinkering is a flight from the hard question, which is the search for remedy. Structure is an alibi for analytical failure. As Bryce wisely reminds us, 'The student of institutions, as well as the lawyer, is apt to overrate the effect of mechanical contrivances in politics.'

Fascinating as constitutional-tinkering may be, like the Rubik cube, let it not divert us from the real task of statecraft. Let us never forget that politics is the high and serious art of solving substantive problems.

PART II

PRESIDENTIALISM IN LATIN AMERICA

11

THE ANGOSTURA ADDRESS

SIMÓN BOLÍVAR

The continuance of authority in the same individual has frequently meant the end of democratic governments. Repeated
elections are essential in popular systems of government, for
nothing is more perilous than to permit one citizen to retain
power for an extended period. The people become accustomed
to obeying him, and he forms the habit of commanding them;
herein lie the origins of usurpation and tyranny. A just zeal is
the guarantee of republican liberty. Our citizens must with good
reason learn to fear lest the magistrate who has governed them
long will govern them for ever. . . .

   I am thoroughly imbued with the idea that the government
of Venezuela should be reformed; and, although many prominent citizens think as I do, not all of them possess the courage
necessary to recommend publicly the adoption of new principles. This consideration obliges me to take the initiative in a
matter of the greatest importance—a matter in which the utmost
audacity is required—the offering of advice to the councillors of
the people. . . .

   The Venezuelan constitution, although based upon the most
perfect of constitutions from the standpoint of the correctness of
its principles and the beneficent effects of its administration, dif-
fered fundamentally from the North American constitution on
one cardinal point, and, without doubt, the most important
point. The Congress of Venezuela, like the North American
legislative body, participates in some of the duties vested in the

Simón Bolívar, excerpted from 'Address Delivered at the Inauguration of the
Second National Congress of Venezuela in Angostura, February 15, 1819',
in *Selected Writings of Bolivar*, comp. by Vicente Lecuna, ed. by Harold A.
Bierck, Jr, transl. by Lewis Bertrand (published by Banco de Venezuela; New
York: Colonial Press, 1951), ch. 70.

executive power. We, however, have subdivided the executive power by vesting it in a collective body. Consequently, this executive body has been subject to the disadvantages resulting from the periodic existence of a government which is suspended and dissolved whenever its members adjourn. Our executive triumvirate lacks, so to speak, unity, continuity, and individual responsibility. It is deprived of prompt action, continuous existence, true uniformity, and direct responsibility. The government that does not possess these things which give it a morality of its own must be deemed a nonentity.

Although the powers of the President of the United States are limited by numerous restrictions, he alone exercises all the governmental functions which the constitution has delegated to him; thus there is no doubt but that his administration must be more uniform, constant, and more truly his own than an administration wherein the power is divided among a number of persons, a grouping that is nothing less than a monstrosity. . . .

Among the ancient and modern nations, Rome and Great Britain are the most outstanding. Both were born to govern and to be free and both were built not on ostentatious forms of freedom, but upon solid institutions. Thus I recommend to you, Representatives, the study of the British constitution, for that body of laws appears destined to bring about the greatest possible good for the peoples that adopt it; but, however perfect it may be, I am by no means proposing that you imitate it slavishly. When I speak of the British government, I only refer to its republican features; and, indeed, can a political system be labelled a monarchy when it recognizes popular sovereignty, division and balance of powers, civil liberty, freedom of conscience and of press, and all that is politically sublime? Can there be more liberty in any other type of republic? Can more be asked of any society? I commend this constitution to you as that most worthy of serving as model for those who aspire to the enjoyment of the rights of man and who seek all the political happiness which is compatible with the frailty of human nature. . . .

The British executive power possesses all the authority properly appertaining to a sovereign, but he is surrounded by a triple line of dams, barriers, and stockades. He is the head of the government, but his ministers and subordinates rely more upon law than upon his authority, as they are personally responsible;

and not even decrees of royal authority can exempt them from this responsibility. The executive is commander-in-chief of the army and navy; he makes peace and declares war; but parliament annually determines what sums are to be paid to these military forces. While the courts and judges are dependent on the executive power, the laws originate in and are made by parliament. To neutralize the power of the king, his person is declared inviolable and sacred; but, while his head is left untouched, his hands are tied. The sovereign of England has three formidable rivals: his cabinet, which is responsible to the people and to parliament; the senate [sic], which, representing the nobility of which it is composed, defends the interests of the people; and the House of Commons, which serves as the representative body of the British people and provides them with a place in which to express their opinions. Moreover, as the judges are responsible for the enforcement of the laws, they do not depart from them; and the administrators of the exchequer, being subject to prosecution not only for personal infractions but also for those of the government, take care to prevent any misuse of public funds. No matter how closely we study the composition of the English executive power, we can find nothing to prevent its being judged as the most perfect model for a kingdom, for an aristocracy, or for a democracy. Give Venezuela such an executive power in the person of a president chosen by the people or their representatives, and you will have taken a great step toward national happiness. . . .

Although the authority of the executive power in England may appear to be extreme, it would, perhaps, not be excessive in the Republic of Venezuela. Here the Congress has tied the hands and even the heads of its men of state. This deliberative assembly has assumed a part of the executive functions, contrary to the maxim of Montesquieu, to wit: a representative assembly should exercise no active function. It should only make laws and determine whether or not those laws are enforced. Nothing is as disturbing to harmony among the powers of government as their intermixture. Nothing is more dangerous with respect to the people than a weak executive; and if a kingdom has deemed it necessary to grant the executive so many powers, then in a republic these powers are infinitely more indispensable.

If we examine this difference, we will find that the balance of power between the branches of government must be distributed in two ways. In republics the executive should be the stronger, for everything conspires against it; while in monarchies the legislative power should be superior, as everything works in the monarch's favour. The people's veneration of royal power results in a self-fascination that tends greatly to increase the superstitious respect paid to such authority. The splendour inherent in the throne, the crown, and the purple; the formidable support that it receives from the nobility; the immense wealth that a dynasty accumulates from generation to generation; and the fraternal protection that kings grant to one another are the significant advantages that work in favour of royal authority, thereby rendering it almost unlimited. Consequently, the significance of these same advantages should serve to justify the necessity of investing the chief magistrate of a republic with a greater measure of authority than that possessed by a constitutional prince. . . .

[L]et us put aside the triumvirate which holds the executive power and centre it in a president. We must grant him sufficient authority to enable him to continue the struggle against the obstacles inherent in our recent situation, our present state of war, and every variety of foe, foreign and domestic, whom we must battle for some time to come. Let the legislature relinquish the powers that rightly belong to the executive; let it acquire, however, a new consistency, a new influence in the balance of authority. . . .

In separating the executive jurisdiction from that of the legislature by means of well-defined boundaries, it is my intention not to divide but rather to unite these supreme powers through those bonds that are born of independence, for any prolonged conflict between these powers has never failed to destroy one of the contenders. In seeking to vest in the executive authority a sum total of powers greater than that which it previously enjoyed, I have no desire to grant a despot the authority to tyrannize the Republic, but I do wish to prevent deliberative despotism from being the immediate source of a vicious circle of despotic situations, in which anarchy alternates with oligarchy and monocracy.

12

EFFORTS MADE BY VARIOUS LATIN AMERICAN COUNTRIES TO LIMIT THE POWER OF THE PRESIDENT

HARRY KANTOR

It was logical for the victorious military leaders to turn towards the US model in setting up their new governments. Many of the new leaders had lived in France and the United States. Some had fought in the French army, and many were admirers of Jefferson, Washington, and other leaders of the new United States. The leaders of the victorious armies in the new Latin American republics seemed to see the need for a strong executive around which they could unite the varied population in their new republics; yet they wanted to check the power of the new presidents, so they took the US system of checks and balances as their model. They thought they would thus have what they were seeking, a strong executive limited by the power of the other branches of government. . . .

Even while the strong executive ran the governments, there always was a current of opposition to the all-powerful executive, and the large number of constitutions adopted by all of the Latin American states is eloquent testimony to the repeated efforts made to limit him. Whether this has been done effectively in any of the Latin American republics is debatable, but there is no doubt that efforts have been made. This paper is an attempt to describe and evaluate the efforts made by various Latin American countries to limit the power of their chief executives. . . .

Harry Kantor, excerpted from 'Efforts Made by Various Latin American Countries to Limit the Power of the President', in Thomas V. DiBacco (ed.), *Presidential Power in Latin American Politics*, Praeger Special Studies in International Politics and Government (New York: Praeger, 1977), ch. 2. Copyright 1977 Praeger Publishers, Inc. Reprinted by permission of Greenwood Publishing Group Inc., Westport, CT.

NO RE-ELECTION

The most successful check upon the presidents has proved to be the denial of immediate re-election. During the past century the practice of *continuismo* was so prevalent that 'no re-election' became the slogan of the Mexican Revolution and was adopted in almost all of the other republics. By now it is part of most of the constitutions that there is no re-election, and where re-election is permitted, it is usually allowed only after one or two intervening terms. While this does not limit the president during his term of office, it puts a time limit upon how long he remains in office. At present only Paraguay and the Dominican Republic permit immediate re-election. Another such mechanism is the long list of relatives of the president and other government officials who are not allowed to run for president. Both of these schemes are infractions upon true democracy, which demands that voters be allowed to vote for whomever they choose, yet no re-election is a widely held opinion, and does seem to keep power limited in time.

THE URUGUAYAN PLURAL EXECUTIVE

The first really well-thought-out scheme for limiting the power of the president came in Uruguay. There José Batlle y Ordóñez, one of the most remarkable political leaders Latin America has produced, came to power in the first years of the twentieth century. He was a typical caudillo, but he also was a deep political thinker. He thought that all of Uruguay's problems were rooted in the excessive power the country's constitution gave to the president. At that time, the Uruguayan president dominated the legislature and the Supreme Court during his term of office, and then selected a successor, whom he installed in office after a managed election. All that the opposition could do was accept the situation or revolt after the new president was installed. Batlle y Ordóñez decided that the cycle of revolutions, disorder, managed elections, and virtual dictatorship could be ended if the president were stripped of his power. The solution Batlle came up with was the substitution of a plural executive for a president as the chief executive.

Uruguay has twice experimented with the plural executive. The 1919 constitution divided the powers of the president into political affairs and non-political affairs. The president, elected for a four-year term, retained management of foreign affairs, national defence, agriculture, and certain other matters. A nine-member national council of administration, serving a six-year term (with three members elected every two years) controlled the administration of education, health, public works, industrial relations, and the preparation of the budget. Further complicating the system, the political party receiving the second highest vote received one-third of the membership of the council. While this system brought the country's two largest political parties into the government and prevented the president from controlling all of the executive departments, it split the administration in such a way that its functioning was poor when crisis struck. When the world depression of the 1930s affected Uruguay, the system broke down and the president used his control of the armed forces to establish a dictatorship in 1933. The plural executive disappeared with the abrogation of the 1919 constitution.

The strong president, either elected or in power by a *coup d'état*, remained the rule in Uruguay until the president elected in 1950 decided that the terrific competition during presidential election campaigns was harmful to Uruguay. He succeeded in having a constitution containing a plural executive adopted in a referendum, and in 1952 the nine-member National Council of Government became Uruguay's executive. This was a true plural executive, for none of the nine members of the council headed the executive departments, each of which was led by a minister appointed by the national council. As in the previous effort, the minority party was given one-third of the seats and the minority faction of the majority party was given one seat. As the system worked, the nine men exercised the powers normally given to a president in a presidential system, with a majority vote needed for decisions.

This was a very interesting experiment. Unfortunately, the experiment failed, probably because the National Party won control of the majority of the executive council in 1959. This was the first time the National Party had come to power in ninety-three years. It was so accustomed to being in opposition that chaos and indecision marked its years in office. As a very severe economic and social crisis hit the country during these years, the demand grew for a strong president, and in 1967 the plural executive was abolished by a referendum. In reaction to the plural executive, the 1967 constitution created a very strong presidency, took away some of the legislature's power to initiate legislation, and provided for automatic approval of bills under certain conditions when the assembly might fail to act.

The Uruguayan experience with the plural executive demonstrates how strong is the desire to limit the power of the president and yet how powerful is the desire to have a strong president. No other country in Latin America has ever tried this solution.

PARLIAMENTARY SYSTEMS

On the other hand, parliamentary government with a cabinet responsible to the legislature has been tried several times with the hope that this would control omnipotent presidents. The most complete system of cabinet government was in Chile from 1891 to 1925; however, this never worked well because no party ever had a majority in the legislature, and so the 1925 constitution reverted to the presidential system.

A limited constitutional monarchy in Brazil from 1824 to 1889 included a parliamentary system, but the emperor was so powerful that the system was not a true parliamentary system and was dropped after the 1889 revolution, when the presidential system was instituted. In 1961, Brazil faced a constitutional crisis after an elected president suddenly resigned, leaving the presidency to a vice-president of a party representing a minority of the voters. Faced by the possibility of civil war, the legislature stripped the new president of his power by creating a parliamentary system. This new effort failed because, although the powers of the executive rested in a cabinet responsible to the Chamber of Deputies, the president had the power to appoint the prime minister. Thus, the president could, and did, appoint prime ministers who worked to destroy the parliamentary system. In one year things became so bad that the parliamentary system was abolished without ever really having had a chance to demonstrate whether it could work to limit the power of the president.

SEMI- OR QUASI-PARLIAMENTARY SYSTEMS

Some writers about Latin American government refer to semi- or quasi-parliamentary systems because many constitutions have contained clauses under which cabinet ministers can attend meetings of the legislature or be questioned by the legislature, or in which the legislature can vote no confidence in a minister or a cabinet, forcing resignation from office. . . .

In Chile the 1925 constitution did not contain a no-confidence rule, but cabinet members could be impeached by the legislature and have been from time to time. The constitutional crisis that led to the present military dictatorship came, in part, because President Allende several times broke the spirit of the constitution, if not the letter, by not removing impeached ministers. What he did was to shuffle the cabinet posts; thus, the impeached minister remained a member of the cabinet.

Similar clauses appeared in many of the constitutions adopted through the years. In all cases, however, the dominance of the presidency kept these constitutional rules from being really important limitations upon the power of the president. As long as he has had the power to appoint and remove ministers, the presidential system has remained the rule.

LEGISLATIVE APPROVAL OF APPOINTMENTS

Many constitutions have included requirements that the legislature approve certain presidential appointments. This has not been a real check upon the presidents because of the general weakness of the legislatures. Another clause found in Peru, Chile, and some other countries is the rule that a president cannot leave the country without the permission of one or both houses of the legislature. Even when this power is exercised, as it was in Chile in 1969 when the Communist, Socialist, and National Parties combined in the Senate to refuse to allow

President Frei to visit the United States, this is not really a limit on what the president can do within the country.

THE SHARING OF EXECUTIVE POWER

The Costa Rican constitution of 1949 made a determined effort to weaken the relative power of the president by strengthening the legislature and the judiciary, and by requiring that executive power be exercised by a president and his ministers acting together. The constitution specifies those powers to be exercised exclusively by the president, those he must exercise jointly with one of his ministers, and those to be exercised in the name of a council of government, which consists of the president and his ministers meeting formally.

Whatever the intentions of the writers of the constitution, the Costa Rican president remains a strong executive with few limits upon his actions, except for the Supreme Court's power to declare his acts unconstitutional and the legislature's power to refuse him funds. The reason for this is that, although the president needs the counter-signature of a minister or the agreement of the entire cabinet, he always gets this because he appoints the cabinet ministers. Ex-President José Figueres told me that he made a deliberate attempt to strengthen the council of government by refusing at times to make his opinion known and asking the group to make a decision. He never succeeded; instead, the group would wait and refuse to make the decision until it found out his opinion. On occasion, Figueres would turn the office over to a vice-president and go to his farm to give the cabinet a chance to make decisions without him. This also failed, he reported, because a constant stream of cabinet officers kept dropping in to tell him they just happened to be driving by, and asking him what he thought about whatever their problem was. Apparently, the tradition of having the president make all important decisions is too strong to be overcome by a change in the wording of a constitution, especially when the essential features of the presidential system are preserved and the president has the exclusive power to appoint and discharge ministers.

The same scheme is found in the present Venezuelan constitution that divides executive power so that part is exercised by the president alone, part by the president together with his council of ministers, and part by the president counter-signed by a minister. As in Costa Rica, this does not limit the president, as he alone has the power to appoint and remove his ministers.

The president in many of the republics must have a cabinet minister counter-sign all presidential decrees and regulations, but as long as the president appoints and removes his ministers as he sees fit, this is no limitation upon his power.

LEGISLATIVE IMPEACHMENT OF THE PRESIDENT

Another attempt to limit the power of the president, copied from the US constitution, is the power of the legislature to impeach the president, thus removing him from office. Practically all constitutions have this clause. In Panama, during the campaign to elect a new president for the 1968–72 term, the legislative assembly voted to impeach President Marco A. Robles, who immediately used the national guard to prevent further meetings of the assembly. The issue went to the Supreme Court, which by a vote of 8–1 decided that the impeachment was illegal.

In 1950 in Colombia, the Liberal majority of the legislature decided to impeach the president for not preserving law and order during the presidential election campaign. The incumbent president, Mariano Ospina Pérez, immediately used the army to prevent the Congress from meeting. It never met again and thus could not vote the impeachment.

As these examples show, impeachment is not an easy method for removing a president from office. There have been some successful impeachments. In Panama in 1951 and 1955, respectively, Presidents Arnulfo Arias and José Ramón Guizado were impeached, but generally this method has failed to control presidents. . . .

THE CREATION OF INDEPENDENT AGENCIES

Another scheme devised to curtail the power of the president has been to have the constitution or the legislature create independent or semi-independent governmental agencies or institutions that are financed by public funds. Usually, each independent agency is controlled by a board of directors that the president has trouble dominating. In Costa Rica, for example, it takes about three years of a president's term before his appointees are the majority of the directing boards of the autonomous agencies. Since the Costa Rican president has a four-year term, he only really influences the activity of these groups during half of his term in office.

The independent agency has proved to be a real check upon the power of the president where constitutional government is the rule. It hampers the president in that he is not able to force the agency to follow his policy, and in some cases the president of the republic and the directors of the independent agencies have found themselves in open opposition on policy.

There seems to be no logical reason why one organization is set up as an independent agency and another is under the control of the president. In Ecuador, for example, from 1952 to 1956 independent agencies spent from 34 to 44 per cent of the total national budget without any direct control by the president. At that time civil aviation, radio, telegraph, telephones, and the post office were under the minister of public works, while roads in the province of Guayas, many ports, the state railroads, and the drinking water in Manta were controlled by decentralized independent agencies.

OTHER SOLUTIONS ATTEMPTED

In order to end a period of extreme political violence, Colombia, in 1958, devised a system of limiting the president's power known as the 'national front'. This was a method of creating a coalition government in which the presidency alternated between the country's two large parties, and all other positions—legislative, cabinet, bureaucratic, and judicial—were divided equally between the two parties. Thus, there were two very great limitations upon the power of the presidency: the difficulty of getting a majority in the legislature and the need to appoint members of the opposing party to 50 per cent of the cabinet positions. While the Colombian national front system did not win universal support, it succeeded in stopping most of the violence it was created to end. . . .

Most of the constitutions give the president some kind of emergency power which enables him to suspend parts of the constitution and declare a state of siege. This is something that was not taken from the US constitution, and it has been used over and over again to allow presidents to wield unlimited power.

CONCLUSIONS

Is there anything that can be done really to limit the power of the president in Latin America? The experience of the last 150 years seems to demonstrate that power can only be checked by power. The way to limit the power of the president, therefore, is to create competing centres of power. The most important step probably would be to end the French system of local government and, through a system of universal suffrage, allow local bases of power to be created. This would strengthen political parties, and with stronger political parties more responsible presidents could be elected, and responsible oppositions created.

A second step would be to strengthen the legislatures, especially by allowing re-election where this is not allowed. All of the constitutional provisions that prevent legislatures from meeting except for limited periods should be removed from the constitutions. Salaries, staff, and offices should be provided to members of the legislatures. Given the crisis atmosphere surrounding the drive, during recent decades, for more rapid economic development, the executive has been supreme because it had almost a monopoly of technology, skills, and financial resources. Giving some of these to the legislatures would enable them to legislate more effectively and allow them truly to check the president.

The creation of an impartial bureaucracy by utilizing a system of merit appointment for the civil service would also be a check upon the activity of the president. In most of the Latin American republics this has not yet been done.

The need to build up other power centres is of the utmost importance. Political parties, trade unions, business groups, and varied interest groups, if strong and active, would be real forces for limiting the power of the president. An independent press, including radio and television, would help to create more alert public opinion. This is recognized by all of the executives whose power we are talking about limiting. That is why the military dictators and the overpowerful presidents refuse to allow a free press and prevent the growth of strong political parties, trade unions, and interest groups.

Eternal vigilance remains the price of liberty, and it is almost impossible to preserve liberty and limit the power of the executive when the press is shackled, trade unions and political parties are harassed and prevented from functioning, and opposition to the president is looked upon as treason. Until such independent centres of power are created, the omnipotent executive will remain the centre of political power in Latin America.

13

PRESIDENTIALISM IN LATIN AMERICA

SCOTT MAINWARING

Although presidentialism has received insufficient attention in the past few decades, this was not always the case. In several Latin American countries, the desirability of presidentialism was the subject of intense political debate for some decades. In the 1940s and 1950s, many US textbooks on Latin American politics included a chapter on the subject. . . .

In retrospect, one of the flaws in most of these earlier analyses of presidentialism was a failure to differentiate sharply between presidentialism in authoritarian polities and in democracies. Many analyses excluded Chile, Costa Rica, and Uruguay from their generalizations about weak congresses and dominating presidents. This exclusion is telling because these three countries had the most democratic traditions in Latin America. Thus the sharpest distinction probably lies between presidentialism in democratic systems and in authoritarian regimes, rather than between US presidentialism and Latin American presidentialism. Presidents in democracies face a number of similar constraints and opportunities, while presidents in authoritarian regimes function in completely different circumstances. For analysts of presidentialism, it would have been more revealing to compare Chile, Costa Rica, and Uruguay with the United States rather than comparing them with Latin American countries under authoritarian rule, or even with new democracies whose procedures were not yet institutionalized.

Scott Mainwaring, excerpted from 'Presidentialism in Latin America', first published in the *Latin American Research Review*, 25/1 (1990), pp. 157–79 (footnotes and references abridged). Reprinted by permission.

This observation is not meant to suggest that presidentialism in Chile, Costa Rica, and Uruguay[1] was the same as in the United States but rather to argue that the more meaningful difference (authoritarian versus democratic context) may have been misperceived as a result of attempts to write about Latin America as a whole. This point is important because it can suggest conclusions that differ markedly from those drawn by most analysts. Focusing on the subset of Latin American democracies might have led observers to question how strong their presidents really were. My own view is that under democratic conditions, most Latin American presidents have had trouble accomplishing their agendas. They have held most of the power for initiating policy but have found it hard to get support for implementing policy. If my analysis is correct, it points to a significant weakness in democratic presidencies. Robert Dix has made a similar point, characterizing the Colombian presidency as 'dominant in comparison to other institutions of government, yet traditionally weak in its ability to effect policy and carry out its decisions'.[2] . . .

The general belief that presidentialism affords stronger executive power than parliamentary systems is questionable. Presidentialism rests on a balance and separation of powers, but this balance often gives rise to immobilism. Samuel Huntington pointed out that most Americans prefer dispersion of power to concentration of power, but that in underdeveloped countries, some concentration is necessary for effective policy co-ordination and implementation.[3] In presidential systems, it is difficult to attain concentration of powers while preserving democracy. Richard Rose argues that even in the more auspicious US context, presidentialism has not fostered effective policy implementation in recent decades, in part because the balance of powers

[1] Uruguay was a special case because of the deviations from classical presidentialism. Some scholars have argued that Uruguay did not have a presidential system between 1919 and 1933 and from 1951 to 1966 because there was a plural executive.

[2] Robert Dix, 'The Colombian Presidency: Continuities and Change', in Thomas DiBacco (ed.), *Presidential Power in Latin American Politics* (New York: Praeger, 1977), p. 72.

[3] Samuel Huntington, *Political Order in Changing Societies* (New Haven, Conn.: Yale University Press, 1968), pp. 1–32, 93–139.

has led to immobilism.[4] This outcome has been a recurring problem in Latin America. Michael Coppedge has argued that even Venezuela, which politically and economically has fared better than most of Latin America, has experienced frequent periods of immobilism.[5]

Effective executive power is almost indispensable if democracy is to thrive, yet the history of presidential democracies in Latin America has often been one of immobilized executives. Immobilism in turn has often contributed to democratic breakdown. Many scholars have insisted on the importance of strengthening congresses in order to bolster democracy in Latin America, but it may be even more important to create effective executives—a point that has received little attention. Unfortunately, in presidential systems, especially those with fragmented party systems, strengthening congress can exacerbate executive immobilism.

But the combination of presidentialism and a fractionalized multi-party system seems especially inimical to stable democracy. Considerable empirical evidence supports this argument. The world has had relatively few presidential democracies that have endured for twenty-five years or more consecutively: Chile, Colombia, Costa Rica, the United States, Uruguay, and Venezuela.[6] Two of these six countries (Colombia and the United States) have consistently had two-party systems. Costa Rica has generally had a dominant-party system or a two-party system but on occasion has had three relevant parties. In

[4] Richard Rose, 'Government Against Sub-Governments: A European Perspective on Washington', in Richard Rose and Ezra Suleiman (eds.), *Presidents and Prime Ministers* (Washington, DC: American Enterprise Institute, 1981).

[5] Michael Coppedge, 'Strong Parties and Lame Ducks: A Study of the Quality and Stability of Venezuelan Democracy', Ph.D. dissertation (Yale University, 1988).

[6] Colombia might be excluded from the group of long-standing democracies on the grounds that no real competition for executive power took place between 1958 and 1974. Whether Colombia is included or excluded has no bearing on my main argument here. Similarly, Uruguay might be excluded from the set of established presidential democracies because of its plural collegial executive. The exclusion of Uruguay likewise does not affect my argument, except to reinforce the point about the difficulty of establishing stable presidential democracy.

Venezuela the two major parties have dominated electoral competition since 1973, and the system has worked essentially along two-party lines. Uruguay had a dominant-party system or a two-party system for most of its democratic history, although it has moved to a three-party (or two-and-a-half-party) format since the early 1970s. Chile is the only case in the world of a multi-party presidential democracy that endured for twenty-five years or more. The rarity of stable presidential multi-party democracy has generally gone unobserved.

The combination of a fractionalized party system and presidentialism is inconducive to democratic stability because it easily creates difficulties in the relationship between the president and the congress. To be effective, governments must be able to push through policy measures, which is difficult to do when the executive faces a sizable majority opposition in the legislature. Parliamentary systems have institutionalized means of resolving this problem: in most cases, the prime minister can call parliamentary elections, and in all cases, the parliament can topple the government. Minority governments do exist in parliamentary systems, but in most countries, they are the exception and are generally not intended to last for a long time. Presidential systems contain no institutionalized mechanisms for dealing with this situation, and conflict between the executive and the legislature is frequent when different parties control the two branches. A prolonged impasse can result that can have potentially damaging consequences for democratic stability. . . .

To avoid this kind of impasse, a president can pursue one of several options, none of which augurs particularly well for democratic stability. First, the president can attempt to bypass congress, but this course of action can undermine democracy. Opposition parties may claim that the president is violating the constitution and invite military intervention. In Colombia presidents have frequently declared a state of siege as a means of governing without checks and balances. Second, the president can seek constitutional reforms in order to obtain broader powers. Frustrated by the difficulties of getting measures through congress, every Chilean president from Jorge Alessandri to Salvador Allende attempted either to bypass congress or to reform the constitution in order to broaden executive power.

President Eduardo Frei (1964–70) ultimately succeeded in the latter course, but as Arturo Valenzuela and Alexander Wilde have noted, the cost was very high: the erosion of spaces of negotiation and compromise.[7] Similar problems of immobilism led to constitutional reforms broadening presidential powers in Colombia in 1968 and in Uruguay in 1967. Third, the president can attempt to form a coalition government. Coalition or consociational government is possible in presidential regimes, as the Colombian experience indicates, but it is considerably more difficult than in parliamentary regimes. Parliamentary regimes require party coalitions for creating governments when no single party obtains a majority, which means most of the time in most parliamentary systems. Presidential systems rarely include such institutionalized mechanisms for establishing coalition rule.

When presidents are incapable of pushing critical legislation through congress, they often create new state agencies as a means of enhancing their power and accomplishing their agendas. This approach explains part of the endemic expansion of the state apparatus and the tendency to pursue policy through state bureaucracies rather than through congress. Circumventing congress can lead to a vicious cycle: expansion of the state apparatus, even if it means duplication of tasks; congressional resentment at being bypassed, leading to further congressional tendency to impose vetoes; and the encouragement of irresponsible behaviour and clientelism on the part of politicians who have no opportunity to play a major role in the polity. Finally, the president can attempt to buy the support of individual politicians from opposition parties, but this option exists only if the parties are malleable. In this case, even if the president manages to obtain a temporary majority, the effects on institution-building, public morality, and legitimacy can be pernicious. This approach to working out presidential–congressional relations has prevailed in Brazil since 1985, but the egregious corruption and plundering of the state apparatus associated with this practice have taken a high toll.

[7] Arturo Valenzuela and Alexander Wilde, 'Presidential Politics and the Decline of the Chilean Congress', in Joel Smith and Lloyd Musolf (eds.), *Legislatures in Development: Dynamics of Change in New and Old States* (Durham, NC: Duke University Press, 1979), pp. 189–215.

Scholars have debated whether the number of parties in the party system affects democratic stability. One reason for the inconclusive results has been that it matters whether analysts are talking about a multi-party presidential system or a multi-party parliamentary system, a distinction that has been consistently overlooked. The fact that parties must agree to form a government gives parliamentary systems an institutionalized mechanism for dealing with a large number of parties, a mechanism lacking in presidential systems. This observation does not imply that a stable multi-party presidential democracy is impossible, but it certainly is more difficult than a two-party presidential democracy or a multi-party parliamentary system.

If this argument is correct, presidential systems face a serious (and, once again, unstudied) dilemma: whether presidential elections should involve a simple or an absolute majority. Current wisdom in some Latin American countries favours the latter. The argument is that where presidents are narrowly elected with a simple majority, their claim to represent the nation may be tenuous, a situation that can undermine legitimacy. Nevertheless, the costs of having a second round of elections to establish an absolute majority may outweigh the benefits because it might encourage fragmentation of the party system. Stephen Wright and William Riker have shown that in US primaries, absolute majority systems with a second round encourage an increase in the number of candidates,[8] and Maurice Duverger argued earlier that systems with a second round generally favour multi-partism.[9] In many Latin American countries, then, a second round is likely to encourage more candidates to run for president and consequently may foster fractionalization of the party system, with the deleterious implications noted above. . . .

Beyond several rather obvious and sometimes misleading generalizations, we know surprisingly little about the nature of the presidency in Latin America. What are the reaches and limits of presidential power in the democratic systems? As noted

[8] Stephen Wright and William Riker, 'Plurality and Runoff Systems and Numbers of Candidates', paper presented at the World Congress of the International Political Science Association (Washington, DC, August 1988).

[9] Maurice Duverger, *Political Parties: Their Organization and Activity in the Modern State* (London: Methuen, 1954), pp. 239–45.

above, the common tendency to characterize Latin American presidents as all-powerful is misleading. Other actors in the system may lack the power to accomplish their agendas and may be overshadowed by presidents, but this situation does not mean that presidents are omnipotent. Hambloch's title, *His Majesty, the President of Brazil* amuses, captures common perceptions and accurately characterizes the presidency in many authoritarian situations, but it does not apply to Latin American democracies.[10]

Particularly in regard to policy implementation, the weaknesses of Latin America's democratic presidents eclipse their strengths, but in some ways, executives have broad powers. Latin American presidents have devised countless means of partially circumventing legislative vetoes and counteracting immobilism. Their constitutional authority in legislating, appointing officials, and enacting emergency measures generally exceeds that of US presidents. Immobilism may not have caused concentration of power in the executive, but it has encouraged presidents to attempt to expand their powers and weaken the legislative and judicial branches.

[10] Ernest Hambloch, *His Majesty, the President of Brazil* (New York: Dutton, 1936).

14

THE PERILS OF PRESIDENTIALISM

JUAN J. LINZ

As more of the world's nations turn to democracy, interest in alternative constitutional forms and arrangements has expanded well beyond academic circles. In countries as dissimilar as Chile, South Korea, Brazil, Turkey, and Argentina, policy-makers and constitutional experts have vigorously debated the relative merits of different types of democratic regimes. Some countries, like Sri Lanka, have switched from parliamentary to presidential constitutions. On the other hand, Latin Americans in particular have found themselves greatly impressed by the successful transition from authoritarianism to democracy that occurred in the 1970s in Spain, a transition to which the parliamentary form of government chosen by that country greatly contributed.

Nor is the Spanish case the only one in which parliamentarism has given evidence of its worth. Indeed, the vast majority of the stable democracies in the world today are parliamentary regimes, where executive power is generated by legislative majorities and depends on such majorities for survival.

By contrast, the only presidential democracy with a long history of constitutional continuity is the United States. The constitutions of Finland and France are hybrids rather than true presidential systems, and in the case of the French Fifth Republic, the jury is still out. Aside from the United States, only Chile has managed a century and a half of relatively undisturbed constitutional continuity under presidential government—but Chilean democracy broke down in the 1970s.

Parliamentary regimes, of course, can also be unstable, especially under conditions of bitter ethnic conflict, as recent

Juan J. Linz, excerpted from 'The Perils of Presidentialism', *Journal of Democracy*, 1/1 (Winter 1990), pp. 51–69.

African history attests. Yet the experiences of India and of some English-speaking countries in the Caribbean show that even in greatly divided societies, periodic parliamentary crises need not turn into full-blown regime crises and that the ousting of a prime minister and cabinet need not spell the end of democracy itself.

The burden of this essay is that the superior historical performance of parliamentary democracies is no accident. A careful comparison of parliamentarism as such with presidentialism as such leads to the conclusion that, on balance, the former is more conducive to stable democracy than the latter. This conclusion applies especially to nations with deep political cleavages and numerous political parties; for such countries, parliamentarism generally offers a better hope of preserving democracy.

PARLIAMENTARY VS. PRESIDENTIAL SYSTEMS

. . . Two things about presidential government stand out. The first is the president's strong claim to democratic, even plebiscitarian, legitimacy; the second is his fixed term in office. Both of these statements stand in need of qualification. Some presidents gain office with a smaller proportion of the popular vote than many premiers who head minority cabinets, although voters may see the latter as more weakly legitimated. To mention just one example, Salvador Allende's election as president of Chile in 1970—he had a 36.2 per cent plurality obtained by a heterogeneous coalition—certainly put him in a position very different from that in which Adolfo Suárez of Spain found himself in 1979 when he became prime minister after receiving 35.1 per cent of the vote . . . Allende received a six-year mandate for controlling the government even with much less than a majority of the popular vote, while Suárez, with a plurality of roughly the same size, found it necessary to work with other parties to sustain a minority government. Following British political thinker Walter Bagehot, we might say that a presidential system endows the incumbent with both the 'ceremonial' functions of a head of state and the 'effective' functions of a chief executive, thus creating an aura, a self-image, and a set of popular expectations which are all quite different from those associated with a prime minister, no matter how popular he may be.

But what is most striking is that in a presidential system, the legislators, especially when they represent cohesive, disciplined parties that offer clear ideological and political alternatives, can also claim democratic legitimacy. This claim is thrown into high relief when a majority of the legislature represents a political option opposed to the one the president represents. Under such circumstances, who has the stronger claim to speak on behalf of the people: the president, or the legislative majority that opposes his policies? Since both derive their power from the votes of the people in a free competition among well-defined alternatives, a conflict is always possible and at times may erupt dramatically. There is no democratic principle on the basis of which it can be resolved, and the mechanisms the constitution might provide are likely to prove too complicated and aridly legalistic to be of much force in the eyes of the electorate. It is therefore no accident that in some such situations in the past, the armed forces were often tempted to intervene as a mediating power. One might argue that the United States has successfully rendered such conflicts 'normal' and thus defused them. To explain how American political institutions and practices have achieved this result would exceed the scope of this essay, but it is worth noting that the uniquely diffuse character of American political parties —which, ironically, exasperates many American political scientists and leads them to call for responsible, ideologically disciplined parties—has something to do with it. Unfortunately, the American case seems to be an exception; the development of modern political parties, particularly in socially and ideologically polarized countries, generally exacerbates, rather than moderates, conflicts between the legislative and the executive.

The second outstanding feature of presidential systems—the president's relatively fixed term in office—is also not without drawbacks. It breaks the political process into discontinuous, rigidly demarcated periods, leaving no room for the continuous readjustments that events may demand. The duration of the president's mandate becomes a crucial factor in the calculations of all political actors, a fact which . . . is fraught with important consequences. Consider, for instance, the provisions for succession in case of the president's death or incapacity: in some cases, the automatic successor may have been elected separately and may represent a political orientation different from the president's; in other cases, he may have been imposed by the president as his running-mate without any consideration of his ability to exercise executive power or maintain popular support. Brazilian history provides us with examples of the first situation, while Maria Estela Martínez de Perón's succession of her husband in Argentina illustrates the second. It is a paradox of presidential government that while it leads to the personalization of power, its legal mechanisms may also lead, in the event of a sudden mid-term succession, to the rise of someone whom the ordinary electoral process would never have made the chief of state.

PARADOXES OF PRESIDENTIALISM

Presidential constitutions paradoxically incorporate contradictory principles and assumptions. On the one hand, such systems set out to create a strong, stable executive with enough plebiscitarian legitimation to stand fast against the array of particular interests represented in the legislature. In the Rousseauian conception of democracy implied by the idea of 'the people', for whom the president is supposed to speak, these interests lack legitimacy; so does the Anglo-American notion that democracy naturally involves a jostle—or even sometimes a mêlée—of interests. Interest-group conflict then bids fair to manifest itself in areas other than the strictly political. On the other hand, presidential constitutions also reflect profound suspicion of the personalization of power: memories and fears of kings and caudillos do not dissipate easily. Foremost among the constitutional bulwarks against potentially arbitrary power is the prohibition on re-election. Other provisions like legislative advice-and-consent powers over presidential appointments, impeachment mechanisms, judicial independence, and institutions such as the Contraloría of Chile also reflect this suspicion. Indeed, political intervention by the armed forces acting as a *poder moderador* may even be seen in certain political cultures as a useful check on overweening executives. One could explore in depth the contradictions between the constitutional texts and political practices of Latin American presidential regimes; any student of the region's history could cite many examples.

It would be useful to explore the way in which the fundamental contradiction between the desire for a strong and stable executive and the latent suspicion of that same presidential power affects political decision-making, the style of leadership, the political practices, and the rhetoric of both presidents and their opponents in presidential systems. It introduces a dimension of conflict that cannot be explained wholly by socioeconomic, political, or ideological circumstances. Even if one were to accept the debatable notion that Hispanic societies are inherently prone to *personalismo*, there can be little doubt that in some cases this tendency receives reinforcement from institutional arrangements.

Perhaps the best way to summarize the basic differences between presidential and parliamentary systems is to say that while parliamentarism imparts flexibility to the political process, presidentialism makes it rather rigid. Proponents of presidentialism might reply that this rigidity is an advantage, for it guards against the uncertainty and instability so characteristic of parliamentary politics. Under parliamentary government, after all, myriad actors—parties, their leaders, even rank-and-file legislators—may at any time between elections adopt basic changes, cause realignments, and, above all, make or break prime ministers. But while the need for authority and predictability would seem to favour presidentialism, there are unexpected developments—ranging from the death of the incumbent to serious errors in judgement committed under the pressure of unruly circumstances—that make presidential rule less predictable and often weaker than that of a prime minister. The latter can always seek to shore up his legitimacy and authority, either through a vote of confidence or the dissolution of parliament and the ensuing new elections. Moreover, a prime minister can be changed without necessarily creating a regime crisis.

Considerations of this sort loom especially large during periods of regime transition and consolidation, when the rigidities of a presidential constitution must seem inauspicious indeed compared to the prospect of adaptability that parliamentarism offers.

ZERO-SUM ELECTIONS

The preceding discussion has focused principally on the institutional dimensions of the problem; the consideration of constitutional provisions—some written, some unwritten—has
dominated the analysis. In addition, however, one must attend
to the ways in which political competition is structured in
systems of direct presidential elections; the styles of leadership
in such systems; the relations between the president, the political
élites, and society at large; and the ways in which power is exercised and conflicts are resolved. It is a fair assumption that
institutional arrangements both directly and indirectly shape
the entire political process, or 'way of ruling'. Once we have
described the differences between parliamentary and presidential forms of government that result from their differing institutional arrangements, we shall be ready to ask which of the two
forms offers the best prospect for creating, consolidating, and
maintaining democracy.

Presidentialism is ineluctably problematic because it operates
according to the rule of 'winner-take-all'—an arrangement that
tends to make democratic politics a zero-sum game, with all the
potential for conflict such games portend. Although parliamentary elections can produce an absolute majority for a single
party, they more often give representation to a number of parties. Power-sharing and coalition-forming are fairly common,
and incumbents are accordingly attentive to the demands and
interests of even the smaller parties. These parties in turn retain
expectations of sharing in power and, therefore, of having a
stake in the system as a whole. By contrast, the conviction that
he possesses independent authority and a popular mandate is
likely to imbue a president with a sense of power and mission,
even if the plurality that elected him is a slender one. Given such
assumptions about his standing and role, he will find the
inevitable opposition to his policies far more irksome and
demoralizing than would a prime minister, who knows himself to be but the spokesman for a temporary governing coalition rather than the voice of the nation or the tribune of the
people.

Absent the support of an absolute and cohesive majority, a

parliamentary system inevitably includes elements that become institutionalized in what has been called 'consociational democracy'. Presidential regimes may incorporate consociational elements as well, perhaps as part of the unwritten constitution. When democracy was re-established under adverse circumstances in Venezuela and Colombia, for example, the written constitutions may have called for presidential government, but the leaders of the major parties quickly turned to consociational agreements to soften the harsh, winner-take-all implications of presidential elections.

The danger that zero-sum presidential elections pose is compounded by the rigidity of the president's fixed term in office. Winners and losers are sharply defined for the entire period of the presidential mandate. There is no hope for shifts in alliances, expansion of the government's base of support through 'national unity' or 'emergency' grand coalitions, new elections in response to major new events, and so on. Instead, the losers must wait at least four or five years without any access to executive power and patronage. The zero-sum game in presidential regimes raises the stakes of presidential elections and inevitably exacerbates their attendant tension and polarization.

On the other hand, presidential elections do offer the indisputable advantage of allowing the people to choose their chief executive openly, directly, and for a predictable span rather than leaving that decision to the backstage manœuvring of the politicians. But this advantage can only be present if a clear mandate results. If there is no required minimum plurality and several candidates compete in a single round, the margin between the victor and the runner-up may be too thin to support any claim that a decisive plebiscite has taken place. To preclude this, electoral laws sometimes place a lower limit on the size of the winning plurality or create some mechanism for choosing among the candidates if none attains the minimum number of votes needed to win; such procedures need not necessarily award the office to the candidate with the most votes. More common are run-off provisions that set up a confrontation between the two major candidates, with possibilities for polarization that have already been mentioned. One of the possible consequences of two-candidate races in multi-party systems is that broad coalitions are likely to be formed (whether in run-offs or in pre-election manœuvring) in which extremist parties gain undue influence. If significant numbers of voters identify strongly with such parties, one or more of them can plausibly claim to represent the decisive electoral bloc in a close contest and may make demands accordingly. Unless a strong candidate of the centre rallies widespread support against the extremes, a presidential election can fragment and polarize the electorate.

In countries where the preponderance of voters is centrist, agrees on the exclusion of extremists, and expects both rightist and leftist candidates to differ only within a larger, moderate consensus, the divisiveness latent in presidential competition is not a serious problem. With an overwhelmingly moderate electorate, anyone who makes alliances or takes positions that seem to incline him to the extremes is unlikely to win, as both Barry Goldwater and George McGovern discovered to their chagrin. But societies beset by grave social and economic problems, divided about recent authoritarian regimes that once enjoyed significant popular support, and in which well-disciplined extremist parties have considerable electoral appeal, do not fit the model presented by the United States. In a polarized society with a volatile electorate, no serious candidate in a single-round election can afford to ignore parties with which he would otherwise never collaborate.

A two-round election can avoid some of these problems, for the preliminary round shows the extremist parties the limits of their strength and allows the two major candidates to reckon just which alliances they must make to win. This reduces the degree of uncertainty and promotes more rational decisions on the part of both voters and candidates. In effect, the presidential system may thus reproduce something like the negotiations that 'form a government' in parliamentary regimes. But the potential for polarization remains, as does the difficulty of isolating extremist factions that a significant portion of the voters and élites intensely dislike. . . .

PARLIAMENTARISM AND POLITICAL STABILITY

This analysis of presidentialism's unpromising implications for democracy is not meant to imply that no presidential democracy can be stable; on the contrary, the world's most stable democracy—the United States of America—has a presidential constitution. Nevertheless, one cannot help tentatively concluding that in many other societies the odds that presidentialism will help preserve democracy are far less favourable.

While it is true that parliamentarism provides a more flexible and adaptable institutional context for the establishment and consolidation of democracy, it does not follow that just any sort of parliamentary regime will do. Indeed, to complete the analysis one would need to reflect upon the best type of parliamentary constitution and its specific institutional features. Among these would be a prime ministerial office combining power with responsibility, which would in turn require strong, well-disciplined political parties. Such features—there are of course many others we lack the space to discuss—would help foster responsible decision-making and stable governments and would encourage genuine party competition without causing undue political fragmentation. In addition, every country has unique aspects that one must take into account—traditions of federalism, ethnic or cultural heterogeneity, and so on. Finally, it almost goes without saying that our analysis establishes only probabilities and tendencies, not determinisms. No one can guarantee that parliamentary systems will never experience grave crisis or even breakdown.

In the final analysis, all regimes, however wisely designed, must depend for their preservation upon the support of society at large—its major forces, groups, and institutions. They rely, therefore, on a public consensus which recognizes as legitimate authority only that power which is acquired through lawful and democratic means. They depend also on the ability of their leaders to govern, to inspire trust, to respect the limits of their power, and to reach an adequate degree of consensus. Although these qualities are most needed in a presidential system, it is precisely there that they are most difficult to achieve. Heavy reliance on the personal qualities of a political leader—on the virtue of a statesman, if you will—is a risky course, for one never knows if such a man can be found to fill the presidential office. But while no presidential constitution can guarantee a Washington, a Juárez, or a Lincoln, no parliamentary regime can guarantee an Adenauer or a Churchill either. Given such unavoidable uncertainty, the aim of this essay has been merely to help recover a debate on the role of alternative democratic institutions in building stable democratic polities.

15

IDEAS AND ATTEMPTS AT REFORMING THE PRESIDENTIALIST SYSTEM OF GOVERNMENT IN LATIN AMERICA

CARLOS SANTIAGO NINO

Among the approximately 200 constitutions with which Latin American countries have experimented—indeed an over-production in this branch of industry—there have been some relevant variations and some different approaches to parliamentarism within a general presidentialist trend. In general, the first constitutional movement in the region consisted of adopting the United States' system with certain modifications addressed at giving the presidency even more strength. To put it another way, the trend was to ascribe more powers to the president with less parliamentary control and to extend the term of office, though with a prohibition on re-election. Afterwards, a contrary movement for attenuating the strength of the president evolved in different countries at various times.

Brazil provides a remarkable case [see Chapter 16 in this volume—Ed.]. . .

Venezuela also adopted a similar attenuation of the presidentialist system. The constitution currently in force, adopted in 1961, calls for many of the powers of the president, such as declaring a state of emergency or negotiating loans, to be exerted in the Council of Ministers. In actual practice, however, the functions of that Council have not been very relevant because the alternation between the two main parties (ADECA and COPEI) has coincided with a similar change in parlia-

Carlos Santiago Nino, excerpted from 'Transition to Democracy, Corporatism and Constitutional Reform in Latin America', *University of Miami Law Review*, 44/1 (September 1989), pp. 129–64. Copyright © 1989 *University of Miami Law Review*. Reprinted by permission.

mentary majority. Thus, the president was never limited by ministers that were independent from him because of their parliamentary connections. In the reform of 1983, another element of parliamentarism was introduced requiring that the president present in the first year of his term of office a programme of social and economic development to be approved by both Houses in a joint session.

A weak system of censure also exists in Costa Rica, whose constitution of 1949 establishes that the ministers may be interpellated by the legislative assembly and may even be censured by two-thirds of the votes of the members who are present if they are found guilty of illegal or unconstitutional acts or acts which cause manifest harm to public powers.

In Uruguay, the constitution of 1966, which has returned to the essentials of the constitution of 1942 after abandoning the collegiate system of government which was in force since 1952, also includes some elements of parliamentarism. The president exercises his executive power with the agreement of the council of ministers, or he may delegate to the appropriate minister. The House may interpellate the ministers, and the general assembly may censure them. Parliament may be dissolved if it affirms by three-fifths of its votes the censure of a minister that the president opposed. In such a case, the president may call for new parliamentary elections so that the electorate arbitrates the conflict.

The system established in Peru by the 1979 constitution goes even further in the parliamentary direction. The president is the chief of state and personifies the nation. He has the power to formulate the general political direction of government, but he must appoint a chief of cabinet who serves as the president of the council of ministers. This species of prime minister proposes to the president the names of the other ministers and presides over meetings of the council of ministers. He has few other relevant powers, however, because most executive functions, including control of the administration, are concentrated in the president. The council of ministers has the functions, among others granted by law, of approving the projects that the president sends to congress, approving legislative decrees, and deliberating over public issues. The house of deputies may affect the political responsibility of the council of ministers or of individual ministers through a vote of censure or no confidence by more than half of the members. The president of the Republic may dissolve the house of deputies if it has censured three councils of ministers. In such cases, the president must hold elections within thirty days.

In Chile, a kind of parliamentary system was in force from 1891 to 1924. The precedent for this system was found in the constitution of 1833, which granted to congress the power to approve periodically some acts of the executive, particularly with regard to expenditures and taxes. Successive reforms led to more limitations of the administration in favour of congress. In 1891, after a conflict over the budget, parliament deposed President Balmaceda, and imposed a parliamentary system simply by full enforcement of all the previous reforms. For instance, the impeachment of ministers by accusation of the house of representatives before the senate was greatly facilitated. This period of Chilean parliamentarianism was characterized by a strong tendency of the plurality of political parties to conciliate and negotiate. It was also a period of stability and respect for legal guarantees of individual rights.

But in 1925, after the forceful termination of congress, a new constitution was enacted establishing a presidentialist system. According to this constitution, the president is elected by the people if he is favoured by more than 50 per cent of the votes, otherwise congress chooses between the two candidates achieving the highest number of votes. The president assumed a large number of powers which were further expanded by the reforms of 1934 and 1970. Indeed, they even granted him the ability to enact decrees with the force of law and to take most economic measures on his own. It is obvious that this plethora of powers and the attempts to exert them might collide with the existing consensus, as occurred under President Allende.

Quite recently, most Chilean political parties formed a commission of constitutional lawyers which analysed the defects of the Chilean presidentialist system—blockages between the parties, the inability of parliament to control the executive, lack of representation due to the multiplicity of parties, and so forth. The commission proposed a plan which would establish a mixed system with a president as chief of state and a prime minister as chief of government, with the latter acting in conformance to a programme approved by the house of deputies. The house may also censure the ministers in a constructive modality. The proposed system also differentiates the functions of both houses of congress so that the senate functions as a review chamber.

A mixed system of government was adopted by Haiti in 1987, closely following the scheme of the French constitution. Most other Latin American countries have strong presidentialist regimes. One extreme version, established by the Mexican constitution of 1917, is still in force.

In the case of Argentina, the constitution presently in force, enacted in 1853, also established a strong presidentialist regime modelled after the United States. But it went even further by providing a rather long term for the president—six years without re-election—excluding the requirement that cabinet members be confirmed by the Senate and granting to the president wide powers, which have been much abused, concerning declaration of a state of siege and intervention in the provinces.

President Perón promoted the enactment of a new constitution in 1949 through a process whose legitimacy was contested by the opposition. This constitution, which amply recognized social rights, further accentuated the presidentialist system, providing for the direct election of the president, allowing the possibility of his re-election and granting to him certain powers, such as declaring a state of alarm and emergency without the intervention of congress. The ensuing military regime annulled Perón's constitution and re-established the 1853 constitution. In 1957, a constitutional convention was elected, with the proscription of the Peronist Party. Its only contribution was the introduction of a clause concerning social rights, which is still in force.

In 1972, a military government decreed reforms to the constitution that remained in force during the constitutional government, which lasted from 1973 to 1976. Among other things, it shortened the presidential term to four years, allowed re-election, unified all the electoral processes, and improved some parliamentary mechanisms. During that Peronist government, an official proposal for reforming the constitution, including the introduction of a prime minister, was never carried out.

In 1986, President Alfonsín requested an advisory body, the

Council for the Consolidation of Democracy, to study a possible revision to the 1853 constitution. The Council issued two reports, one in 1982 and one in 1987, proposing, among other things, the adoption of a mixed system of government [see Chapter 21 in this volume—Ed.]. The reports also sought to differentiate further the functions of both houses of congress, to adopt mechanisms of direct popular participation, to strengthen federalism, and to recognize some social rights. The ruling Radical Party adopted these proposals, and they engaged in conversations with opposition parties, mainly the Peronist, to achieve the necessary consensus for initiating the formal procedures of constitutional reform. The electoral confrontation which occurred during the presidential elections of 14 May 1989 prevented the achievement of a consensus among the parties on this issue. Thus, the same factors which contribute to the weakness of the presidential system—particularly political competition among parties—have stopped its reform.

16

PRESIDENTIALISM AND PARLIAMENTARISM IN BRAZIL

BOLÍVAR LAMOUNIER

Unlike all other Latin American countries, Brazil retained the monarchical form of government upon independence in 1822. Under King Dom Pedro II (1840–89), the country thus came to know a parliamentary form of government. Historians disagree, however, on how parliamentary Brazil really was at that time, given the oligarchical character of the political system and the important powers the king reserved for himself. With the establishment of the republic in 1889, parliamentary sentiment gradually declined but never disappeared completely. The existence of a parliamentary 'dissidence' partly explains why parliamentary proposals have often come to the fore—most notably during the crisis of 1961 which led to a brief parliamentary interlude (1961–3), and again since 1986 when a Constitutional Congress was convened in order to reorganize the country's institutions after twenty-one years of military rule.

The arguments for presidentialism can be divided into three categories. There are, first, the classical arguments according to which a fixed-term presidency provides greater stability and programmatic unity in the federal government. Second, it is argued that, after 100 years, there is an identifiable presidentialist 'tradition' and—more importantly—that this tradition is congruent with the style of authority embedded in the country's political culture. It is also held to be congruent with features of Brazil's institutional structure, such as federalism, bicameralism, and especially the fact that Brazilian federalism has led to an overrepresentation of the poorer and less populous states in the lower chamber. Thus the strong presidency is the 'progressive' counterweight to the 'conservative' Chamber of Deputies. The third and most recent argument is that resistance to military rule was closely linked to the idea of direct presidential elections; the huge mobilization of 1984, called *diretas-já* or 'direct elections now', was the symbolic climax. Redemocratization became virtually synonymous with the voters' right to choose a president with full powers, and hence a shift to parliamentary government would be regarded as a fraud with immense risks for the very legitimacy of democratic government.

The arguments favouring parliamentarism fit the same three categories. First, there is the classical argument that the institutional flexibility of parliamentary government avoids the escalation of political crises into fully-fledged institutional crises that are likely to lead to structural breakdown and dictatorship. The Brazilian case provides ample evidence for this argument. In particular, the lack of fit between fixed presidential terms and 'real' political time has had dangerous consequences. For example, President Getúlio Vargas's attempts to retain his office resulted in the *Estado Novo* dictatorship in 1937 and in his removal from office by the military in 1945 (so that regular elections could be held). Less visible but no less dangerous have been the crises caused by presidents who lost virtually all authority early in their terms, like João Figueiredo around 1982 and José Sarney after the failure of his anti-inflationary plan in 1986.

The second set of arguments concerns the so-called 'presidentialist tradition'. Called upon to reorganize the country after twenty-one years of military rule, the Constitutional Congress (1986–8) provided the opportunity for a thorough re-examination of the republic's first century. Some major exceptions to this tradition came to light. The period known as the First Republic (1889–1930) hardly qualifies as a regular presidential democracy because of its highly oligarchical character. Theoretically chosen by direct elections, the President was in fact the delegate of the country's regional oligarchies. In nine of the eleven direct elections during this period, there was no true competition at all; only in the last election (1930) did the number of voters reach 5 per cent of the total population. These figures compare unfavourably even with the nineteenth-century monarchy when some 10–12 per cent of the non-slave population did go to the polls. From 1930 on, as the electorate expanded, the crisis-prone nature of Brazilian presidentialism became evident. There were three major violent interventions leading to authoritarian rule: the revolution of 1930, the Vargas dictatorship of 1937, and the military coup of 1964. Between 1945 and 1964, three of the five presidents were unable to finish their terms of office: re-elected in 1950 but once again threatened with removal from office in 1954, Vargas committed suicide; Janio Quadros, alleging that he did not have sufficient congressional co-operation, resigned in 1961; and João Goulart was deposed by a military coup in 1964, fifteen months after a plebiscite had ended the parliamentary interlude and had conferred full presidential powers back on him. On the basis of this record, a growing number of Brazilians have been coming to the conclusion that the presidentialist 'tradition' is not only very shallow but also dangerous to democracy.

The above re-examination has been reinforced by a third set of contemporary arguments focusing on the link between presidentialism and ungovernability. The idea that democratic legitimacy is linked with a charismatic president entrusted by the voters with a major mandate for change is an extrapolation from only a single case—that of Vargas's 1930–45 presidency—and not even a purely democratic case. Vargas was indeed a superpresident, and left government in 1945 as an extremely popular leader because this was a time of nation- and state-building, of a growing public sector, and (in spite of dictatorial rule) of expanding citizenship rights—in short, a time of modernization and progress. Under Brazil's contemporary conditions —those of a mass society with sharp income inequalities and extremely high inflation rates—the probability that such a superpresident will again emerge and will remain popular for long periods appears to be extremely low. As in Alfonsín's and Menem's Argentina, what we see today is a sharp and quick erosion of presidential popularity—and hence presidential authority—leading to institutional instability and ungovernability.

As suggested above, the parliamentarist idea has distant roots in Brazilian history, but it has grown remarkably since the mid-1980s. The Constitutional Congress defeated the parliamentarist proposal by 344 to 212 votes in March 1988, but it also decided, in one of the 'transitional clauses' of the new constitution, that a plebiscite will be called to settle the matter in 1993. Hence there is a clear constitutional mandate that the issue must be subjected to further examination. Conventional opinion polls do not reflect the evolving public debate very well because of the inevitably large number of 'don't knows' on such a complex institutional question. Results have often shown roughly 60–40 margins in favour of presidentialism—a meagre majority if we recall that presidentialists always invoke a deeply rooted 'tradition'. At the élite level, there are clear indications of a growing preference for parliamentarism. The 344–212 vote in the Constitutional Congress can be cited as evidence of this. Considering that the presidential option was favoured by the incumbent president (Sarney) and by the leaders of the two largest parties (which nominally accounted for 70 per cent of the seats at the beginning of the Congress in late 1986), the 212 votes cast for parliamentarism are very impressive.

If parliamentarism prevails in the 1993 plebiscite, which model of parliamentarism is likely to be adopted? Here the presidentialist arguments do carry some weight. Probably impressed by the demand for direct elections in recent years, most parliamentarists favour an adaptation of the French semi-presidential (or semi-parliamentary) model—albeit with a considerably stronger parliamentary component. For instance, the proposal defeated in March 1988 makes explicit provision for both a popularly elected head of state (president of the Republic) and a head of government (prime minister) approved by and accountable to the chamber of deputies; the president cannot freely appoint or dismiss the prime minister. In this respect, the Brazilian formula is more parliamentary than the Gaullist constitution. But the president *must* be chosen by direct elections and retains substantial formal prerogatives (notably as Supreme Commander of the Armed Forces) as well as symbolic functions (as the final 'arbiter' in the governmental structure). This French-inspired parliamentary model may evolve further in the next few years, but it is likely that parliamentarist proposals will retain at least minor elements of presidentialism.

PART III

SEMI-PRESIDENTIALISM AND OTHER INTERMEDIATE FORMS

17

THE BAYEUX MANIFESTO

CHARLES DE GAULLE

The nation and the French Union are still awaiting a constitution which is made for them and of which they can fully approve. Actually, although we may regret that the structure remains to be built, everyone certainly agrees that a success slightly postponed is more valuable than a quick, but imperfect, achievement.

In the course of a period which does not exceed twice a man's lifetime, France was invaded seven times and was governed by thirteen different regimes—to the detriment of our unfortunate people. Because of so many upheavals, poison has accumulated in our public life, and this has had an intoxicating effect on our old Gallic inclination to dissension and strife.

The unprecedented trials that we have just lived through have obviously only aggravated this state of affairs. Because of the present world situation in which the powers between which we find ourselves confront each other behind opposing ideologies, we must not permit the element of impassioned confusion to enter our internal political struggles. In short, the rivalry between the parties betrays one of our fundamental characteristics—that of always questioning everything and thus too often obscuring the highest interests of the country. This is an obvious fact which is based on the national temperament, the vicissitudes of history, and the present turmoil; but it is indispensable to the future of our country and of democracy that our governmental institutions take this fact into consideration and protect themselves, in order to preserve respect for the

Charles de Gaulle, excerpted from 'The Bayeux Manifesto' [address delivered 16 June 1946], in Arend Lijphart (ed.), *Politics in Europe: Comparisons and Interpretations* (Englewood Cliffs, NJ: Prentice-Hall, 1969), ch. 11. French text copyright © French Press and Information Services. Translation © 1969 Eva Tamm Lijphart.

laws, the cohesion of the governments, the efficiency of the administration, and the prestige and authority of the state. . . .

To be sure, it is the very essence of democracy that opinions are expressed, and that they endeavour, by means of the right to vote, to guide public action and legislation accordingly. But all principles and all experience also require the powers of the state—legislative, executive, and judicial—to be clearly separated and well balanced, and a national arbitration— capable of maintaining the highest degree of continuity in the midst of intrigues—to be established above political contingencies.

It is clearly understood that the final vote on the laws and the budgets belongs to an assembly elected by universal and direct suffrage. But the first actions of such an assembly do not necessarily involve perspicacity and complete serenity. Therefore it is necessary to give to a second assembly, elected and composed in a different way, the function of examining publicly that which the first has taken under consideration, of formulating amendments, and of proposing plans. . . .

It goes without saying that the executive power cannot emanate from a parliament composed of two chambers and exercising legislative power without the danger of leading to a confusion of powers in which the government would soon be reduced to nothing but a gathering of delegations. In the present period of transition it was undoubtedly necessary for the constituent National Assembly to elect the president of the provisional government because, with a clean slate, there was no other acceptable method of selection. But this can only be a temporary arrangement. Truly, the unity, the cohesion, and the internal discipline of the French government must be sacred, or else the very leadership of the country will rapidly become powerless and disqualified.

But how could this unity, this cohesion, and this discipline be maintained in the long run, if the executive power emanated from the other power, with which it must be in balance, and if each member of the government, which is collectively responsible to the entire national representation, held his position solely as the delegate of a party?

Hence the executive power ought to emanate from the chief of state, placed above the parties, elected by a body which includes the parliament but which is much larger and is composed in such a manner as to make him the president of the French Union, as well as of the Republic. The chief of state must have the responsibility to reconcile, in the choice of men, the general interest with the direction given by the parliament; he must have the task of appointing the ministers, and first, of course, the premier, who will have to direct the policy and the work of the government; the chief of state must have the function of promulgating laws and issuing decrees, because it is towards the state as a whole that these obligate the citizens; he must have the task of presiding over meetings of the government and of exercising that influence of continuity there which is indispensable to a nation; he must serve as arbiter above political contingencies, either normally through the council or, in moments of grave confusion, by inviting the country to make known its sovereign decision through elections; he must have the duty, if the Fatherland should be in danger, to be the guarantor of the national independence and of the treaties concluded by France.

18

A NEW POLITICAL SYSTEM MODEL: SEMI-PRESIDENTIAL GOVERNMENT

MAURICE DUVERGER

In 1970, the idea was conceived of comparing the French political system established between 1958 and 1962 with that of the other countries in Europe where a president of the republic, elected by universal suffrage and given personal powers, co-exists with a government resting on the confidence placed in it by parliament. At the same time it was suggested that these forms of government intermediary between presidential and parliamentary systems should be called 'semi-presidential'. In addition to that of Paris, there were then five: four operating in Finland, Austria, Ireland, and Iceland, with the last having operated in Germany from 1919 to 1933 under the Weimar Republic. Since then, another has been set up in Portugal by the constitution of 1975. . . .

The concept of a semi-presidential form of government, as used here, is defined only by the content of the constitution. A political regime is considered as semi-presidential if the constitution which established it combines three elements: (1) the president of the republic is elected by universal suffrage; (2) he possesses quite considerable powers; (3) he has opposite him, however, a prime minister and ministers who possess executive and governmental power and can stay in office only if the parliament does not show its opposition to them. . . .

THE DIVERSITY OF SEMI-PRESIDENTIAL PRACTICES

Constitutions which lay down semi-presidential governments are relatively homogeneous. It will be seen that they show con-

Maurice Duverger, excerpted from 'A New Political System Model: Semi-Presidential Government', *European Journal of Political Research*, 8/2 (June 1980), pp. 165–87 (footnotes omitted). Reprinted by permission of Kluwer Academic Publishers.

siderable differences with regard to the powers of the head of state. These differences, however, remain secondary in relation to the general physiognomy of the system. They are far less important than the variety of political practices, which is the essential feature revealed by comparative analysis of the seven countries concerned. Similarity of rules, diversity of games: such is the two-fold aspect of the pleiad formed by the seven countries to which the model applies. In three of them, the president is in practice a figurehead; in one, he is all-powerful; in the other three, he shares authority with the prime minister.

Three Countries with a Figurehead Presidency: Austria, Ireland and Iceland

The constitutions of Austria, Ireland, and Iceland are semi-presidential. Political practice is parliamentary. Although elected by universal suffrage and endowed with personal powers by right of law, the head of state normally behaves in each of these countries like the modern Italian and German presidents or like the queen of England: that is to say, he ratifies all the decisions which the government puts forward to him, his only real prerogative being in his choice of the prime minister, in so far as his choice is not dictated by the result of the elections. However, several differences between the three countries can be observed. In practice, the president uses his personal powers more in Ireland than in Iceland, and more in Austria than in Ireland. . . .

A Country with an All-powerful Presidency: France

Amended in 1962 by the introduction of universal suffrage for the presidential election, the French constitution of 1958 does not give great personal powers to the President of the Republic, except in its Article 16 which allows him to be a veritable temporary dictator in exceptional circumstances: if 'the institutions of the Republic, the independence of the nation, the integrity of its territory or the fulfilment of its international commitments are seriously and directly threatened and if the normal operation of the constitutional Public Powers is interrupted'. These conditions are not easily found together, particularly the second, which presupposes an insurrection, an invasion, or an atomic attack. Article 16 has been invoked only once, in 1961, after the Algerian military coup of General Challe. It can be disregarded, although much ink has been spilt over its symbolic value.

Apart from Article 16, the President of the French Republic can make decisions on his own, without the counter-signature of the Prime Minister, and without the agreement of the government or of the parliamentary majority, in four cases only: (1) to dissolve the National Assembly, with no further dissolution possible within the same year; (2) to refer to the Constitutional Council laws or international commitments which he judges to be opposed to the constitution; (3) to appoint three members and the president of the Constitutional Council, on the expiry of the term of office of their predecessors; (4) to address messages to parliament.

Furthermore, the President can refuse his signature to the ordinances and decrees discussed in the Council of Ministers. The ordinances are texts having the force of law, adopted by the government, which is authorized to do so by a plenipotentiary law. The decrees concern the appointment of senior officials: Counsellors of State and Counsel-Masters at the Audit Office, prefects, ambassadors, generals, rectors, and directors of central administrations. All the other decrees can be made by the Prime Minister on his own, for he has executive and statutory power. As for the enactments made by parliament, the President is forced to promulgate them after a fixed period, during which he can refer them should he so wish to the Constitutional Council. He can also send them back to the House for a second reading; this decision is subject, however, to a counter-signature, that is to say it cannot be taken without the agreement of the Prime Minister. The President can also refuse to resort to a referendum even though he is asked to do so by the government or parliament. He cannot have recourse to the referendum, however, without the initiative of one or the other.

It will be noted that the principal powers of the President of the French Republic have a spasmodic character. Apart from participation in the appointment of senior officials, they are not, like legislative and governmental powers, normal prerogatives in general use, but exceptional powers which can be used only infrequently. Furthermore, the majority are not powers of decision. They tend either to prevent a decision in order to submit it to a fresh examination and have its legitimacy checked, or to submit the decision to the French people (dissolution, referendum). They correspond to the concept of arbitration, as referred to in Article 5 of the constitution.

In practice, the French President exerts much greater powers. On 31 January 1964, General de Gaulle interpreted the constitution in a highly debatable manner, by proclaiming 'that the indivisible authority of the State is entrusted completely to the president by the people who elected him, that there existed no other authority, either ministerial, civil, military or judiciary which has not been conferred and was not being maintained by him, and finally that it was his duty to adapt the supreme domain, which is his alone, to fit in with those, the control of which he delegates to others'. These fine phrases fail to take into account that the National Assembly is elected by the people, like the President, and that like him it is a repository of national sovereignty. They ignore the fact that no organ of the state, even though it holds supreme power, has the right to define its own competence and that of the others in relation to itself, since both are laid down by the constitution, which must be observed by all. They also ignore the fact that the government and its head must keep the confidence of the parliamentary deputies in order to remain in office and to exercise their powers, which limits the choice of the President, and the fact that the latter cannot dismiss the Prime Minister, as the General himself had stated to Paul Reynaud.

However, General de Gaulle's successors have exercised almost the same powers as he did. They have exercised directly the prerogatives conferred on them by the constitution. They have exercised indirectly the prerogatives of their prime ministers and governments, by reducing the latter to obedience. They have thus become supreme heads of the executive and real heads of the government. . . .

Three Countries with a Balanced Presidency and Government: The Weimar Republic, Finland, and Portugal

Semi-presidential constitutions lay down a governmental dyarchy. By establishing a president put into office by universal suffrage and endowed with personal powers alongside a prime minister and a government resting on parliament and charged with executive power, such constitutions introduce dualism into the heart of the state. This dualism, however, remains purely apparent in four cases out of seven, as the president is confined to symbolic functions in Iceland, Ireland, and Austria, while the prime minister in France is reduced to the role of chief of staff. In contrast, dualism operates or has operated in a real sense in Finland, Portugal, and the Weimar Republic. . . .

THE ANALYTICAL MODEL OF
SEMI-PRESIDENTIAL FORMS OF GOVERNMENT

As an analytical model, the purpose of the concept of semi-presidential government is to explain why relatively homogeneous constitutions are applied in radically different ways. It has only four parameters: the actual content of the constitution; the combination of tradition and circumstances; the composition of the parliamentary majority; and the position of the president in relation to this majority. . . .

A scale of semi-presidential regimes can be drawn up according to the powers which the constitution confers on the president. The prerogatives of the head of state are depicted in the first column of Figure 1, in descending order from Finland to Ireland; the irregular spaces give a (very approximate) idea of the magnitude of the differences. Juxtaposed (in the second column of Figure 1) is a scale of the powers in fact exercised in the countries concerned. Comparison of the two is revealing.

It shows two aberrant cases, those of France and Iceland. The French president exercises in practice much stronger powers than his counterparts, although very few are granted him by the constitution, since he appears sixth in order, or the penultimate, in this respect. In contrast, the Icelandic president appears second with regard to legal powers, just behind his Finnish colleague, but comes last with regard to prerogatives actually exercised, just after, or on the same level as his Irish colleague. Apart from these aberrant cases, the other countries are classified in the same order on the two scales, but not on the same level, except for Portugal since the initiatives undertaken by President Eanes in 1978. In Finland and in the Weimar Republic, practice

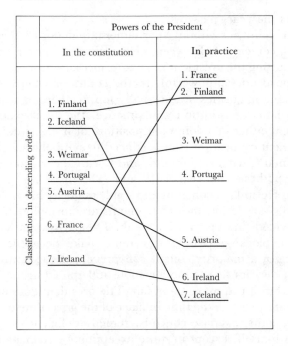

	Powers of the President	
	In the constitution	In practice

Classification in descending order

In the constitution:
1. Finland
2. Iceland
3. Weimar
4. Portugal
5. Austria
6. France
7. Ireland

In practice:
1. France
2. Finland
3. Weimar
4. Portugal
5. Austria
6. Ireland
7. Iceland

FIG. 1 The powers of the president in semi-presidential regimes

goes a little beyond the constitutional rules. In Austria and in Ireland, it falls behind.

Although the constitution plays a certain part in the application of presidential powers, this role remains secondary compared to that of the other parameters; the cases of France and Iceland show this in an undeniable way. . . .

This leads to discussion of the second parameter, formed by the combination of tradition and circumstances, which are indissolubly linked to each other. In law, the practices of a regime do not really create statute law, unless a general consensus is established in this respect through the course of history. . . . Legal rules which are unapplied, are not dead. They hibernate, and the person who has the necessary skill can always bring them to life again.

The practices of a regime, however, create a factual tradition, which makes it increasingly difficult to restore dormant legal rules as the years pass by. . . .

In the countries without a parliamentary majority, there is the greatest coincidence between the constitution and practice, the latter putting the president in an intermediary position, neither figurehead nor all-powerful. In the countries where coherent and stable majorities are normally found, there is a disparity between the constitution and practice, the latter placing the president either in a dominant position, or in the situation of a parliamentary head of state, reduced to symbolic status.

Weimar Germany, Finland, and Portugal correspond to the first hypothesis. Between 1919 and 1933 in Berlin, and since 1919 in Helsinki, a coherent and stable majority has never been formed. As a result, the governments are normally ephemeral and divided, in other words, weak. The parliament has a formidable blocking power. It cannot make decisions, in the absence of a majority, but it can prevent the executive from making decisions. It cannot promote and uphold strong governments, but it can make them fall. The president does not have the means to act all the time in place of the government. He can give impetus, exercise controls, remedy deficiencies, but not govern himself, except in quite exceptional circumstances. In law, this dyarchy is somewhat similar to that of the blind man and the lame.

Nevertheless, the head of state possesses a considerable superiority over governments which stem from parliament. He is on his own, and he has durable power. If essential and urgent decisions must be taken and the cabinet, paralysed by the division of the parties which support it, cannot take them, the citizens naturally turn to the president. . . .

In the four countries with a majority or a quasi-majority [France, Austria, Ireland, and Iceland—Ed.], the presidents have in common a practice far removed from constitutional rules. This distancing, however, is done in opposing directions. In France, a very powerful president plays a much more important role than that provided for by the written constitution. In Austria, Ireland, and Iceland, figurehead presidents play a far smaller role than that allowed by their constitutional prerogatives. The difference depends on the position of the head of state in relation to the parliamentary majority. If he is at the head of it, he becomes all-powerful, like the French presidents.

If he is a member of it, without being its head, he becomes a figurehead like the present Austrian president or the majority of the Irish presidents. If he is outside the majority, whether as an opponent or as a neutral figure, he is in a regulatory position, and his actual powers then correspond to the outline of the constitution.

19

CABINET GOVERNMENT IN THE UNITED STATES

WOODROW WILSON

The apparently necessary existence of a partisan executive presents itself to many as a fatal objection to the establishment of the forms of responsible cabinet government in this country. The President must continue to represent a political party, and must continue to be anxious to surround himself with cabinet officers who shall always substantially agree with him on all political questions. It must be admitted that the introduction of the principle of ministerial responsibility might, on this account, become at times productive of mischief unless the tenure of the presidential office were made more permanent than it now is. Whether or not the presidential term should, under such a change of conditions, be lengthened would be one of several practical questions which would attend the adoption of a system of this sort. But it must be remembered that such a state of things as now exists, when we find the executive to be of one party and the majority of Congress to be of the opposite party, is the exception, by no means the rule. Moreover, we must constantly keep before our minds the fact that the choice now lies between this responsible cabinet government and the rule of irresponsible committees which actually exists. It is not hard to believe that most presidents would find no greater inconvenience, experience no greater unpleasantness, in being at the head of a cabinet composed of political opponents than in presiding, as they must now occasionally do, over a cabinet of political friends who are

Woodrow Wilson, excerpted from 'Cabinet Government in the United States', in Ray Stannard Baker and William E. Dodd (eds.), *College and State: Educational, Literary and Political Papers (1875–1913) by Woodrow Wilson* (New York and London: Harper and Brothers, 1925; New York: Kraus Reprint Co., 1970), i. 19–42. The essay was first published in the *International Review*, 6 (August 1879), pp. 46–163.

compelled to act in all matters of importance according to the dictation of standing committees which are ruled by the opposite party. In the former case, the President may, by the exercise of whatever personal influence he possesses, affect the action of the cabinet, and, through them, the action of the Houses; in the latter he is absolutely helpless. Even now it might prove practically impossible for a President to gain from a hostile majority in the Senate a confirmation of his appointment of a strongly partisan cabinet drawn from his own party. The President must now, moreover, acting through his cabinet, simply do the bidding of the committees in directing the business of the departments. With a responsible cabinet—even though that cabinet were of the opposite party—he might, if a man of ability, exercise great power over the conduct of public affairs; if not a man of ability, but a *mere* partisan, he would in any case be impotent. From these considerations it would appear that government by cabinet ministers who represent the majority in Congress is no more incompatible with a partisan executive than is government by committees representing such a majority. Indeed, a partisan President might well prefer legislation through a hostile body at whose deliberations he might himself be present, and whose course he might influence, to legislation through hostile committees over whom he could have no manner of control, direct or indirect. And such conditions would be exceptional.

20

THE GAULLIST SYSTEM IN ASIA: THE CONSTITUTION OF SRI LANKA

A. JEYARATNAM WILSON

The criteria for determining whether a constitutional structure adheres to the Gaullist model are: in the first place the will to develop a united and strong nation state which is under the direction and supervision of a powerful and independent executive; secondly the continuance of parliament, but in an attenuated form and in a subordinate capacity, its principal functions being to articulate particular interests and adjudicate when there are conflicts between competing interest groups; finally there must be an emphasis on citizen participation so that the chief executive will be able to conduct a dialogue with the electors and consult them through the instrument of the referendum on important policy matters. . . . The Second Sri Lankan Republic conforms to these standards and could therefore be fairly accurately described as a Gaullist system. . . .

ORIGINS OF THE GAULLIST SYSTEM

The chief architect of the Second Republic, J. R. Jayewardene, was, as with de Gaulle and the French Fifth Republic, a single-minded individual of long-standing political experience, but until the penultimate hour, without much support for his cause. There were two propositions, really interconnected, which engaged Jayewardene's attention. Firstly there was a search for executive stability. Secondly there was an anxiety to create and maintain consensus politics. Both were intended as devices to pull the country out of its economic morass. There was the conviction that Westminster-style politics had merely stabilized instability, governmental majorities always being precarious and even when comfortable, systematically eroded. More importantly, the state of the economy, after each general election, seemed to be in a worse plight than after the one immediately preceding it. The major contenders were merely auctioning away the limited assets of a society which was traversing the road to economic ruin. To this architect therefore, there were two ways of remedying the situation—the adoption of a strong presidential system and the formation of national governments based on broad agreement on the critical issues of the times. Neither of these obtained support when they were put forward.

In December 1966, Jayewardene delivered an important seminal address to the twenty-second annual sessions of the Ceylon Association for the Advancement of Science. Hindsight suggests that the speech was as significant as the one made by General de Gaulle at Bayeux . . . It was indicative of the route that constitution-making would possibly take in the decade to follow. Regarding stable executive government, Jayewardene observed:

Our cabinet, the executive government, is chosen from the legislature and throughout its life is dependent on its maintaining a majority therein. We have followed the British Constitution in this respect. In some countries, the executive is chosen directly by the people and is not dependent on the legislature during the period of its existence, for a specified number of years. . . . The new French Constitution is a combination of the British and the American systems. Such an executive is a strong executive, seated in power for a fixed number of years, not subject to the whims and fancies of an elected legislature; not afraid to take correct but unpopular decisions because of censure from its parliamentary party. This seems to me a very necessary requirement in a developing country faced with grave problems such as we are faced with today.

On the subject of consensus politics, without actually stating that the existing first-past-the-post system of single-member constituencies had given rise to two polarized coalitions involved in open confrontation, Jayewardene suggested proportional representation under which 'the voter votes for a party and not for a particular candidate'. The existing system, he said, precludes the best equipped men and women from taking part in our political life. . . .

The Gaullist influence was not the only dominant theme throughout the process of constitution-making. The framers were mindful of the fact that Westminster-style government had come to stay and that they must therefore somehow endeavour to devise a structure which would draw from American, British, and Gaullist practices. Jayewardene took care to point out in his speech on the second amendment to the constitution on 22 September 1977, when introducing the Gaullist-type presidential system,

the new departure we are making from the extant constitution, from the constitution of the United Kingdom, from the constitution of the United States of America, even from the constitution of France because under the French Constitution the ministers are not chosen from the Legislature but from outside. We say they must be from the legislature because I personally believe that a minister being in the House, subject to question, subject to adjournment time, subject to the control of the House, is one of the essential features of the House being representative of the sovereignty of the people.

It will thus be seen that the progenitor of Gaullism in Sri Lanka was seeking not a wholesale imitation of the constitutional instruments of the Fifth French Republic but an adaptation of its presidential style with British parliamentarianism as well as some of the committee practices of US congressional government. What was sought to be fashioned out was a unique constitutional structure related to the particular needs of Sri Lanka's social and economic system. Jayewardene did not desire to discard those features of parliamentary politics to which he had been accustomed during the greater part of his career. . . .

THE EXECUTIVE PRESIDENCY

There is little doubt that the framers of the constitution had in view the example of the Fifth French Republic when they planned on the powers and position of the elected executive

President. The Chairman of the Select Committee on the Revision of the Constitution at the time, J. R. Jayewardene, made allusions to the French example . . .

At one stage the Chairman remarked that 'France is doing pretty well now' and in the course of the same proceedings he said: 'We must try and marry the two ideas—the Executive elected by the people and the Parliament elected by the people.' In his speech on the Second Amendment to the constitution of the First Republic, J. R. Jayewardene admiringly noted that de Gaulle 'saved the French Constitution, because before that the prime minister was elected by the House and there were changes of government three or four times a year'. In other words, what Jayewardene was after was a stable executive which would not be easily swayed by pressures from within the legislature or outside. The outcome in the end was a president who in many ways can, in certain given circumstances, be more powerful than his French counterpart.

The President is elected for a six-year term. He cannot be elected for a total of more than two terms. He combines both the dignified and active aspects of the office. For he is head of the state, head of the executive and of the government, and commander-in-chief of the armed forces. His term commences on the fourth day of February next succeeding the date of his election.

As head of the executive, he wields powers of considerable importance, powers which make it absolutely clear that he is in effect far more powerful than a prime minister could have been under the former system. Firstly he is no longer *answerable* to the legislature; the constitution only makes him *responsible* to parliament. Then there is the fact that the standing orders of the House do not permit any reference to be made to him or his conduct questioned except on a substantive motion. Furthermore the Prime Minister, members of the cabinet and other ministers are entirely dependent on the President for their offices. For Article 43(2) recognizes the President as head of the cabinet. It is he who appoints the Prime Minister, determines the number of ministers that should be in the cabinet and assigns subjects and functions to such ministers. In all this he may or may not consult the Prime Minister; and he could at any time, on his own responsibility, even without consulting his Prime

Minister, change the assignment of subjects and functions and the composition of the cabinet of ministers (Article 44(3)). This section therefore empowers the President to even dismiss his Prime Minister and/or reshuffle his cabinet without consultations with the former; because it states that 'such changes shall not affect the continuity of the Cabinet of Ministers, and the continuity of its responsibility to Parliament'. In addition there is also provision for the President to appoint ministers outside the cabinet, from among members of parliament, and to assign subjects and functions to them with or without consulting the Prime Minister. Most important, the President has the right to assign to himself any subject or function and what is more the residuary of those functions and subjects not specifically assigned to any minister shall be in his charge. He may also determine the number of ministries that should be in his direct charge. In all these areas, he, as a member and as head of the cabinet is together with the Cabinet 'collectively responsible and answerable to Parliament' (Article 43(1) and (2)). There is nevertheless a very significant proviso to Article 43(2); it states that the President shall continue in office notwithstanding the dissolution of the cabinet of ministers.

There are certain implications that flow from these constitutional provisions. The President is head of the cabinet but he will not be affected by an adverse vote of confidence against the government in the legislature. In other words the cabinet goes but the President remains. Furthermore it is the President who appoints ministers and assigns subjects and functions to them and in all this he may or may not consult the Prime Minister. . . .

The Sri Lankan system . . . approximates to the French in that there is the ever-present prospect of a president and a majority in parliament being hostile to each other. The system presupposes a president and a legislature working in harmony. But if there is conflict or a direct confrontation, then the President would be faced with a serious dilemma. A number of possibilities might be envisaged given the various provisions in the constitution of Sri Lanka. There could be a reversion to prime-ministerial government with the President functioning as a constitutional head. Or the President can appeal to the people by dissolving parliament. If the same result ensues, the President will have no option but to resign, or come to an understanding with the Prime Minister that he will not interfere with the workings of the government.

21

CONSTITUTIONAL REFORM IN ARGENTINA

COUNCIL FOR THE CONSOLIDATION OF DEMOCRACY

The main point of the institutional transformation proposed by the Council is to change our presidential system of government to a 'mixed' system. . . .

PROBLEMS OF THE PRESIDENTIAL SYSTEM

In the course of our research, we have uncovered at least four focuses of problems a presidential system harbours.

The first is caused by its inability to channel political tensions as an adequate institutional system should. In the last fifty years of Argentine history, there has often been a recourse to solutions outside the system. Currently, the concentration of power and the expectations in the President causes him or her to be the central figure in times of crisis. Thus the solution to crises may require in some instances his or her abandonment of office. It is obvious that such a resignation must be traumatic; this is not only because of the sense of failure, but also because the inability to complete his or her tenure is caused by pressure groups which are certainly less in number than the people who brought him or her to power.

A possible remedy to ameliorate tensions within the current framework would be the impeachment of the President. But this remedy is almost impracticable. Not only is it difficult to establish sufficient evidence of misconduct, but also it seems

Consejo para la Consolidación de la Democracia, excerpted from *Reforma Constitucional: Segundo Dictamen del Consejo para la Consolidación de la Democracia* (Buenos Aires: EUDEBA, 1987), Sintesis en Inglés (summary in English). Copyright 1987 Editorial Universitaria de Buenos Aires.

implausible that a legislative majority will support these proceedings for members of the President's party would have to be part of it.

In contrast, in a 'mixed' system the solutions for those kinds of problems are less traumatic because the prime minister and the government serve as 'circuit-breakers' that 'break' in cases of tension. This is due to the dependence of the prime minister and the government on the confidence of the President and the representatives.

The removal of the prime minister and his or her cabinet, which a parliamentary or mixed system provides, is not the only escape valve in a crisis situation. There are others resulting from the fact that this system multiplies the number of main political players; the system also gives each a 'trump card' which can be used when others have failed. For instance, recourse can be had to the dissolution of the house of representatives and the call for new elections by the President, the latter's intervention in serious governmental problems utilizing the prestige earned by him or her in the exercise of constitutional powers, the calling for a plebiscite and the recourse to the Council for Constitutional Affairs when conflicts among the branches of government are at issue and so forth.

The second focus of problems is caused by the personalization of power promoted by the amount of powers and discretions vested in the President of the nation.

This personalization of power makes the system vulnerable because expectations are centred on the President. Thus when the President is politically or physically impaired, the entire system is adversely affected. . . .

The third focus of problems revolves around the relations among the branches of the state. Numerous difficulties arise in a system with an electoral regime and an organization of parties that put a premium on party cohesiveness which in turn prevails over the legislators' desire to maintain independent bases of electoral support.

Some scholars, such as Juan Linz, compare this type of system to a zero-sum game, in which everything gained by a player is lost by the others. In Argentina this occurs in so far as predetermined majorities in the legislature are created by party discipline.

When that predetermined majority belongs to the President's party, the function of Congress is undermined. Given the control exercised by the President as leader of the party, the legislators, under the threat of hampering their political fortunes, feel the need automatically to support presidential initiatives.

When the opposite situation occurs, a 'frozen majority' tries to obstruct executive tasks and ideas, for only with the fall of the government can it hope to enact its own agenda. Even if the executive's proposals are palatable, the opposition's legislators must stay 'in line'. . .

In a mixed system these patterns of behaviour are considerably reduced. The system has an inherent flexibility which alternatively emphasizes presidential or parliamentary aspects, depending on the prevailing majorities in the congress.

If the President names a prime minister from his or her own political family, the system would take on the most important traits of presidential systems: no great contradictions in the execution of policy can be expected among them, especially if one keeps in mind that the President may always remove the prime minister.

When the majority in the lower house belongs to another party, the President is compelled to name a prime minister from that party. He or she will be forced therefore to vest a number of important tasks in the prime minister in order to maintain an efficient government. Of course, if the President thinks that he or she has sufficient support to carry out his or her policies, the lower house may be dissolved and new elections called for.

In short, the proposed system would improve the relations among the branches of the state, and between government and opposition. This would have a decisive influence in the formulation and implementation of policy. Further, by shielding the President from day-to-day politics, he or she would be regarded as a more impartial interlocutor by the nation.

The fourth focus of problems arises out of the fact that presidentialism disfavours the generation of coalitions and multi-party convergences because of the nature, rigidity, and extension of the presidential mandate. The above infringes on democratic pluralism, raises questions of legitimacy and breeds 'movimientos', among other unpleasant results.

A mixed system, in turn, allows for the formation of the said alliances while maintaining the personalities of the parties involved—and consequently democratic pluralism—due to the temporary nature of the agreements. . . .

THE EXECUTIVE BRANCH

In semi-presidential systems, it is of utmost importance to delineate precisely the functions of the President and those of the prime minister and his or her government. . . .

It is recommended that a clause be included in the constitution to assign to the prime minister all the necessary powers for the realization of national policy. All those powers relating to the maintenance of institutions and the continuity of the nation should be explicitly assigned to the President; for instance, the nomination of judges, ambassadors, and the highest military officers.

The President has to be the custodian for the compliance by the government with the programme agreed to by the house of representatives. Although he or she may not directly intervene in the implementation of the said programme, some 'red buttons' should be in place if the programme is distorted or is in danger. That is why he or she should have the power to dissolve the lower house and so forth.

In the end, such a system should promote a better relationship among all those involved in the government of the state, providing sufficient incentives for co-operation and avoiding the risks of a zero-sum game.

22

DUAL LEADERSHIP IN THE CONTEMPORARY WORLD

JEAN BLONDEL

Dualism has so far been studied very little, except in the special cases of the French Fifth Republic, Finland, and Portugal. Yet the development is far from confined to those countries; almost a third of the national executives are currently organized on a dual basis and they include traditional monarchical governments as well as communist systems, authoritarian semi-presidential systems as well as liberal regimes. . . .

How then should a dual leadership be defined? A dual leadership system is one in which two, and only two, men or women share formally, effectively, and in a continuous manner in the general affairs of the government. [One of] such persons would usually be a monarch or president. It excludes the cases in which the head of state has a symbolic role only, and it also excludes the cases in which a council or a junta of more than two persons constitutes the collective leadership. Such councils are exceptional; rarely do more than two persons become involved in a continuous manner in the conduct of governmental affairs.

Within the context of an arrangement in which two men share effectively the general running of the affairs of the state, however, there is ample scope for variations in the manner in which this sharing takes place. The leaders may be more or less equal in status and influence, or they may be unequal; they may decide to oversee jointly all the major policy decisions, or they may decide, formally or informally, to divide the burden according to fields or even degree of importance. The division of responsibility is also likely to vary over time. Thus the dual leadership system is most flexible; it is indeed this flexibility which constitutes one of the attractions of the arrangement, although a process of institutionalization may none the less be taking place.

WHERE DUAL LEADERSHIP OCCURS

The number of dual leadership systems has increased markedly in recent years, especially in the 1970s; but the geographical spread is not uniform. Western countries have rarely shown any desire, or felt any need to adopt it. Before 1958, Finland was the only example. Then came the French Fifth Republic and, in 1974, Portugal, but the last may be in the process of reverting to parliamentary rule, although the president is attempting to retain some influence. In Spain, dual leadership prevailed for a while at the end of the Franco regime and at the beginning of the new monarchy, but power had been transferred wholly to the prime minister; the period of dual leadership was there truly transitional and transitory—transitory in that it lasted less than a decade, transitional in that it enabled Spain to move from Franco's dictatorship to a fully-fledged parliamentary demo-cracy in the smoothest of manners.

Nor has dual leadership been popular in Latin America, where Peru provides the only long-standing and not altogether felicitous example, although, as we shall see, the system might benefit the countries of the subcontinent. However, elsewhere in the world, dual leadership has truly flourished. It has been widely adopted in the communist countries; it has existed for substantial periods in some monarchies and it has been main-tained or re-introduced occasionally when these monarchies were replaced by republics; and it has been adopted in a substantial number of African and Asian countries that had previously been presidential (and occasionally parliament-ary): this is where the arrangement has proved to be truly popular . . .

Dual Monarchies

The most traditional form of dual leadership is the one which now is the least common—the dual monarchy. The king and prime minister system, which has existed in Britain, Sweden, and some other western European countries since the eighteenth or nineteenth centuries, has been adopted, in the course of the twentieth century, by a number of non-European monarchies, such as Egypt, Iraq, Jordan, Ethiopia, Nepal, and Morocco. But most of these states became republics in the course of the post-war period; Jordan, Nepal, and Morocco are the principal cases of dual monarchies in the 1980s. Although a similar system has begun slowly to be introduced in the monarchies of the Arabian Peninsula (Kuwait, United Arab Emirates), most of the countries in the area are ruled by a king or emir who also holds the position of prime minister. . . .

Communist Systems

If dualism has been transitional in monarchies, it does not have this character any longer in communist systems. In European and north Asian communist countries at least, it has become a near-universal rule for the positions of party secretary and of prime minister to be held by two different men. This has reversed a trend which seemed at one point to prevail in the Soviet Union and in some other communist states and which suggested that dual or collective leadership corresponded only to the scramble for power in the aftermath of a change of leader. In fact, there were already in the early post-war years several exceptions to the single leadership of the party secretary, for example China, North Vietnam, or Albania; since the 1950s and 1960s, however, dual leadership has become the norm. . . .

Semi-presidential Republics

While there was always a potential for dual leadership in communist countries in view of the division between party and state and while the evolution of monarchies seems to lead naturally to at least a period of dual leadership, only recently has such an arrangement been widely adopted in republican regimes; traditionally, republics were presidential in the strict constitutional sense, occasionally parliamentary, and, if they were not liberal, purely and simply absolutist. In the late 1940s, there were only six cases of semi-presidential dualist systems—in Finland, Peru, the Lebanon, Syria, South Korea, and Indonesia; a quarter of a century later, over two dozen republics were of this type. Although the number of independent countries markedly increased during the period, the expansion of dual leadership was more than proportional.

Black Africa is the area where the change from single presidential rule to a dual leadership system occurred most frequently. In the early 1960s, only Zaire and Somalia had a dual system; elsewhere, a form of parliamentary or prime-ministerial system was often adopted at first, soon to be transformed into strong presidential rule. From the early 1970s, in many countries, this presidential rule became somewhat modified by the appointment of prime ministers, both in civilian and in military regimes. Sometimes the appointment was short-lived and the post of prime minister quickly abolished, but the arrangement survived in about a dozen black African countries. Meanwhile, similar developments, though not quite on the same scale, occurred in north Africa, the Middle East, and south Asia; thus Tunisia, Algeria, Burma, and Sri Lanka, for instance, acquired a dual system. In Sri Lanka, the change occurred after decades during which a parliamentary system had functioned relatively smoothly and in a pluralistic context; thus dualism is making inroads in liberal Commonwealth countries as well as in more authoritarian or 'charismatic' presidential polities.

Dual leadership has thus ceased to be primarily a transitional arrangement by which monarchs gradually lose power to the people's representatives; it has become a mechanism used by many presidents of new states—both civilian and military—to devolve some of their powers to someone of their choice who continues to depend on them, but who none the less may exercise considerable influence. By doing so, these presidents begin to institutionalize the national executive, even if it is only to a limited extent and, in the early period in particular, even if the institutionalization remains weak. This cannot but have some effects on the president's power and freedom of manœuvre; one can see why the experiment is sometimes abandoned, indeed at times very quickly, while the return to single-man rule may also occur after many years, as in Senegal. But, in the majority of cases, the new institutional arrangement is maintained. The repeated occurrence of this phenomenon in such diverse countries and regimes surely suggests that leaders are conscious of a need and that some problems can be solved by the appointment of a prime minister. What is the nature of this need and does dual leadership appear able to meet it?

THE *RAISON D'ÊTRE* FOR DUAL LEADERSHIP

It is of course difficult to know why, in each case, a dual arrangement is set up. In the French example, the best documented of all, there was little consciousness of the change which was taking place. De Gaulle did not state categorically in 1958 what the relationship between president and prime minister was to be; French politicians seemed content to leave the matter in a state of some obscurity, as there was fear that the post of prime minister might be abolished and a fully-fledged presidential system instituted. There was probably much relief in many quarters that de Gaulle did not go further and settled for a halfway system. In other countries the specific motivations of leaders are even less well known. But, if these cannot be fully assessed, one can at least discover from the way the political system developed since the introduction of dualism a number of reasons that singly or in combination provide a case for a dual system.

Five such reasons stand out as most important. The first results from the existence of a variety of political constituencies which no leader alone can control and which have to be represented jointly at the top. The second, which may over time lead to the first, stems from the need to manage groups of politicians outside the government (for instance in an assembly). The third reason relates to the desire to administer the country more efficiently, while the fourth comes from the need felt by the head of state to allow his probable successor to familiarize himself with the decision-making process. Finally, dual leadership may also result, in a more diffuse manner, from the desire of the head of state to keep some distance apart from 'ordinary' politics.

Existence of Two Political Constituencies

The first two reasons relate generally to the characteristics of the broader political system. In one case, however, there are groups, ethnic, religious, or political, which have to be represented at the top, while, in the other, the head of state needs an 'agent' who will manage for him the wider political world. In the first case, the two leaders are equal or near-equal; the prime minister is indispensable. His removal might lead to such difficulties that it becomes in practice unthinkable. Indeed, the arrangement may become wholly institutionalized; in the Lebanon, which is, however, the only example of a clear-cut division of this type, the prime minister represents the Moslems and the president represents the Christians. Such a division has been or was relatively harmonious in that country until the Palestinian issue arose, but, elsewhere, arrangements of this kind have tended to be unstable, as they have corresponded to moments in the fights of various tribal or ethnic groups to exercise predominance: Zaire, Uganda, or Burundi at the time of independence are good examples of such situations.

A division among political constituencies can also be said to exist, at least after a period, in dual monarchies. Originally, prime ministers are appointed in these countries as agents of the monarch and with a view to ensuring the loyalty of politically relevant groups; the increased role of parliaments and of the representative process, however, tends to lead to a cleavage between the political support for the monarch and the political support for the prime minister. . . .

Political Management

While the prime minister may ultimately acquire a constituency of his own in a dual monarchy, the political *raison d'être* for the creation of his office is typically different; it is to manage the political élite. This was clearly the case in Britain in the eighteenth century; this is also the case in several semi-presidential republics of the contemporary world, in particular France. The role of the prime minister is to help the king or president to ensure that some political groups which either might be hostile or, more often, might show signs of declining loyalty are kept within the fold. . . .

Administrative Management

Dual leadership also exists for reasons of administrative management. Indeed, prime ministers were appointed by monarchs in the past in part in order to achieve better co-ordination between the ministries: in England and Sweden this administrative role was at least as prominent as the political role. With the modern expansion of government services, heads of state are likely to feel that they have neither the time nor the technical competence to supervise and give impetus to ministers and civil servants.

Thus, almost certainly, the requirements of administrative management are at the root of most, if not all, the dual leadership arrangements which exist in the contemporary world. This is particularly true in communist states where the division of the whole decision-making structure into a party and a state hierarchy makes the existence of the office of prime minister logical, if not necessary. The demands for co-ordination are obviously particularly pressing in a governmental system in which the public sector comprises a large number of activities, especially industrial. It would therefore be unrealistic to expect the party leader, whether or not he is also head of state, to be effectively in charge of co-ordination; this is indeed the main function of the prime minister, although he will collaborate, in these matters as in others, with the party secretary.

Administrative management is also the *raison d'être* for the existence of the office of prime minister in semi-presidential republics. In the early years of the French Fifth Republic, de Gaulle did point out that this was indeed the main role of the prime minister, thereby also reminding the head of the government that he was not to be too deeply involved in what might be called 'high politics'. This situation changed somewhat after de Gaulle left power; the division between two levels—'high politics' and administration—has consequently become more blurred, in part because French presidents have been markedly involved in matters of administrative management, but in part also because French prime ministers have been seen to be deeply interested in questions both of defence and of foreign policy (especially with respect to Europe). None the less the function of administrative management does remain one of the main aspects of the activities of the prime minister. . . .

The Succession Process

The fourth *raison d'être* for dual leadership is to help smooth the succession process. Leaders have long attempted, with more or less success, to play a part in the selection of those who follow them. The hereditary mechanism was obviously the best means of achieving that goal. But, with the virtual ending of the hereditary principle as a means of appointing rulers, a more circuitous route has had to be discovered. Thus leaders who wish to have an influence on their country's policies after they leave office try and prepare the ground by placing someone whom they trust in a key position which comes to be recognized as a natural stepping-stone to the office that they hold. They can meanwhile train this potential successor in the problems they will face when they become ruler. The office of prime minister tends naturally to fit this type of strategy; it seems more flexible than that of vice-president, which is sometimes used, however, to select future presidents, as occurred for instance in Kenya. Prime ministers can be appointed and dismissed without ceremony, while vice-presidents, who are normally elected for a specific term, cannot be easily changed if they appear unsuited to become successors. Moreover, prime ministers are naturally more involved in governmental affairs than are vice-presidents; there is a supernumerary and at most a purely political character to a vice-presidential office which the position of prime minister does not display. . . .

Standing Aloof

Finally, the head of state might wish to appoint a prime minister in order to be relieved from the burden of daily politics. This may be particularly the case with older leaders whose interest in political life has declined and who may wish to concentrate on a limited range of matters—foreign affairs, for example. But even newer and younger leaders may like to be able to keep some distance from current problems; they may especially wish to avoid having to adjudicate between ministers on secondary issues which are likely to undermine their authority. Admittedly, even in single-leadership presidential systems, there are 'filters' which stop many matters from coming to the chief executive. But, if the persons involved in the dispute are influential, if, for example, they are ministers, the presidential aides who act as 'filters' may not be able to prevent the matter from reaching the leader. A prime minister is better able to act because he holds a formal position.

The case for dual leadership is thus strong. Although the result must be a reduction in the ability of monarchs and presidents to exercise full discretion, some substantial advantages accrue to them. Indeed, the appointment of a prime minister may seem inevitable in the context of the growth and increased complexity of government services. It may therefore not be surprising that the arrangement should have currently become popular and should appear to serve the interests of many rulers. How far, however, do these advantages also contribute to a genuine improvement of the political process? Does dual leadership have a measurable and positive impact on the characteristics of political life?

THE VALUE OF DUAL LEADERSHIP

. . . Clearly, dual leadership systems have, to a greater or lesser degree, helped some Western countries to achieve better results. France is the outstanding example; dual leadership brought about, somewhat unexpectedly, a major improvement in the political stability and indeed responsiveness of the government. But similar conclusions can be drawn, though in a less clear-cut manner, about Portugal; the president's intervention has probably prevented party divisions from leading to a crisis of regime—indeed, parties have occasionally come closer together in order to avoid leaving the president with an open field for intervention. In neighbouring Spain, the authority of the king has given strength to the early governments of the new democracy and helped the development of a responsible party system.

In general, however, dual leadership systems have not been used so far consciously to promote a stable liberal system. This is almost certainly because the arrangement is not normally viewed as a 'system' in its own right, to be compared to the parliamentary—or prime-ministerial—system and to the presidential system, which are the only two types of arrangements commonly regarded as able to ensure a working liberal regime. Yet it is worth examining the potential of dual leadership in view of the clear inability of both parliamentary and 'constitutional' presidential systems to make substantial inroads in the Third World.

While the parliamentary system has worked satisfactorily in most of western Europe, in the Old Commonwealth and, indeed, in parts of the New Commonwealth, it has clearly not been successful elsewhere; even in the Commonwealth, especially in Africa, it has been abandoned for varieties of 'charismatic' presidential regimes. Outside the Commonwealth, except in Japan and Israel, the parliamentary system has usually not been adopted at all or it has quickly been replaced, often by a *coup*, by authoritarian presidential regimes as well.

For genuine motives or not, the parliamentary system has been blamed by those who have abolished it for being unable to provide strong leadership and for fostering divisions among irresponsible legislators. This, of course, is not true of all parliamentary systems, but an effective and streamlined party system is needed if these consequences are to be avoided. The French pre-1958 experience, as well as that of other southern European states, shows that, without such a party system, parliamentarism does give rise to semi-anarchic 'assembly rule' and to ineffective government. *Coups* are therefore possible or even likely. This has been the usual scenario in Third World countries where parliamentary government was at first established. It has been avoided in some Commonwealth countries not merely because of luck but because of the establishment of strong party systems in the British tradition (India, Malaysia, Jamaica, Mauritius).

As it is not possible suddenly to engineer a pluralistic party system which has no roots in the society, the only liberal alternative appears to be the setting up of a constitutional presidential system. This seems to have advantages, as presidentialism does not rely so directly on a party system since the president is elected directly and for a fixed term. But the experience of Latin America and of the few other countries in which constitutional presidentialism was introduced (Philippines) shows that there are other defects which may even be more dangerous to the maintenance of liberal government. Presidentialism extols the prestige of the chief executive. He can exercise leadership, but as there are limits to presidential power (such as the right to stand for a second or third term, the power of the legislature which he cannot control), the temptation is great to use his 'leadership' to bypass the system. If it embodies the principle of separation of powers with no provision for a constitutional mechanism to bring about a solution (such as the right of dissolution or the censure motion), the presidential system will tend to lead to an escalation in the struggle between the 'powers' and, ultimately, to 'caesarism' because of the elevated position in which the chief executive is placed by the constitution itself.

Thus neither parliamentarism nor constitutional presidentialism can be expected to bring about a solution to the problems of a country in which efforts are made to set up a pluralist system but where the party configuration is weak or insufficiently streamlined. A dual leadership system, on the other hand, may be able to provide a combination of authority and flexibility which can create the necessary conditions for a more stable liberal regime. In a parliamentary system, the president needs the support of the majority of the chamber to keep his government in office; this may be difficult to achieve if the party system is inchoate. But, as the president is elected for a substantial period by universal suffrage, he has authority and can be expected to rally at least some of the political waverers to himself and to his government. The party system may then become better organized. The system is not foolproof, but it gives the executive a breathing-space as well as some means of exercising pressure on the chamber, for instance through dissolution and a share in the government.

23

REPORT ON THE 1848 DRAFT
CONSTITUTION OF SWITZERLAND
CONSTITUTIONAL REFORM COMMITTEE

The President of the Federal Council shall be the President of
the Confederation. As such he shall enjoy precedence over the
Presidents of the National Council and of the Council of
States even during the session of the Federal Assembly, because
there must be unity and foreign governments must know who
represents the country.

However this supreme magistrate shall have no special prerogatives, such as those . . . enjoyed by the President of the United
States of America. While recognizing the advantages offered by
such an office from the point of view of the unity and continuity
of the administration as well as from that of the faithful expression of the national will and of the responsibility of the government, the committee could not think of proposing the creation
of an office so contrary to the ideas and habits of the Swiss people
who might see therein evidence of a monarchical or dictatorial
tendency; in Switzerland one is attached to councils. Our democratic feeling revolts against any personal pre-eminence. A part
of the committee would have preferred to see the President and
the other members of the Federal Council elected by the people,
in order to place their authority on a more secure and on a
broader basis. . . . The cantons, it is true, would have had no
voice in the choice of the government. . . . The majority
therefore decided to entrust the election of the executive to
the two houses assembled. It proposes this solution first in order
to secure the co-operation of the cantons and of the people,

William E. Rappard, excerpted from 'Documents on the Government of
Switzerland', in William E. Rappard, Walter R. Sharp, Herbert
W. Schneider, James K. Pollock, and Samuel N. Harper (eds.), *Source Book
on European Governments: Switzerland, France, Italy, Germany, the Soviet Union*
(New York: van Nostrand, 1937), ch. II.

secondly because it is in the interests of the unity of the state and of the subordination of the executive to the supreme authority of the legislature, thirdly because it is the practice of most of the cantons and finally because a popular election would present certain difficulties.

24

A COLLEGIAL EXECUTIVE
FOR URUGUAY

JOSÉ BATLLE Y ORDÓÑEZ

We tend to think of the executive power as a warrior's power. It is force, action, swiftness in attack, single-minded foresight in defence. Whoever exercises it must always be ready to leave his house at any hour, even in the middle of the night, to shoot at an adversary, to lead a skirmish, or to take command of an army. His voice must be resonant, his carriage imposing, his gestures crisp and threatening. On foot, he should carry himself as if marching, and on horseback or in a coach the shoes of his charger should raise sparks from the pavement. The holder of executive power is not readily thought of in any other form.

We should recognize that such a manner of feeling and thinking has deep roots in history. Societies, in primitive times and even, for the most part, in modern times, have rallied around a figure of this type. Law has been primarily the absolute will and sovereignty of one man. The most astute or intelligent, the most determined, the most audacious, the most valiant, he who knows how to deliver the best-aimed blow, who can best direct a battle, has been the chief naturally and by necessity. Strong men, kings, caesars and emperors have had no other origin.

We do not criticize this. Humanity tends to develop slowly. The idea of governments ever more democratic, in which the will of all is substituted for the will of individuals, could not fully develop without repeated trials and a long period of gestation . . . As the greatest problems always pertained to the

José Batlle y Ordóñez, excerpted from 'El Poder Ejecutivo colegiado', *El Día* (Montevideo), 18 December 1911. Translation © John M. Carey. Used by permission.

establishment and maintenance of order and the defence of independence, public authority fell to those men who could exercise power without limitation.

Without a doubt, some of the most advanced peoples of every age have at some point in time recognized the drawbacks of domination by one man and have experimented with a collective executive. Athens, Rome, and Venice reached their grandeur under governments of this type; revolutionary France vested the defence of its independence in a committee, and when it was felt the moment had arrived to construct a permanent body, the government was given to another committee—the Directorate. At the dawn of our own independence, our ancestors constructed a government by junta which assumed charge of their interests; and another junta was formed in Buenos Aires to prepare the emancipation of that part of the Americas. Such institutions were more or less ephemeral, evolving towards personal domination not only out of the competition among interests and passions that besiege all governments, of whatever form, that are established without sufficient political experience; but also, and above all, by the prejudice bred in our spirits by almost all experience that governmental power ought to be exercised by one person.

The greatest challenge to this mode of thought has been the establishment of constitutional monarchies and of republics in the most advanced countries in the world. Still, the argument is launched against the constitutional regime and against the republic that power is best exercised by a single head and a single hand; the speed of action, the potential for secretiveness, the single-mindedness, the unity and resolve of command—all are invoked in defence of the old order. Nevertheless, the most important governmental decisions are made by law. The most crucial legislation, instead of being dictated in a fit of passion, is submitted to prolonged deliberation. Absolute power has been limited; and the conservative spirit of regimes in which the will of one was the will of all could never have conceived of the potential of the institutions that now move society.

This reform could have been more complete. Since the disadvantage of conferring on one person the entire power of government has been recognized, the disadvantage of conferring on one person any important part could also have been recognized. But revolutions are never made in their entirety. Human thought is imperfect and flawed, and never deduces all at once all of the conclusions logically implied by its principles. What is more, reality resists conforming to an ideal. It was necessary to compromise with kings to get them to abandon a good part of the government. Republics imitated constitutional monarchies, preserving the monarchs, whom they called president, substituting election for the obvious injustice of inheritance, and reducing more or less the term during which elected officials could exercise power.

The idea, nevertheless, is on the march. In the Swiss federation the executive faculties are entrusted to a council of seven citizens, who are elected every three years and can be re-elected. One of them holds the title of president, but his mandate lasts only one year and his powers are extremely limited, such that the true government is the Council. No catastrophe has occurred in that country as a result of its institutions. On the contrary! There is no happier country in Europe. And not because of its size or power. Its territory is a third of ours. Its population is only three times our own . . .

In France, the executive power is exercised by a committee. The role of the President of the Republic is merely symbolic. He is the representative of the nation. He visits friendly nations, receives sovereigns and emissaries; he attends national celebrations and ceremonies, makes speeches, and so on, but he does not govern. It is the council of ministers that governs, a committee which in turn is subordinate to a more numerous committee—the legislative body. Under the direction of such a government, France has been reborn from its immense disaster of 1870. Knowledge has flourished there. And with prudence and patriotic energy a people that seemed to have been defeated for ever is today, more than ever, a power of the first order, with strong friends and allies, capable of defending its interests and independence with much more certainty and energy than when its destiny was decided by the unfettered will of one individual.

PART IV

PARLIAMENTARISM AND
PRESIDENTIALISM IN AFRICA,
ASIA, AND EUROPE

25

REPORT ON THE DRAFT
CONSTITUTION OF NIGERIA
CONSTITUTION DRAFTING
COMMITTEE

EXECUTIVE PRESIDENCY FOR THE FEDERATION

7.1-1. The subcommittee on the Executive and the Legislature recommended as follows:

There shall be a President and a Vice-President of the Republic who shall be elected on the same ticket. The President shall be head of state and head of government of the federation and commander-in-chief of the armed forces of the federation.

7.1-2. The subcommittee thus clearly rejected the system of separation between the head of state on the one hand and the head of government on the other, and the plural executive of the cabinet system in which government rests with a cabinet of ministers headed by a prime minister.

7.1-3. The separation of the head of state from head of government involves a division between real authority and formal authority. The division is meaningless in the light of African political experience and history. The tendency indeed of all people throughout the world is to elevate a single person to the position of ruler. In the context of Africa the division is not only meaningless, it is difficult to maintain in practice. No African head of state has been known to be content with the position of a mere figurehead. The experience of Nigeria, Uganda, Lesotho, and Swaziland testifies to this. In these countries, the system has resulted in a clash of personalities and of interests, a conflict of authority, and an unnecessary

Constitution Drafting Committee, excerpted from *Report of the Constitution Drafting Committee Containing the Draft Constitution* (Lagos: Federal Republic of Nigeria, Federal Ministry of Information, Printing Division, 1976), i. ch. 7.

complexity and uncertainty in governmental relations. The system presupposes a non-political head of state, but the lesson of African experience with the system is that if non-political heads of state are not already in existence, mere constitutional provisions alone will not bring them into being.

7.1–4. A constitution should be adapted to the needs of the country and to the aspirations of its citizens. The paramount need of Nigeria is for development. We want to be able to develop our economy, to modernize and integrate our society, to secure and promote stability in the community, and to safeguard civil liberty. While it may be arguable whether an executive presidency or the system of separation *per se* conduces more to economic and social development, the effect of the latter on national integration and social stability is positively detrimental. The clashes and conflicts inherent in the system produce instability in government and in society, and also endanger national unity. The system of separation clearly fails to provide a clear focal point of loyalty, which is indispensable to national integration.

7.1–5. The dangers of separation are complemented by the disadvantages of plurality. The single executive has the merit of unity, energy, and despatch. Energy in the executive, it has been rightly said, is a leading character in the definition of good government. The unity of a single executive clearly conduces more to energy and despatch than the disunity of many wills. This is not, of course, to deny the virtue of collective discussion and consultation in bringing the views and experiences of different people to bear upon a problem or upon the determination of policy. Yet it is essential to effective leadership in government that there should be a single individual in the capacity of a chief executive who can decide and act promptly when despatch is demanded, and who can impose his will when differences of opinion among cabinet members threaten to paralyse the government.

7.1–6. Another demerit of the plural executive is that it undermines responsibility. It does this in two ways: first, through the weakened authority of the prime minister to enforce collective responsibility, and secondly, by making it difficult to determine on whom the blame or punishment for error should fall. One of the factors that has discredited cabinet government in the developing countries of the Commonwealth was the inability of the prime minister to control the actions of ministers and to enforce the requirements of collective responsibility.

7.1–7. The Westminster system hampers effective government in yet another respect. The parliamentary character of the executive means that the right of the executive to govern derives from the legislature. Government under the system is the rule of the legislature, hence it is called parliamentary government. What justifies this description is the fact that the right to govern flows through the legislature to the executive. There is only one popular election—that for members of the legislature. No separate popular election is held for the executive. Thus the only popular mandate for the government is that conferred by the votes that elected the members of parliament. Since that mandate is the only authority for government, the authority belongs to the legislature. The legislature, in theory at least, makes and unmakes the government. The need to consider parliamentary majorities cannot [but] hamper vigour and decisiveness in government. Under the presidential system recommended by the subcommittee, on the other hand, the president will be elected directly by the people, a fact that gives him an independent right to govern. The right flows directly from the people who elect him. It is not being suggested that the president under this system should ignore the wishes of the legislature. As we have already pointed out, he would have to depend on the legislature for legislation to implement his policies and for funds to execute his measures. The success and effectiveness of the system demand co-operation between the two organs.

7.1–8. It was argued by some members that an executive presidency such as is recommended by the subcommittee concentrates too much power in the hands of one person. A president with such wide powers and armed with the organized forces of the state could easily become a dictator, and could dismiss the legislature which, as an institution, has no organized force under its control and no machinery for preventing usurpation of power by the executive. The stage is then set for personal rule by the president. The great tragedy of personal rule is its inhibiting effect on personal liberty. Every challenge to any act of government might be viewed as a challenge to the state and to the entire political system. Even vigorous party-politicking becomes a threat to the state.

7.1–9. The danger of dictatorship is recognized. However, the ultimate sanction against usurpations of power is a politically conscious society jealous of its constitutional rights to choose those who direct its affairs.

THE MIDDLE WAY: THE PRESIDENT
WITH LIMITED POWERS

7.1–10. It was also suggested that the dangers of personal dictatorship might be minimized under a system which, while not unduly weakening the efficacy of the executive, shares executive power between a president and a vice-president. The line of division should be between functions that sustain the state and those that relate to routine day-to-day administration; the former should be the responsibility of the president while the latter should vest in the vice-president. More specifically, it is suggested that the president should have the following matters under his control:

National Defence Council
Police Service Commission
Nigeria Police Council
National Security Council
Civil Service Commission
Judicial Service Commission
National Population Commission
Electoral Commission
Council of State
Prerogative of mercy
Assent to bills (federal and state)
Legal aid to prosecute or enforce fundamental rights
Accreditation of diplomats
Prisons
Adjudication over issues that relate to compliance with fundamental objectives and the directive principles of state policy.

The vice-president shall appoint his ministers and preside over his Federal Executive Council. He shall run the ministries and, in addition, the following:

National Economic Commission
National Council on Establishments
Fiscal Review Commission
National Economic Council

7.1-11. In so far as this arrangement divides executive functions between the president and the vice-president the majority of us consider that it is fraught with the same dangers of clash of personalities and of interests, and of conflict of authority. The only way to avoid such conflict is to provide that in such an event the will of one is to prevail. That would lead back to the need to have a paramount functionary as proposed in the recommendation.

7.1-12. At the end of the debate on this question we decided to accept the recommendation of the subcommittee. We were however conscious of the very wide powers being conferred on the president under this constitution and we feel that it is desirable that a person should have widespread support throughout Nigeria before he can assume that office. A good deal of our time was spent on working out the rules for determining when a person can be declared duly elected as president and these rules will be found in section 111 of the draft constitution.

MINISTERS

7.2-1. An executive presidency of the type proposed by the Committee implies a somewhat rigid separation between the executive and the legislature. The two are mutually independent of each other. The president is of course the executive. The question is whether the separation and the independence should be confined to the president, or whether it should also extend to the ministers. The committee decided to extend it to the ministers. This means that ministers should not be members of the National Assembly, though they should have a right to attend and speak at meetings of the Assembly in order to be able to explain government policies and actions.

7.2-2. Some members felt that membership of the legislative house by ministers has a cardinal merit in bringing the government and the legislature into close and regular contact. The real value of this is not just that their membership enables them to participate in the work of the legislature, to answer questions from members, and generally to explain the actions of the government; it lies more importantly in the fact that, since the ministers are the leaders of the parliamentary parties, their legislative membership and participation enable them to rally to the government the support of the majority of members of the legislative house. Their ministerial offices give them the authority which the legislative party leaders in America do not have. Together the ministers give guidance and leadership to the members of the legislative house, thereby maintaining the parties' authority over them and checking an undue assertion of independence, such as characterizes American Congressmen. Modern government should be a co-operative, co-ordinated effort, and not a tug-of-war between the principal organs of the government. The cardinal defect in American government is the mutual antipathy and antagonism between the President and Congress, resulting from the rigid separation of powers. This is not of course an argument against any kind of separation of power. On the contrary, some separation of executive and legislative functions is necessary and desirable if limited government and individual liberty are to be secured, but certainly not a rigid separation.

26

FOR A DIRECTLY ELECTED
PRESIDENT OF INDIA

VASANT SATHE

It is of utmost importance first to consider the national scene so
as to find out if there is any need for a change or modification
in our constitution. The next question would be whether such
a change can be brought about within the framework of our
existing constitution.

As to the national scene, the very concept of nationhood of
India in the modern sense of a political entity is of comparatively
recent origin and any threat to this concept arising out of
regional, parochial, linguistic, or communal urges can prove
perilous to the very concept of our nation, and national integrity
and unity will be in serious jeopardy. The apprehension is no
longer imaginary because it is on the cards for everyone to see
that in the forthcoming elections to the parliament the likelihood
is that no single party, including the Congress(I), may emerge
with an absolute majority. The divisive and fissiparous forces
that have been raising their ugly heads have already shown their
fangs and it is only an utterly complacent or naïve person who
can close his eyes to this reality. It will, therefore, be foolhardy
to think that we can afford to experiment with coalitions at the
national level. One can easily imagine how a coalition with a
slender majority would not be able to tackle problems like that
of terrorists and subversion in Punjab. . . .

The issue, therefore, is not whether we should have the
parliamentary form or presidential form, but whether within
the framework of our present constitution we can have a provi-

Vasant Sathe, excerpted from 'For a Directly Elected President', in
A. G. Noorani, *The Presidential System: The Indian Debate* (New Delhi: Sage
Publications, India Pvt. Ltd, 1989), app. II. Copyright Centre for Policy
Research, 1989. Reprinted by permission of the publisher.

sion whereby we could ensure the stability of the government at the national level. Once we start arguing as to whether we should have a presidential form or not, we then ask ourselves whether it should be the American or the French variety and then get into the examination of those two systems and thus invariably land ourselves into a barren debate. We have had enough experience now of the working of our own constitution to know where our weakness lies and how to go about setting it right. It is not necessary for us to find analogies or support from other systems.

It must be remembered that after independence the framers of our constitution clearly visualized India as one nation and a democratic republic. The very preamble of our constitution makes this clear. It has been clearly stated that the objective was to establish a 'sovereign socialist secular democratic republic' and to secure to all its citizens justice, liberty, equality and to promote among them all fraternity, assuring the dignity of the individual and the unity and integrity of the nation.

Having resolved to constitute India as a nation, the framers of the constitution also provided for a democratic pattern. It is pertinent to note that the words 'a parliamentary democracy' are not mentioned anywhere in the constitution. However, for the sake of clarity of understanding one can say that the framers of the constitution visualized three major wings of democracy, namely, legislature, executive, and judiciary, and assigned to them distinct functions. Under this system they thought of a parliament consisting of two houses, namely, the house of the people and the council of states. The house of the people was to consist of members of parliament elected by their respective constituencies and the council of states was to consist of representatives elected indirectly by the members of state legislatures as well as members of parliament.

As for the executive, the head of state in whose name all executive actions are to take place is the president who appoints the council of ministers with the prime minister at the head to aid and advise the president. In terms of the constitutional provisions, it is only by convention that the leader of the majority party is called upon to be the prime minister and head of the council of ministers but there is no article or rule which makes this mandatory. It is because the prime minister and the council of ministers are to be collectively responsible to the house of the people and because a minister has to be a member of either house that a system has been evolved in which parliament exercises control over the executive. It is in this sense that we describe our constitution and government as one having parliamentary form.

Now, therefore, if the above essential features are kept intact, namely, that the executive shall remain collectively responsible to the house of the people, then it would not be possible to allege or contend that the parliamentary form has been altered.

As long as there is a guarantee of stable government at the national level, the present system of parliament, consisting of elected representatives from all over the country electing the leader of the majority as prime minister, can continue to function without much difficulty, as indeed it has for the last thirty years. The problem arises when one visualizes a state of affairs at the national level where, in the absence of clear-cut alternatives, a thin majority consisting of a coalition of more than one political party, including regional parties, emerges at the national level. It is clear that under such circumstances, where every leader would want to be the prime minister, no government could be stable, defections would be encouraged, and, unlike a situation where in case of any instability in the states a stable national government can intervene, it would become a precarious situation because there would be no popular authority to intervene in case of instability at the national level itself.

One thing about which everyone seems to be clear is that we want a democratic republican structure and on this we are not going to compromise. We also want that the supreme law-making body at the national level should be a parliament consisting of the elected representatives of the people which will ensure the republican character and that the executive should be collectively responsible to this parliament. Today the president is, even in terms of our constitution, the chief executive under Article 53, and is elected under Article 54 indirectly by an electoral college consisting of elected members of both houses of parliament and the elected members of the legislative assemblies of the states.

The point for consideration is whether he could be directly

elected by the entire electorate of the country subject to his securing more than 50 per cent of the votes cast. With this single amendment and some other incidental amendments as may be necessary, we can retain all other essential features of the existing constitution, including the collective responsibility of his council of ministers to the parliament, subject to a modification that every minister may not be required to be a member of either house, etc. All other essential powers, including that of impeachment and those of the judiciary, could be retained with one essential change, namely, that the president thus elected with a mandate of clear majority of the entire people of India as head of the executive would not then depend on the vagaries of majority or minority in the parliament. Thus, we will ensure the stability of the national government headed by a president directly elected by the people which will be an even more democratic way than the present indirect election and yet we will retain all the essential and basic features of our present constitution and its parliament.

This one small but important change will have another salutary impact. It is the very essence of parliamentary democracy that it should provide clear-cut alternatives to the people in the form of political parties whereby they can make a clear choice of a political party which could give them a stable government. And the bigger the nation which has an inherent federal character, the greater the need for such clear-cut national alternatives. Unfortunately, during the last thirty years such political alternatives have not emerged at the national level. And because it was not imperative, regional forces have grown and the one national party, that is, the Congress(I), has also eroded in its national impact. Once we have the need for electing the national chief executive by the entire people of the country, it will automatically become imperative to have political parties emerge on the national scene as a cohesive force. This will be a healthy development. Another hopeful advantage in this change would be that having secured stability of sovereign authority at the national level, we could then afford to give greater powers to the states for their economic growth because that would not have any tendency to threaten or weaken the national authority.

27

THE CASE FOR A DIRECTLY ELECTED PRIME MINISTER IN THE NETHERLANDS

J.P.A. GRUIJTERS

The basic idea of the parliamentary system is that the cabinet must have the confidence of parliament . . . It is this form of government that must be regarded as one of the principal causes of the poor operation of the Dutch political system. Although the basic rule of parliamentary confidence is meant to ensure the supreme authority of the people's representatives, in practice these representatives are more and more enfeebled.

The reason is that the cabinet can threaten to make issues 'matters of confidence'. If the cabinet wants to have its way on a certain question, it states that it will regard a contrary decision by the Second Chamber [the lower house of parliament—Ed.] as a lack of confidence.

This has two disastrous consequences. The cabinet gets what it wants with regard to many matters that a majority of the Chamber would have preferred to decide otherwise. The people's representatives shrink from overthrowing a cabinet—and for good reasons. The formation of a new cabinet paralyses all governmental and parliamentary work for many weeks or even months, because it is inevitable that complicated and lengthy negotiations have to be conducted to put together a new cabinet coalition. Therefore, when the Chamber is faced with a 'question of confidence', it will usually submit to the will of the cabinet. The painfully constructed parliamentary majority supporting the cabinet with its confidence tends to remain a supportive majority even with regard to many questions where,

J. P. A. Gruijters, excerpted from *Daarom D'66* (Amsterdam: Uitgeverij De Bezige Bij, 1967), ch. 3. Translation by Arend Lijphart. Reprinted by permission of the author.

in terms of substance, the majority has already fallen apart. It is not surprising that the term 'blackmail' is used in order to describe the pressure that the cabinet can exert on the Chamber by means of the 'question of confidence'. If, nevertheless, the Chamber has the courage to resist this pressure and not to yield to 'blackmail', it produces the other evil of a new cabinet formation. . . .

Whichever way one looks at it, a system in which the cabinet's existence depends on the confidence of parliament has great disadvantages. These are minimized when the party system is simple and tends to a two-party system, but even then they do not disappear: they enfeeble the people's representatives, and 'the people' in their capacity as voters have too little input.

Therefore, [the new party—Ed.] Democrats '66 has decided to propose the direct election of the prime minister. The cabinet, which will consist of the popularly elected prime minister and the ministers he appoints, will no longer need the confidence of parliament. Its democratic legitimacy will be directly based on the electorate.

The voters will have the opportunity to elect, for a three-year or four-year term, a prime minister who will emerge from an election campaign in which both he and his programme will be tested. He will face a parliament that is also elected, for the same period, by the same voters who have chosen the prime minister.

But, the critics are saying, what will happen if these two powers, both founded on the popular will, come into conflict with each other? They will be unable to dismiss or dissolve each other, and, so the argument goes, the conflict will remain unresolved.

In the above criticism, the idea of 'confidence' remains the point of departure. If one gives up this assumption, however, then the criticism turns out to be utterly erroneous: cabinet and parliament will each have their own tasks which in many cases they will have to carry out in mutual co-operation. But, depending on the questions at stake, sometimes the one power and sometimes the other will have the final word. . . .

The head of state will no longer play a role in the formation of the cabinet. This removes the last remnant of the autocratic system of the nineteenth century—a logical development of the radical democratization that Democrats '66 champions. However, to remove this remnant of autocracy has never been the main goal of the reforms advocated by Democrats '66. There is—this needs to be stated emphatically—no reason to do so. But just as British constitutional and political practice recently resulted in virtually terminating the monarch's role in the formation of cabinets—when the Tories, too, decided that their party leader had to be elected, without exception, by the Tory members in the House of Commons—the reform propagated by Democrats '66 will have the same effect. However, as in the British case, the abolition of the monarchy is not the intention.

28

DIRECT ELECTION OF THE PRIME MINISTER

INTERNATIONAL FORUM OF THE ISRAEL-DIASPORA INSTITUTE

In [the] discussion about the system of directly electing the prime minister it was agreed by the Israel-Diaspora Institute's International Forum that a two-ballot system, such as the one used in electing the president of France, is the best method. The first ballot will be unlikely to produce an absolute majority for any one candidate. In that case, the two candidates who receive the most votes shall face each other on the second ballot. This system ensures the victorious candidate of having won the support of a majority of the electorate. . . .

The deliberations of the Israel-Diaspora Institute's International Forum on the system for direct election of the prime minister are summarized in the following list of advantages and disadvantages.

ADVANTAGES OF DIRECT ELECTIONS

1. Direct election of a prime minister awards electoral choice to the voter. This alone has intrinsic democratic value. The elector would be able to choose his prime minister rather than find a prime minister chosen for him after prolonged coalition negotiations of dubious repute. The citizen would know the morning following the election who was to be prime minister.

International Forum of the Israel-Diaspora Institute, excerpted from *Electoral Reform in Israel: A Report of the First Working Session of the IDI International Forum on Electoral Systems held from March 28–April 2, 1989 at the Dan Caesarea Hotel*, ed. by Dr Yoram Peri (Tel Aviv University Campus, Ramat Aviv 69978: Israel-Diaspora Institute, 1989), chs. B.2, B.3. Reprinted by permission of Dr Yoram Peri.

Moreover, a directly elected prime minister would have the clear support of the majority of voters. This is in contrast to the present system by which the candidate of the largest minority party—which may have received less than 40 per cent of the vote—almost certainly attains the premiership. The need for national unity governments would thus be obviated and the deep political disagreements in Israeli society would once again be represented by a strong government and a strong opposition.

2. Popular election of the prime minister would curtail the prolonged post-election period of coalition bargaining. This period only serves to undermine public confidence in the democratic system. While direct elections will not eliminate coalition bargaining altogether, they will alter the whole context of these negotiations: they would now be held either before the elections—as the small parties throw in their lot with one candidate or the other in a public fashion and thus identify themselves with that candidate's platform—or after the government has already been formed (since the prime minister would no longer be dependent on coalition partners in order to begin to govern). In the latter case, the prime minister could leave certain cabinet seats vacant for potential members of his government.

3. To be elected, a candidate would have to enjoy considerable popular support; he or she could not be a mere party functionary. The prime minister would be directly accountable to the electorate—rather than to the party—for government policies and their execution. Political responsibility would be clearly focused.

4. In reality, collective responsibility is a source of weakness in the Israeli government, producing government on the lowest common denominator. A directly elected prime minister's enhanced prestige and power would successfully replace collective responsibility with his own accountability. Discipline within the government would be improved, as would the government's performance.

5. Direct election of the prime minister would strengthen the incipient bipolarity in the Israeli party system. With a two-ballot system of election competition would most probably be centripetal, the second ballot setting a candidate of the moderate left against a candidate of the moderate right. Because the

floating vote in the centre of the political spectrum would be the key to victory, the strength of extremist parties would be reduced.

6. In a system which more clearly separates winners from losers, the latter will also need a better-defined role, suggesting that a more effective parliamentary opposition will come into being.

7. The new public nature of coalition negotiations would strengthen the probity of political life and improve the image of politicians. There might very well be beneficial implications for Israel's political culture.

8. Having a prime minister serving a fixed term of office would introduce greater stability in the country's foreign affairs. In their dealings with Israel other governments would be negotiating with a prime minister whose presence on the scene was semi-permanent and whose legitimacy and authority clearly derived from popular support.

9. If elections to the Knesset followed those for the prime minister, voters (already knowing the identity of the prime minister) would then have the opportunity of electing a Knesset of the same party as the prime minister—thus producing a strong government—or a Knesset controlled by the opposition—leading to a more power-sharing, consensual style of government.

10. The Knesset would be free to fill its watchdog role over the executive. Votes on legislation would not, as they are now, be confused with the survival or defeat of the government.

11. A prime minister with a power base independent of the parties could appoint ministers to his cabinet not solely on the basis of their relative political standing in their parties or in the coalition. Cabinet ministries would be depoliticized and ministers would more closely resemble their American counterparts: administrative heads of departments. This would improve the professionalism and raise the level of government in general.

DISADVANTAGES OF DIRECT ELECTIONS

1. Political power is based on persuasion and bargaining. The strength of the prime minister is a function of his/her authority

vis-à-vis the Knesset and the political parties and should not derive from a popular mandate. (Presidential systems do not guarantee strong executives.) Thus, a presidential system where the prime minister is nominated by a party would be no different than the current system. On the other hand, if a candidate were to run independently of the party machine, he would later experience problems leading the government, as well as the parties in the Knesset.

2. Direct election of the prime minister would not moot the problem of coalition formation; the problem would only present itself under another guise. The direct election of the prime minister may actually increase coalition bargaining since the process of electing a government would be spread out over several elections (first round, run-off, Knesset).

3. Effective government would still rely on a parliamentary majority and a crisis of authority will still occur in the absence of such a majority.

4. There is a real danger of two poles of democratic legitimacy developing within the same society—the prime minister and the Knesset—which would lead to paralysis and deadlock.

5. Extremist candidates might triumph rather than be eliminated in a popular vote. It is most dangerous to have a populist in power in Israel because the government lacks a system of checks and balances. In societies with successful presidential types of government—namely the United States, whose presidential system is uniquely successful—there exist additional layers of authority between the central government and the citizen—for instance, strong local governments in a federal system. No such structure exists in Israel. And those 'mediating agencies' which do exist in Israel (the Knesset, political parties, and, yes, the governmental coalition) and which have a moderating influence on government would actually be weakened by a system of directly electing the prime minister.

6. The excessive personalization of politics expected from direct election of the prime minister will lower the quality of political leaders. And once elected there would be no procedure for recalling an incompetent prime minister or one who has entirely lost public support. The much-touted advantage of

directly electing a prime minister—namely, its stabilizing nature—may, in such a case, become a debilitating inflexibility in the system.

7. A majoritarian (a plebiscitary) system of electing the national leader is unsuitable for a society as heterogeneous as Israel. The almost existential problems and issues facing Israel today require a broader base of consensus than can be commanded by a prime minister who could be elected by a bare majority of the eligible voters.

Would the creation of bipolar politics be such a positive development? Is Israel really interested in replacing her tradition of consensus rule with majoritarian government?

8. There would be a weakening of ministerial accountability to the Knesset and, thus, of Knesset influence over the cabinet.

9. The direct election of the prime minister would result in the intentional weakening of small parties even though small parties are not the principal hindrance to the effective operation of Israeli politics. They have always been part of the Israeli political landscape, even in times when the government suffered no crisis of authority. It is the relation between the two major parties that has brought on the current stalemate.

10. We must ask ourselves whether such an ambitious reform as direct election of the prime minister solves chronic structural problems, or whether it only addresses an immediate crisis. It would be a mistake to make conclusions based only on the results of the last two general elections and to propose a major reform on this basis alone. Will such a change have substance and functionality in 1998, or in 2048? Would we be solving yesterday's problem at the cost of real reform?

11. The government could be dangerously weakened if it becomes completely subservient to the dominating will of a single individual, the prime minister. Ministers could be stripped of their autonomy, becoming second-class executives and their positions could be used to further the interests of the prime minister rather than broader professional aims.

12. Three separate, nationwide elections within a short space of time—two for the prime minister and one for the Knesset—could induce voter fatigue, apathy, polarization, and alienation. A second (and third) round of voting could only serve to over-stimulate the ideological ferment which already characterizes

Israeli elections to an unhealthy extent. The disadvantages to the country would be both emotional and economic.

13. Such a reform is not a minor alteration but a major change in Israel's system of government, one which few democracies have ever undertaken and which is contrary to the anti-presidential spirit of the age. (Electoral reform as practised around the world today favours parliamentary types of systems over presidential ones.) A parliamentary system successfully functions in all the European democracies; this alone is proof of its workability. Why, then, abandon it? There is no precedent for such a radical change.

14. It is a fallacy to think that a single component of a political system can be changed without then having to overhaul it entirely. Such an ambitious reform as this one could not possibly be insulated from other features of the Israeli governmental system. A direct election of the prime minister would entail wide-ranging change in the relations between executive and legislature and between executive and judiciary. There would be a need to re-define the respective roles of the prime minister and the Knesset, the conditions for dissolution of the latter and recall of the former. An authority would have to be established in order to resolve constitutional disputes between the prime minister and the Knesset.

In short, direct election of the prime minister could necessitate the introduction of a codified constitution. There would be a need to review almost all of the Basic Laws. The piecemeal work of building a constitution through the Basic Laws would be undone.

15. The nominating process of prime-ministerial candidates within the parties would have to be regulated. This would involve the state in the workings of political parties, which are essentially voluntary organizations.

16. There is no guarantee that a presidential system will always produce a powerful executive.

17. The personalization of power is inherent in authoritarian regimes and it is easier to slide into autocracy from a presidential system. This has not happened in the United States only because a formal constitution and a federal system—not to mention two hundred years of democratic tradition—counteract the tendency. Israel's situation is quite different.

18. A president has a double function: he is both the chief executive and the head of state, a symbol of national unity. A directly elected prime minister in Israel would fulfil only the former function since Israel already has a president who fills the symbolic function. In lacking this second source of authority a directly elected prime minister would have more difficulty realizing the prospective power of his position.

19. Electoral reform could achieve all the necessary improvements in the prime minister's status (by reducing the number of parties and speeding coalition formation).

PART V

SYSTEMATIC EVIDENCE: BROADLY COMPARATIVE AND MULTIVARIATE ANALYSES

29

COMPARING DEMOCRATIC SYSTEMS

DONALD L. HOROWITZ

In 'The Perils of Presidentialism' [Chapter 14 in this volume—
Ed.], Professor Juan Linz makes the claim that parliamentary
systems are 'more conducive to stable democracy' than are
presidential systems. 'This conclusion,' he continues, 'applies
especially to nations with deep political cleavages and numerous
political parties.' . . .

Linz's claims, however, are not sustainable. First, they are
based on a regionally skewed and highly selective sample of
comparative experience, principally from Latin America.
Second, they rest on a mechanistic, even caricatured, view of
the presidency. Third, they assume a particular system of
electing the president, which is not necessarily the best system.
Finally, by ignoring the functions that a separately elected president can perform for a divided society, they defeat Linz's own
admirable purposes.

PRESIDENTIALISM AND POLITICAL INSTABILITY

As frequent references to Brazil, Colombia, Venezuela, and
Chile attest, Linz believes that presidentialism has contributed
to instability in Latin America. If, however, his focus had been
on instability in post-colonial Asia and Africa, the institutional
villain would surely have been parliamentary systems. Indeed,
Sir Arthur Lewis argued twenty-five years ago in his lectures on
'Politics in West Africa' that the inherited Westminster system
of parliamentary democracy was responsible for much of the
authoritarianism then emerging in English-speaking Africa.

Donald L. Horowitz, excerpted from 'Comparing Democratic Systems',
Journal of Democracy, 1/4 (Fall 1990), pp. 73–9.

What Lewis emphasized was the winner-take-all features of the Westminster model, in which anyone with a parliamentary majority was able to seize the state.

Lewis's understanding conforms to that of many Africans seeking to restore democratic rule. The most impressive efforts at re-democratization, those of Nigeria in 1978–9 and again at the present time, involve adoption of a presidential system to mitigate societal divisions. Under the parliamentary system inherited at independence, a cluster of ethnic groups from the north had managed to secure a majority of seats and shut all other groups out of power. This game of total inclusion and exclusion characterized Nigerian politics after 1960, precipitating the military *coups* of 1966 and the war of Biafran secession from 1967 to 1970. By choosing a separation of powers, the Nigerians aimed to prevent any group from controlling the country by controlling parliament.

Now it is possible that parliamentary systems helped stifle democracy in Africa while presidential systems helped stifle it in Latin America, but there are grounds for doubt. Linz refers to the emergence of conciliatory practices in the presidential systems of Colombia, Venezuela, and Brazil, but he dismisses them as 'deviations'. Chile under Salvador Allende, on the other hand, is regarded as closer to the norm, with presidentialism exacerbating social conflict. Yet at least some research by Arturo Valenzuela suggests that, before Allende, many Chilean presidents actually bolstered centrist, moderating tendencies. The experience of the presidency in the United States, where the presidency was invented, is also explained away as 'an exception'. Consequently, Chile's exacerbated conflict is traced to its presidency, while the moderated conflict of the United States is said to have other roots. Political success has, so to speak, many parents; political failure, only one: the presidency. . . .

Before responding to these claims, it is necessary to underscore a central assumption of the Linz analysis: that the president will be elected under a plurality (first-past-the-post) system or a majority system, with a run-off election if necessary. From this assumption follow most of Linz's complaints. Consequently, it needs to be said clearly that presidents do not need to be elected on a plurality or majority run-off basis. In divided societies, as I shall explain shortly, presidents should be elected by a different system, one that ensures broadly distributed support for the president. This greatly alleviates the problem of the narrowly elected president who labours under the illusion that he has a broader mandate. Winner-take-all is a function of electoral systems, not of institutions in the abstract.

MODES OF PRESIDENTIAL ELECTION

. . . In the Nigerian Second Republic, which began in 1979, a presidential system was created. (The same presidency and electoral system will be used in the Third Republic, scheduled to begin in 1992.) To be elected, a president needed a plurality plus distribution. The successful candidate was required to have at least 25 per cent of the vote in no fewer than two-thirds of the then nineteen states. This double requirement was meant to ensure that the president had support from many ethnic groups. To put the point in Linz's terms, the aim was to shut out ethnic extremists and elect a moderate, centrist president. That is precisely the sort of president the Nigerians elected under the new system. The extremists, in fact, were elected to parliament, not the presidency. Nor was there any of the polarization that Linz associates with majority run-offs. Carefully devised presidential-election arrangements can bolster the centre and knit together the rent fabric of a divided society. In choosing a presidential electoral system with incentives for widely distributed support, the Nigerians were rejecting winner-take-all politics. They aimed instead for a president bent on conciliation rather than on conflict. They succeeded.

In 1978, Sri Lanka also moved to a presidential system. Its principal purpose was to create a political executive with a fixed term that would permit the incumbent to make unpopular decisions, particularly those concerning the reduction of ethnic conflict. A majority requirement was instituted. Since most candidates were unlikely to gain a majority in Sri Lanka's multi-party system, a method of alternative voting was adopted. Each voter could vote for several candidates, ranking them in order of preference. If no candidate attained a majority of first preferences, the top two candidates would be put into what amounted to an instant run-off. The second preferences of voters for all other candidates would then be counted (and likewise for third preferences) until one of the top two gained a majority. It was expected that presidential candidates would build their majority on the second and third choices of voters whose preferred candidate was not among the top two. This would put ethnic minorities (especially the Sri Lankan Tamils) in a position to require compromise as the price for their second preferences. So, again, the presidential system would rule out extremists, provide incentives to moderation, and encourage compromise in a fragmented society. . . .

CHOOSING AMONG DEMOCRATIC INSTITUTIONS

Although the sharp distinction between presidential and parliamentary systems is unwarranted, Linz's disquiet is not. He has genuine cause for concern about the institutions adopted by democratizing states, particularly those with deep cleavages and numerous parties. He is right to worry about winner-take-all outcomes and their exclusionary consequences in such societies. Nevertheless, it is Westminster, the Mother of Parliaments, that produces such outcomes as often as any presidential system does.

As this suggests, Linz's quarrel is not with the presidency, but with two features that epitomize the Westminster version of democracy: first, plurality elections that produce a majority of seats by shutting out third-party competitors; and second, adversary democracy, with its sharp divide between winners and losers, government and opposition. Because these are Linz's underlying objections, it is not difficult to turn his arguments around against parliamentary systems, at least where they produce coherent majorities and minorities. Where no majority emerges and coalitions are necessary, sometimes—but only sometimes—more conciliatory processes and outcomes emerge. As a result, Linz's thesis boils down to an argument not against the presidency but against plurality election, not in favour of parliamentary *systems* but in favour of parliamentary *coalitions*.

30

THE CENTRALITY OF POLITICAL CULTURE

SEYMOUR MARTIN LIPSET

Juan Linz and Donald Horowitz are to be commended for reviving the discussion of the relationship between constitutional systems—presidential or parliamentary—and the conditions that make for stable democracy. Linz, basing himself largely on the Latin American experience, notes that most presidential systems have repeatedly broken down. Horowitz, a student of Asia and Africa, emphasizes that most parliamentary systems, particularly those attempted in almost all African countries and some of the new nations of post-war Asia, have also failed. He could also have pointed to the inter-war collapse of democratic parliamentarism in Spain, Portugal, Greece, Italy, Austria, Germany, and most of eastern Europe. Conversely, in addition to the successful parliamentary regimes of northern Europe and the industrialized parts of the British Commonwealth, countries such as France under the Fifth Republic, pre-Allende Chile, Costa Rica, and Uruguay (for most of this century) offer examples of stable and democratic presidentialism.

Clearly, it is not obvious that constitutional variations in type of executive are closely linked to democratic or authoritarian outcomes. As Linz emphasizes, parliamentary government (especially where there are several parties but none with a clear majority) gives different constituencies more access to the decision-making process than they would enjoy in presidential systems, and presumably helps bind these constituencies to the polity. Under presidential government, those opposed to the president's party may regard themselves as marginalized, and thus may seek to undermine presidential legitimacy.

Seymour Martin Lipset, excerpted from 'The Centrality of Political Culture', *Journal of Democracy*, 1/4 (Fall 1990), pp. 80–3.

Because presidential government entrusts authority and ultimate responsibility to a single person, some scholars regard it as inherently unstable; failures can lead to a rejection of the symbol of authority. Power seems more diversified in parliamentary regimes.

The reality is more complicated. Given the division of authority between presidents and legislatures, prime ministers and their cabinets are more powerful and may pay less attention to the importunings of specific groups. A prime minister with a majority of parliament behind him has much more authority than an American president. Basically, such parliaments vote to support the budgets, bills, and policies that the government presents. Government members must vote this way, or the cabinet falls and an election is called. Unlike members of a legislative branch, opposition parliamentarians, though free to debate, criticize, or vote against the policies set by the executive, rarely can affect them.

The situation is quite different in a presidential system. The terms of the president and cabinet are not affected by votes in the legislature. As a result, party discipline is much weaker in, say, the US Congress than it is in the British parliament. In the United States and other presidential systems, the representation of diverse interests and value groups in different parties leads to cross-party alliances on various issues. Local interests are better represented in Congress, since a representative will look for constituency support to get re-elected and can vote against his president or party. An MP, however, must go with his prime minister and his party, even if doing so means alienating constituency support.

The fact that presidencies make for weak parties and weak executives, while parliaments tend to have the reverse effect, certainly affects the nature of and possibly the conditions for democracy. But much of the literature wrongly assumes the opposite: that a president is inherently stronger than a prime minister, and that power is more concentrated in the former. I should emphasize that a condition for a strong cabinet government is the need to call a new election when a cabinet loses a parliamentary vote. Where parliament continues and a new cabinet is formed from a coalition of parties, no one of which has a majority, parliamentary cabinets may be weak, as in the

Weimar Republic, the Third and Fourth French Republics, or
contemporary Israel and India. . . .

THE CULTURAL FACTOR

The question remains, why have most Latin American polities
not functioned like the US political system? The answer lies in
economic and cultural factors. If we look at the comparative
record, it still suggests, as I noted in 1960 in *Political Man*, that
long-enduring democracies are disproportionately to be found
among the wealthier and more Protestant nations. The 'Fourth'
or very undeveloped world apart, Catholic and poorer countries
have been less stably democratic. The situation has of course
changed somewhat in recent times. Non-Protestant southern
European countries like Greece, Italy, Portugal, and Spain have
created parliamentary democracies, while most Catholic Latin
American countries have competitive electoral systems with
presidential regimes.

I will not reiterate my past discussions of the diverse social
conditions for democracy, other than to note that the correla-
tions of democracy with Protestantism and a past British connection point up the importance of cultural factors. In this
connection, it may be noted that in Canada the 'Latin' (French-
speaking and Catholic) province of Quebec seemingly lacked
the conditions for a pluralistic party system and democratic
rights until the 1960s, while the anglophone and Protestant part
of the country has had a stable multi-party system with democratic guarantees for close to a century. In seeking to explain
in 1958 why 'French Canadians have not really believed in
democracy for themselves', and did not have a functioning
competitive party system, political scientist Pierre Trudeau,
who would later serve as prime minister of Canada for sixteen
years, wrote, 'French Canadians are Catholics; and Catholic
nations have not always been ardent supporters of democracy.
They are authoritarian in spiritual matters; and . . . they are
often disinclined to seek solutions in temporal matters through
the mere counting of heads.'[1]

[1] Pierre Elliott Trudeau, *Federalism and the French Canadians* (New York:
St Martin's, 1968), p. 108.

Trudeau mentioned other factors, of course, particularly those inherent in the minority and economically depressed situation of his linguistic compatriots, but basically, as he noted, Canada had two very different cultures and political systems within the same set of governmental and constitutional arrangements. Quebec, like most of South America, may be described as Latin and American, and its pre-1960 politics resembled that of other Latin societies more than it did any in the anglophone world, whether presidential or parliamentary. Quebec, of course, has changed greatly since the early 1960s, and now has a stable two-party system. But these political developments have occurred in tandem with major adjustments in the orientation and behaviour of the Catholic Church, in the content of the educational system, and in economic development and mobility, particularly among the francophones. What has not changed is the formal political system.

Islamic countries may also be considered as a group. Almost all have been authoritarian, with monarchical or presidential systems of government. It would be hard to credit the weakness of democracy among them to their political institutions. Some writers claim that Islamic faith makes political democracy in a western sense extremely difficult, since it recognizes no separation of the secular and religious realms. Such claims should not be categorical, since, as with Christianity, doctrines and practices can evolve over time.

This emphasis on culture is reinforced by Myron Weiner's observation that almost all of the post-war 'new nations' that have become enduring democracies are former British colonies, as are various others, such as Nigeria and Pakistan, which maintained competitive electoral institutions for briefer periods. Almost none of the former Belgian, Dutch, French, Portuguese, or Spanish colonies have comparable records. In the comparative statistical analyses that I have been conducting of the factors associated with democracy among the Third World countries, past experience with British rule emerges as one of the most powerful correlates of democracy.

Cultural factors deriving from varying histories are extraordinarily difficult to manipulate. Political institutions— including electoral systems and constitutional arrangements —are more easily changed. Hence, those concerned with enhancing the possibilities for stable democratic government focus on them. Except for the case of the Fifth French Republic, and the barriers placed on small-party representation in West Germany, there is little evidence, however, that such efforts have had much effect, and the latter case is debatable.

31

THE VIRTUES OF PARLIAMENTARISM

JUAN J. LINZ

I agree with Professor Horowitz that the study of democratic regimes cannot be separated from the study of electoral systems, and acknowledge that my analysis does not cover all possible methods of presidential election. The Nigerian system represents a unique method of presidential election that might be applicable in federal states, particularly multi-ethnic ones, but I doubt very much that one could justify it in more homogeneous societies, even in the federal states of Latin America. My analysis concentrates on the two most common methods of election: the simple majority or plurality system, and the two-candidate run-off. The case where an electoral college may make a decision irrespective of the popular vote is left out, as is the very special case of Bolivia. The Bolivian congress chooses among presidential candidates without regard to their popular vote totals, a practice that has certainly not contributed to either political stability or accountability in that country. I also refrained from mentioning the practice of directly electing a plural executive or a president and vice-president to represent two different constituencies (of Greek and Turkish Cypriots, for example). My argument concerns the *likelihood* of certain patterns of politics in the most common types of presidential systems, and does not attempt an exhaustive analysis of all types of directly elected executives. The patterns in question are likely to contribute to instability or difficulties in the performance of presidential executives. I use the word 'likelihood' to stress that those consequences need not be present in each and every presidential system, or lead to the breakdown of democracy itself. On the contrary, recent

Juan J. Linz, excerpted from 'The Virtues of Parliamentarism', *Journal of Democracy*, 1/4 (Fall 1990), pp. 84–91.

experience shows that even rather inept democratic regimes stand a good chance of surviving simply because all relevant actors find the non-democratic alternatives to be even less satisfactory.

Horowitz stresses that the majoritarian implications of presidentialism—the 'winner-take-all' features that I have emphasized—may also be present in parliamentary systems with plurality elections in single-member districts, especially under the two-party systems that so often go together with Westminster-style parliamentary government. In societies that are polarized, or fragmented by multiple cleavages, a multi-party system with proportional representation may allow the formation of alternative coalitions (as in Belgium, for example), and thus forestall dangerous zero-sum outcomes.

As for parliamentary systems with plurality elections, Mrs Thatcher is certainly a first above unequals, like a president, and probably has more power than an American chief executive. Certainly, parliamentary democracies in which a single disciplined party obtains the absolute majority of all seats find themselves in what is close to a 'winner-take-all' situation. But this is not the most frequent pattern in parliamentary systems, particularly when there is proportional representation. Indeed, Horowitz implies that I should probably extend some of my concerns about the style of politics in presidentialism to take in the case of such majoritarian prime ministers, and that I might have a slight bias in favour of stable coalition government. I must once again note that I am dealing with ideal types that cannot subsume all of the possible varieties of political systems; indeed, I deal only with the more frequent tendencies in those ideal types. Nevertheless, while the actual situation of a powerful prime minister like Mrs Thatcher might be comparable to that of a president with a legislative majority, the *de jure* difference is still significant. If Mrs Thatcher were to falter or otherwise make herself a liability, for instance, the Conservative majority in the House of Commons could unseat her without creating a constitutional crisis. There would be no need to let her linger ineffectually in office like former presidents Raúl Alfonsín of Argentina or Alan García of Peru. Parliamentary elections may be called not only to benefit from popularity, but also when governing becomes difficult because of a lack of cohesion among the parliamentary majority. That was what happened in Spain in 1982, when Prime Minister Leopoldo Calvo Sotelo's dissolution of the Cortes allowed Felipe González to assume power at the head of a Socialist majority. Moreover, in cases where the parliamentary majority remains intact but the prime minister becomes discredited or exhausted (like Spanish premier Adolfo Suárez in 1981), he can resign without having to wait for the end of his term or a *coup* to remove him from office.

The 'winner-take-all' character of the presidential election and the 'unipersonal' executive (to use Arend Lijphart's term) does not rule out either weak presidents in particular or a weak presidency in general, Horowitz's suggestion to the contrary notwithstanding. The 'all' that the winner takes may not include much effective power, especially if congressional support is not forthcoming. This is doubly so if popular support ebbs as the next election approaches. Presidents, especially those who come to power after a plebiscitarian or populist campaign, often find that the power they possess is hopelessly insufficient to meet the expectations they have generated. Constant presidential efforts to obtain new powers or invoke emergency authority are reflections of this fact. . . .

Horowitz tends to overstate my position by ignoring the necessarily qualified nature of my analysis. I was merely trying to evaluate the existing evidence and offer an estimate of probabilities; I would never place myself in the absurd position of claiming certitude about matters that remain only partly understood.

VARIETIES OF PRESIDENTIALISM

Horowitz further claims that my sample is skewed and highly selective, drawing as it does mostly on Latin American cases. I did not do a quantitative analysis, but the presidential systems of Latin America, together with those of the Philippines and South Korea (which I also had in mind), comprise almost all of the world's pure presidential regimes; the only exceptions are the systems of the United States, Nigeria, and Sri Lanka. Horowitz bases much of his argument on these last two countries.[1] I did not limit my generalizations to Latin America, since I think them largely valid for South Korea and the Philippines as well. The South Korean presidential election of 1987, for instance, saw Roh Tae Woo of the Democratic Justice Party (DJP) win office with 36.6 per cent of the vote—almost the same percentage of the vote (34.7) as Adolfo Suárez's UCD garnered in Spain in 1977. Roh's victory frustrated opposition leaders Kim Young Sam and Kim Dae Jung, who had insisted on a direct presidential election and then split 55 per cent of the vote between them.

As for Africa, close attention to the post-colonial history of that continent does not sustain Horowitz's claim that 'the institutional villain would surely have been parliamentary systems'. It was not simply parliamentarism, but rather demo-cratic institutions as a whole—alien and weakly rooted as they were—that failed in Africa. The British Westminster model has winner-take-all features, to be sure, but these were even more prominent in presidential systems. Indeed, the emergence of authoritarian regimes in countries like Ghana, Uganda, and Senegal coincided with and was consolidated by 'constitutional change from a parliamentary to a presidential system, with extreme concentration of power in the presidency and marked diminution of legislative authority'.[2] . . .

Horowitz's third claim—that I did not deal with each and every possible system for electing a president—is accurate enough, though I did cover the predominant ones (with the exceptions he presents). As for his fourth point, concerning the functions that a separately elected president can perform

---

[1] Horowitz also refers to Colombia as a more successful case of presiden-tialism, but that country's transition to and early maintenance of presidential democracy was made possible only by the *Concordancia* of 1958, an arrange-ment under which the two major parties agreed to suspend their electoral competition for the presidency and accept alternating terms in power instead. While this helped to stabilize the country after a period of civil war and dictatorship, it can hardly be considered a model of democratic politics, or a method for making government accountable to the voters. To call it a deviation may be too mild.

[2] Larry Diamond, 'Introduction: Roots of Failure, Seeds of Hope', in Larry Diamond, Juan J. Linz, and Seymour Martin Lipset (eds.), *Democracy in Developing Countries*, vol. 2: *Africa* (Boulder, Col.: Lynne Rienner, 1988), p. 3.

in a divided society, I concede that under certain very special circumstances (like those of Nigeria and perhaps Sri Lanka), a president *might* be able to help build political consensus. Still, there are counter-examples like Cyprus and Lebanon (to mention two other presidential systems) which show that presidentialism cannot overcome certain types of cleavages. Moreover, in view of the failure of Nigeria's Second Republic and the transition from military rule to a presidential Third Republic that is now under way, the jury is still out on the Nigerian presidency. The same might be said about Sri Lanka, where ethnic violence continues to rage and the deterioration of democratic institutions and liberties has yet to be reversed. The political problems of multi-ethnic societies under whatever system of rule (democratic or authoritarian, for that matter) present complexities that I could not address within the confines of a short essay.

Horowitz insists that a presidential electoral system with incentives for seeking widely distributed support (as in Nigeria) can obviate the winner-take-all politics that prevail in most presidential systems, particularly those with a weak separation of powers, no true federalism, and no strong judiciary. I have no doubt that requiring each candidate to gain, say, at least 25 per cent of the vote in no fewer than two-thirds of the states will tend to produce a president with broad support across ethnic-cum-territorial divisions, thereby reducing ethnic polarization. But in any event, none of this did much to mitigate the winner-take-all aspect of Nigeria's presidential system. That system twice gave a minority party the exclusive right to constitute the executive branch, and helped to undermine democracy by spurring the massive rigging of the 1983 presidential election. Such a system can also backfire by leading to the election of a weak compromise candidate. Perhaps I overgeneralized from the cases included in my analysis, but to make contrary generalizations on the basis of highly unusual arrangements seems to me even less satisfactory. I still wonder how easy it is for Sri Lanka's president to make the sorts of unpopular decisions of which he is supposed to be capable (thanks to a method of election that aggregates second and subsequent preferences) in the face of a hostile legislative majority.

32

PRESIDENTIALISM: A PROBLEMATIC REGIME TYPE

FRED W. RIGGS

On 25 May 1787, a quorum of seven states (out of thirteen) having been obtained, the Constitutional Convention started 100 days of debate, in Philadelphia, producing agreements on an American constitution that remains in effect to this day. On 25 May 1987 the city of Philadelphia opened a six-month celebration of this historic event. Thomas Ferraro of United Press International reported from that city that every state in the USA would celebrate 'to salute the enduring document, which has served as a model for national constitutions around the world' (*Honolulu Advertiser*, 25 May 1987: A-8).

Ferraro's journalistic euphoria mirrors the complacency of most American political scientists who tend, similarly, while analysing the experience and problems of governance in America, to take for granted the essential viability of its constitutional design.[1] They sometimes complain about the racism and sexism supported by the founders, but they regard the longevity of the system as irrefutable evidence of its superiority and its export value as a model for emulation by would-be democracies. If American politics were to be studied within the context of comparative politics, however, such complacency could not be defended.

Fred W. Riggs, excerpted from 'The Survival of Presidentialism in America: Para-constitutional Practices', *International Political Science Review*, 9/4 (October 1988), pp. 247–78. At the author's request, two new footnotes (nos. 1 and 5) were added.

[1] This design, based on the 'separation of powers', requires only that the head of government (who also serves as head of state) must have a fixed term of office and cannot be removed for political reasons by a congressional vote of no confidence.

A PAROCHIAL AGENDA

Sad to say, most Americanists know little, in depth, about other systems of government, and American comparativists typically ignore American politics. Without further inquiry I dare not say that this limitation applies to comparativists working outside the United States. However, I submit that comparisons based on the higher survival rate of Third World regimes which emulate 'parliamentary' and 'one-party' models as compared with the disasters universally experienced by those who follow the American model do raise fundamental questions that are almost always ignored. American political scientists usually start their inquiries by studying issues that appear on the agenda of the American Congress, President, courts and political parties. Although this agenda sometimes includes complaints about the constitution, it rarely challenges the basic viability of the system, or it directs attention to marginal changes—e.g. amendments (the fourteenth and fifteenth) designed to overcome its original blindness to slavery and current proposals to enhance the status of women by adopting an 'Equal Rights Amendment'.

When Americanists analyse the constitution, as they do in the opening chapters of any textbook on American government . . ., they focus on issues debated by the 'founding fathers', or they analyse the class, racial, and sexist biases inherent in the design. Although they often take up problems of interpretation, they ignore fundamental constitutional questions that contemporary comparative studies might raise. When they do compare the American regime with alternative models, they seek to explain the differences—or perhaps to register a preference for the British system—but never, I believe, to explain why the American constitution survives. . . .

A Flawed Prescription

One starting-point for analysis might be the proposition that some thirty-three Third World countries (but only one in the First or Second!) have adopted presidentialist constitutions. Almost universally these polities have endured disruptive catastrophes, usually in the form of one or more *coups d'état* whereby conspiratorial groups of military officers seize power, suspend the constitution, displace elected officials, impose martial law, and promote authoritarian rule: recent examples in Korea, South Vietnam, Liberia and many Latin American countries come to mind. Sometimes an elected president dissolves congress and rules by martial law, as Ferdinand Marcos did in the Philippines. Very exceptionally, a popular revolution terminates a presidentialist regime, as in Nicaragua. No country following a presidentialist model, except the USA, has been able to avoid at least one such disruptive experience. In many, the disruptions are frequent.[2]

By contrast, almost two-thirds of the Third World countries which adopted parliamentary constitutions, usually based on British or French models, have maintained their regimes and avoided the disruptions typical of all American-type systems.[3] This does not mean that they were well governed but only that somehow they were able to avoid military domination. It also means that one-third of these polities did experience military interventions. No doubt other factors were also important. However, I doubt that cultural peculiarities explain why some parliamentary regimes survive and others collapse. A more significant factor is the relatively great power of career bureaucracies (military and civil) in many new states by contrast with the weakness of their institutions for self-government.

Incidentally, the democratic constitutions found in western

[2] Thirty Third World countries with presidentialist regimes have experienced disruption by *coup d'état* since 1945: of these, twenty-one are in Latin America, seven in Africa, and two in Asia. Three others have been disrupted by other means. Not one has been able to sustain an uninterrupted series of constitutionally prescribed presidential and congressional elections. See Fred W. Riggs, 'Bureaucratic Power and Administrative Change', unpublished manuscript, 1985, p. 34. The US did, of course, experience a major threat to its survival during the civil 'war between the states'. Nevertheless, the federal government in Washington and the authority of President and Congress persisted throughout this highly traumatic period.

[3] Forty-three Third World countries had parliamentary regimes when they were liberated from imperial rule: of this number, twenty-nine remained intact as of 1985, and thirteen experienced disruption by *coup*. Grenada, an exceptional case, apparently had a 'revolution': Riggs, 'Bureaucratic Power', p. 32.

Europe, all of which were established after the American Revolution, uniformly rejected presidentialism in favour of some kind of parliamentarism. No doubt parliamentary systems have their own inherent weaknesses, especially when they become highly polarized by the multiplication of parties. The purpose of this inquiry, however, is not to compare presidentialist with parliamentary regimes, but only to use such comparisons to highlight features of the American system that have contributed to the survival of its constitution.

Third World polities which opted for one-party regimes, following the Soviet model, have perpetuated their systems even more successfully than have the parliamentary types.[4] Mere survival, of course, is not the only important consideration and we much prefer multi-party competition to one-party conformity. None the less, it is important to understand why one type of democratic constitution works so much better than another in Third World countries—and why a system that works so wretchedly elsewhere has nevertheless survived in the United States.

Explaining Failures and Successes

Although American political scientists are well aware of the many catastrophes experienced by other presidentialist regimes, especially in Latin America, they usually look for external variables to explain them—cultural or religious differences, educational and economic levels, ethnic problems, imperialism, or dependency. They scarcely consider the relative success of parliamentary regimes, or even of single-party regimes, as evidence of the basic fragility of presidentialist systems based on the American model.

In so far as similar contextual and environmental conditions prevail in all Third World countries, students of comparative politics might have asked why some regime types are much more unsuccessful than others. This question might also have led them to ask: 'If presidentialism works so badly elsewhere,

---

[4] Thirty-four new states opted for a single-party regime when they became independent: of these, only five succumbed to coups: Riggs, 'Bureaucratic Power', p. 37.

why has it nevertheless survived in the United States for 200 years?' Moreover, if we could discover the reasons for the American 'success', this might help us identify some variables that account for the failures in other presidentialist countries.

Two general kinds of explanation are needed. One is environmental, or contextual, and the other is systemic. A good example of a contextual variable is the legal culture of a society—thus common law prevails in the USA, whereas codified civil law is normal in Latin America. Some say that North American culture is more conducive to conflict management and Latin culture more likely to accentuate confrontations—but this is surely an oversimplification. The Roman Catholic Church was established in most Latin American countries, whereas Protestantism and the separation of church and state became the norm in the United States. The open frontier and opportunities for social mobility available to Americans contrast with the more aristocratic or quasi-feudal social structure found in other presidentialist regimes. Do such differences explain success or failure? No doubt many contextual/environmental variables and historical accidents helped the fragile American presidentialist constitution survive. But can we prove that they were necessary—even if not sufficient—conditions for the survival of the American constitution?

A more fruitful line of inquiry, especially in a short article, may evolve if this analysis is limited to systemic variables, because they might be substantiated by comparative inquiry. By investigating the failures of presidentialist regimes it may be possible to discover if their breakdowns were linked with the lack of systemic features whose presence may be viewed as part of the explanation for the survival of the American system.[5]

Although the focus of this article is on the American constitution, its real goal is to promote a new (institutionalist) mode of

[5] In subsequent work, I have identified seven crucial practices which seem to me to explain in large measure the survival of American presidentialism, while their absence probably accounts for the failure of other presidentialist regimes. Sadly, these practices may be faulted as anti-democratic and, perhaps, their absence elsewhere reflects the impact of pro-democratic reforms. The reformers simply failed to recognize how the reforms undermined the viability of the presidentialist model for representative government.

comparative government that explicitly includes both American and non-American systems. We need to transcend the existing dichotomy between research on the Third World and studies of the industrialized countries, and we must overcome the ethnocentric assumption that the American formula for democratic self-governance can and should be emulated elsewhere.

33

CONTEMPORARY DEMOCRACIES: PARTICIPATION, STABILITY, AND VIOLENCE

G. BINGHAM POWELL, JR

Theoretical expectations vary about the impact of executive–legislative arrangements on democratic performance. The only clear expectation is that presidential systems should be more stable—as measured by the tenure of the chief executive—than ministerial ones. The greater and more autonomous presidential resources make such stability likely. They do not, however, ensure party or policy compatibility between legislature and executive.

Expectations about effects on participation are less clear-cut. On the one hand, direct participation of citizens in the election of a strong chief executive might encourage citizen involvement. On the other hand, the separate electoral bases of president and legislature may weaken the national party systems, as the organizing and co-ordinating power of parties is not needed to choose a prime minister; individual candidates may be more important than party labels; weaker party organizations may mean lower turnout. Finally, a single major prize in the presidential contest may encourage party alliances and consolidation, with unknown consequences for participation.

Expectations about violence are also conflicting. The presidential system's stability and concentration of emergency powers may make it easier to clamp down on violent outbreaks, but the divided legislative–executive relations may make it more difficult to respond quickly and positively to policy demands

G. Bingham Powell, Jr, excerpted from *Contemporary Democracies: Participation, Stability, and Violence* (Cambridge, Mass., and London: Harvard University Press, 1982), ch. 4 (footnotes abridged). Copyright © 1982 the President and Fellows of Harvard College. Reprinted by permission of the publisher.

from citizens. Moreover, the independently elected single executive, often with limited individual re-election possibilities, lends itself to less accommodative reactions to discontent.

Bases of Legislative Representation

A well-developed body of theory exists to link the constitutional bases of legislative representation to party-system configurations and indirectly to government performance. It was long argued that elections using proportional representation and multi-member electoral districts would encourage multi-party systems, while plurality elections and single-member districts (as in the United States and Britain) would encourage two-party systems. . . . For our purposes here the inference seems reasonably clear that the proportional representation (PR) systems with multi-member districts would be expected to lead to less stability and fewer situations of government control of the legislature, because they encourage the existence of more than two political parties. . . .

Expectations about aspects of democratic performance other than government stability are mixed or conflicting. Supporters of PR tend to believe that the inherently more equitable system of representation will encourage legitimate participation and limit violence. . . . Proponents of single-member districts, by contrast, believe that the propensity of such systems to create clear-cut elected majorities will encourage voter involvement, because the choice of the government is more directly shaped by the election returns. Strong majorities may also be better able to deal with citizen discontent. Following the language of the literature on this subject, I shall use the term 'election laws' to refer to the legislative rules of representation.

CONSTITUTIONAL DESIGN AND POLITICAL PERFORMANCE

The Constitutional Types

Expectations about the two major dimensions can be combined into a single typology with resultant predictions. As the only unambiguous theoretical predictions have to do with government stability, and as these emphasize the presidential resources first, followed by the impact of electoral systems on legislative majorities and multi-partism (where legislatures are important for stability), the typology combines all the presidential systems. Regardless of the legislative or party fractionalization, we expect government stability where we find presidential executives. But majority control of the legislature is more doubtful. It depends on simultaneous election of party majorities from different electoral bases in the presidential systems. Within the parliamentary systems the constitutional arrangements emphasizing single-member districts, or at least a few members per district and perhaps cut-off exclusion of small parties, are expected to be more stable than their fully proportional counterparts. . . . From these expectations, the parliamentary systems with single or a few representatives per district are designated 'majoritarian parliamentary systems', while the others are designated 'representational parliamentary systems'. . . .

Constitution and Performance

We can now classify the democracies by their constitutional features. The seven presidential systems are listed at the top of Table 1. Six of them were presidential throughout the period of this study, while Uruguay adopted a presidential constitution in a referendum in 1966 and chose its first contemporary president in 1967, at the beginning of the second decade of our analysis. The lower two groupings of countries distinguish the majoritarian and representational parliamentary systems. After the name of each country appears the number of representatives per legislative district in the popular legislative chamber, which is the primary basis for distinguishing among the types. As suggested by F. A. Hermens, I have not classified a system as having a fully representational constitution unless it has at least five representatives per district.[1] . . . West Germany, Ireland, and Japan also have other less representational features accompanying their two to four representatives per district.

---

[1] F. A. Hermens, 'The Dynamics of Proportional Representation', in Andrew J. Milnor (ed.), *Comparative Political Parties* (New York: Thomas Y. Crowell, 1969), p. 220.

TABLE 1. Constitutional types[a] and political performance

Country	Representatives per district[b]	Median voting turnout, %	Median executive durability, months	Median majority control, %	Median yearly riots/million 1958–67	Median yearly riots/million 1967–76	Median yearly deaths/million 1958–67	Median yearly deaths/million 1967–76
Presidential systems								
Chile	6							
Costa Rica	8							
France	1	71	36	72	0.14	0.15	0.18	0.53
Philippines	1							
US	1							
Uruguay	5							
Venezuela	9							
Majoritarian–parliamentary systems								
Australia	1							
Canada	1							
Ceylon	1							
West Germany	2							

India	1	73	33	94	0.07	0.03	0.01	0.30
Ireland	4						
Jamaica	1						
Japan	4						
New Zealand	1						
UK	1						
Representational-parliamentary systems							
Austria	6						
Belgium	7						
Denmark	10						
Finland	13						
Italy	19	87	22	64	0.10	0.02	0.03	0.00
Netherlands	150						
Norway	8						
Sweden	8						
Turkey	7						

[a] Switzerland's unique constitutional arrangements exclude it from this analysis. Uruguay became presidential in 1967. Greece and Israel would be classified as representational–parliamentary, but are not shown as data are not available for the second decade. Executive durability and majority control are for 1967–76 only.

[b] These are the number of legislators in the popular house of the legislature, divided by the number of electoral districts, in the late 1960s. In 1971 Austria decreased the number of districts, increasing the number of representatives per district to nearly 20. Sweden increased to 12 after 1970.

Here they are shown in the majoritarian group, but in multi-variate analysis they will be assigned an intermediate status. The unique Swiss multi-party, strong, collective executive does not appear in the table.

Despite the concern about constitutional complexities, we can see in the table that the expectations about government performance are realized quite effectively. The presidential systems are designed to produce executive stability, and they do so. In fact, only in the United States was a president (Nixon in 1974) forced from office by political pressures in less than three years. In Chile and Uruguay military intervention did remove an incumbent or render him largely powerless before his term expired. But certainly the presidential systems provided more executive stability than either of the other designs. At the same time, the separate election of the president and the legislature often led to minority presidents; a majority of the presidential systems faced a divided legislative/executive situation for over two years in the decade. Moreover, as in the United States, the quite different constituencies to which president and legislature were responsible often made for difficult collaboration between the president and his own legislative party when it was in the majority. . . . The presidential systems also were characterized by rather low levels of citizen electoral involvement, another respect in which the United States is typical of presidential systems.

Table 1 shows that the majoritarian parliamentary constitutions were the most effective at avoiding minority governments, with half of them experiencing less than seven months of minority prime ministers, and were quite effective in generating executive stability. The median duration of the cabinet in such systems, before either being defeated or having to call an election, was around 33 months of the 36-month maximum. The representational parliamentary systems, by contrast, experienced considerable problems with both stability and effective majorities. The average tenure of their chief executives was only around 22 months, and minority governments were quite common.

The representational systems did mobilize very high levels of voting turnout. . . .

While the nature of the constitutional design yields fairly clear expectations about government stability and effectiveness, the implications for the containment of violence are not so obvious. On the one hand, the presidential and majoritarian parliamentary systems should have chief executives capable of dealing vigorously with violence. On the other hand, the representational systems are designed to allow discontented citizens easy access into the political system, thus perhaps taking the pressure off suppressed grievances. Table 1 shows the median riots and deaths per capita for the different constitutional types.

Although we cannot reach any final conclusions before we look at environmental factors, the data in Table 1 speak well for the representational strategy. Rioting was most frequent (per capita) in the presidential systems, although not very strongly related to constitutional types. Deaths by violence were much more clearly associated with constitutional arrangements, with the presidential systems manifesting the most deaths and the representational ones the fewest. This pattern is very clear in both time periods. . . .

CONSTITUTION AND CULTURE

Constitutions are man-made designs. These designs reflect the constitution-makers' values, their expectations of the consequences of various arrangements, their often laboriously negotiated compromises.[2] In so far as constitution-makers have tried to make their constitutions responsive to local needs and conditions, and to avoid negative consequences, associations between constitutional type and democratic performance may reflect those initial efforts, rather than reflect ongoing consequences of the incentives and costs created by the constitution itself. In so far as the constitution embodies values widely held in a society, both constitutional type and performance pattern may be products of political culture—the configuration of

---

[2] In some cases these designs were worked out at a single constitutional convention, as in the United States, or by a single piece of parliamentary legislation, such as the British North America Act (for Canada), or by a designer and his advisers, as in de Gaulle's constitution for the Fifth Republic of France. In other cases, as in Britain, the constitution reflects a long history of experience and re-working.

attitudes and beliefs held by citizens and élites in a society—
rather than one being a cause of the other.

The inability to measure political culture directly is a grievous
limitation of a statistical analysis such as this one. But Table 2
shows how powerful the relationship is between general culture
and constitutional type.

TABLE 2. Culture and constitutional arrangements

Cultural influence	Predominate constitution type	Countries fitting type	Exceptions or mixed
American or American-dominated	Presidential executive and majoritarian legislature	USA Philippines	West Germany Japan
British or British-dominated or educated	Parliamentary and majoritarian legislature	UK Australia Canada Ceylon India Jamaica New Zealand	Ireland
Continental western Europe and Scandinavia	Parliamentary and representational legislature	Austria Belgium Denmark Finland Israel Italy Netherlands Norway Sweden	France Switzerland
Latin America	Presidential executive and representational legislature	Chile Costa Rica Uruguay Venezuela	pre-1967 Uruguay
Other	Parliamentary and representational legislature	Greece Turkey	

Clearly the fit between cultural background and constitutional type is very strong. Britain and [six] of its ex-colonies are marked by the majoritarian parliamentary type, with Ireland, as a country once part of Britain, the only (partial) exception through the period covered by the study. The Latin American countries are all characterized by presidential executives and representational legislatures, except for pre-1967 Uruguay (a collective executive representation system). The United States and its long-time colony the Philippines have presidential systems and single-member-district legislatures. The nations of western Europe and Scandinavia, as well as Israel whose initial leaders were primarily continental Europeans from the early days of the Zionist movement, typically have parliamentary systems with proportional representation and large multi-member legislative districts. France—where de Gaulle installed a presidential system in 1958 to improve stability—and collective executive Switzerland are the exceptions. Japan and West Germany, whose constitutions reflect both some indigenous traditions and American or Anglo-American influence during post-Second World War reconstruction, are, appropriately, hybrids of representational and majoritarian patterns. . . .

SOCIO-ECONOMIC AND CONSTITUTIONAL EFFECTS

. . . As some types of constitutional arrangements are found more frequently in countries with more favourable environmental conditions, we need to examine the association between constitutional types and performance while controlling for the environmental advantages enjoyed by some of the democracies. Some of the associations found so far in this chapter may be spurious effects of environment.

Table 3 presents the results of a multivariate regression analysis of environmental advantages and constitutional arrangements. For each measure of performance the table lists the variance explained and then the standardized regression coefficients for the variables of population size, level of economic development, and ethnic homogeneity. . . . Immediately below the first row of regression coefficients appear the coefficients that emerge when variables for constitutional arrangements

TABLE 3. Regression analysis of environmental advantages, constitutional arrangements, and political performance (standardized regression coefficients)[a]

Performance dimension	Variance explained, %	Environmental advantages[b]			Constitutional arrangements[c]		
		Small population	Economic development	Ethnic homogeneity	Presidential executive	Majority electoral laws	Switzerland dummy
Voting participation, 1958–76	21	0.05	0.22	0.33*	–	–	–
	58	0.11	0.32**	−0.09	−0.26**	−0.44**	−0.62**
Executive durability, 1967–76	1	0.13	0.04	−0.09	–	–	–
	44	0.18	0.03	0.32*	0.42**	0.64**	0.38**
Majority control, 1967–76	12	0.22	−0.11	−0.32	–	–	–
	41	0.24	−0.26	−0.06	−0.42**	0.40**	0.22
Low rioting,[d] 1958–67	71	0.87**	0.06	−0.11	–	–	–
	72	0.90**	0.05	−0.03	0.06	0.10	0.05

Low rioting,[d] 1967–79	61	0.80**	0.12	−0.12	–	–	–
	64	0.80**	0.09	−0.13	−0.17	−0.02	−0.03
Low deaths,[d] 1958–67	76	0.34**	0.47**	0.38**	–	–	–
	81	0.28**	0.45**	0.32**	−0.19*	−0.11	0.01
Low deaths,[d] 1967–76	61	0.27**	0.64**	0.10	–	–	–
	64	0.24*	0.62**	0.01	−0.13	−0.20	−0.04

[a] Standardized regression coefficients are shown for two equations explaining each dependent variable. The first equation includes all environmental variables that were significant in the [earlier] analysis. In the second equation, the constitutional variables are added. Comparing the first and second equations shows the additional explanatory power of the constitutional variables.

[b] Population size and GNP/capita are logged.

[c] From Table 1. The majoritarian electoral laws variable is coded: single-member districts = 3; Germany, Ireland, Japan = 2; other = 1. Presidential executive variable coded: presidential system = 1; other = 0.

[d] Again, extreme outliers on the riots and deaths variables have been truncated to the ninetieth percentile values to prevent bias. A log transformation yields similar results. For voting, 28 cases are used; all 1967–76 analysis uses 27 cases; all 1958–67 analysis uses 26 cases.

* F level over 1.7 (significant at 0.10).
** F level over 3.0 (significant at 0.05).

are added to the simultaneous regression equation. Comparing the variance explained by the two equations shows how much additional explanatory power is added by considering constitutional differences.

The coefficients for presidential executives and majoritarian representation laws indicate how these relate to each performance measure and how powerful they are. I should point out that the analysis uses the constitutional properties, not a strict dummy variable analysis of the types of constitutions. This approach allows us to see more clearly the separate effects of executive arrangements and legislative election laws, and to make finer distinctions than is possible with the threefold typology.

This analysis emphasizes that the constitutional variables have a strong impact on voting and on the government performance measures but a limited impact on the measures of political order. When we enter the constitutional variables, the percentage of variance explained jumps very sharply for the measures of voting turnout, government stability, and majority control, but increases only slightly for the violence measures. Moreover, some of the coefficients for the environmental advantages change notably in the full explanation of voting and government performance but are hardly altered in the violence equations.

In explaining voting turnout, only the level of economic development remains significant as an environmental advantage: even with constitutional factors considered, the more economically developed countries have higher turnout. As expected from the theoretical discussion, both presidential executives and majoritarian election laws are sharply negatively related to turnout. The representational parliamentary systems manifest the highest voting participation, even with size, economic development, and ethnicity controlled. . . .

In explaining government stability and majority control, the constitutional variables dominate the equations, and act just as was predicted theoretically. Both presidential executives and majoritarian election laws are strong predictors of executive durability. The Swiss multi-party executive is also very durable. At the same time, the majoritarian election laws indeed promote majority governments, in which the same party or coalition of parties controls both the executive and the legislature. But the presidential executive arrangements are associated with substantial periods of minority government. The consideration of these relationships with controls does not change, then, the conclusion drawn from Table 1.

In the analysis of violence, the constitutional differences do not add much to the environmental effects. The variance explained increases only slightly, and few of the coefficients for constitutional variables are significant. To put it another way, most of the advantages of the representational systems discussed early in this chapter, which appear very strong in Table 1, seem to be artefacts of the location of these systems in more economically developed societies. However, we must not overstate this conclusion. In considering deaths by political violence, *all* the coefficients for presidential executives and majority legislative representation are associated with more deaths. Presidential executives are significantly associated with such violence in the first decade, even after the environmental controls are in the equation. Such executives are also associated with more riots in the second decade, although the relationships are not significant. There remains a tendency for the representational constitutions, with their parliamentary executives and multi-member districts, to perform better in maintaining political order.

34

GOVERNING BY COMMITTEE: COLLEGIAL LEADERSHIP IN ADVANCED SOCIETIES

THOMAS A. BAYLIS

The literature on small groups and organizations . . . suggests that there are both virtues and drawbacks to making decisions 'by committee'. On the one hand, groups are likely to require more time to reach decisions than individuals; group decisions are apt to tend toward the cautious and incremental, while innovative responses to novel or difficult problems face the danger of being denied consensus support. On the other hand, a greater range of information and a larger number of options are apt to be considered in the group's deliberations, and the decisions reached may be more widely accepted and efficiently executed. Early critics like Weber, Hamilton, and Mill emphasized primarily the drawbacks of collegial bodies: delay and decision-avoidance, internal division and thus an absence of unity towards the outside world, and the tendency to conceal faults and make impossible the fixing of responsibility. . . .

If we examine quantitative measures of the performance of those regimes that tend towards the higher end of our scale of collegial sharing in decision-making, it is not easy to find any evidence suggesting that their record is inferior to that of more nearly monocratic regimes. The difficulty of finding adequate and widely agreed-upon measures of regime performance is, of course, formidable.[1] Furthermore, if the most serious problem

Thomas A. Baylis, excerpted from *Governing by Committee: Collegial Leadership in Advanced Societies* (Albany: State University of New York Press, 1989), ch. 7 (footnotes abridged). Copyright 1989 State University of New York. Reprinted by permission.

[1] See G. Bingham Powell, *Contemporary Democracies: Participation, Stability, and Violence* (Cambridge: Harvard University Press, 1982), pp. 8–10.

TABLE 1. National executives grouped according to collegiality

5 (collegial)	Switzerland, Yugoslavia
4 |	Netherlands, Norway, Japan, West Germany,
|	USSR
3 |	Great Britain, East Germany, Austria
2 |	Italy, Israel, Canada
1 (monocratic)	United States, France, Romania

collegial regimes face is indeed that of adapting to substantial or sudden changes in their economic, political, or social environments, finding appropriate measures becomes still more difficult. What appears to be reasonable performance over time as revealed in statistical measures may conceal the incapacity of a system to respond to crisis. I know of no clear evidence suggesting that collegially led countries are less effective in responding to crises than monocratic ones. Such a proposition is difficult to test, however, since systemic crises appear to be relatively rare among the more collegial polities listed in Table 1.

The success of regimes, justly or unjustly, is often assessed in terms of their *economic* performance. Here, what differences exist between the collegial regimes that we considered, taken as a group, and the monocratic ones appear to favour the former (see Table 2).[2] To be sure, almost all of the polities examined, with the exception of some of the communist ones, belong to the wealthiest nations of the world. Two of the countries whose GNP per capita can be found at or near the top of industrialized nations, the United States and Switzerland, are at opposite ends of the monocratic–collegial scale. On the average, however, the Western collegial polities (in categories 4 and 5) have a substantially higher GNP per capita than the monocratic ones (categories 1 and 2), owing largely to the presence of Italy and

---

[2] Calculated from Charles Lewis Taylor and David A. Jodice, *World Handbook of Political and Social Indicators*, 3rd edn. (New Haven: Yale University Press, 1983), i. 110–13; United Nations, *Monthly Bulletin of Statistics*, 38/9 (September 1984), pp. 220–7, and 38/12 (December 1984), pp. 17–20; US Department of Commerce, *International Economic Indicators*, December 1984, p. 63; Statistisches Bundesamt, *Statistisches Jahrbuch für die Bundesrepublik Deutschland* (Stuttgart u. Mainz: Kohlhammer, 1984), p. 660.

TABLE 2.   Collegiality and economic performance

Collegiality Rank (N)	GNP per capita 1978, $	GNP 1960–75, %	Growth 1970–8, %	Unemployment 1977–83, %	Inflation (1970 = 100)	Income share, %	Days lost in strikes
4,5 (5)	9,950	4.2	3.3	3.8	236.0	18.8	10,492
3 (2)	6,620	3.2	2.8	5.9	336.2	18.9	128,922
1,2 (5)	7,130	3.9	2.4	7.1	370.1	15.4	190,677

Communist systems are excluded from these figures. GNP growth and unemployment figures are annual averages. Israel is not included in the inflation (consumer price) index. Income share data are for the bottom 40% of population; no data are available for Switzerland, Austria, or Israel; data for individual countries are for varying years between 1963 and 1973. Days lost through strikes is the number per million population per year from 1980 to 1982. Overall averages are of individual country figures without weighting for population. For sources, see note 2.

Israel in the latter group. The difference persists on a lower level if the communist states are included. Average *growth* rates of GNP were similar in collegial and monocratic countries between 1960 and 1975, while the collegial ones performed slightly better in the crisis-ridden period between 1970 and 1978.

We might expect collegially ruled nations to be more sensitive to problems of unemployment than monocratic ones, in so far as the first place greater emphasis on themes of 'social partnership', and in fact the average unemployment rate between 1977 and 1983 was nearly twice as high in the more monocratic Western countries as in the more collegial ones. Median inflation rates (since 1970), however, are also substantially lower in the collegial polities, even if we exclude the spectacularly high rate of Israel in the monocratic group. Because of the number of northern European welfare states whose regimes tend toward collegiality, we might expect collegially ruled states to do relatively well on measures of income and wealth equality. In fact, for those countries for which we have data, the collegial polities appear to be significantly more egalitarian (as measured by the proportion of income going to the bottom 40 per cent of the population). The usefulness of this finding is vitiated, however, by the absence of data for Switzerland and Israel. The 'social partnership' component might lead us to expect collegially ruled nations to have a lower rate of strikes than monocratically governed ones, and in fact that appears to be the case with the more monocratic states losing something like eighteen times as many work days per capita through strikes as the more collegial ones.

If we turn to political variables we find few significant differences.[3] Given the comparatively closed, 'élitist' aura attaching to collegial cabinets and the populist qualities often associated with monocratic leadership, we might expect the former to rank lower in measures of political participation than the latter. In terms of percentage of voter turnout that is not the case: the two countries with the worst turnout records in national elections—the United States and Switzerland—are at opposite

---

[3] Calculated from Taylor and Jodice, *World Handbook*, i. 76–7, ii. 16–60; Arend Lijphart, 'Measures of Cabinet Durability', *Comparative Political Studies*, 17 (July 1984), pp. 272–3.

TABLE 3.   Collegiality and Political Performance

Collegiality Rank (N)	Voter turnout, %	Durability		Protest demos.	Political strikes	Riots	Armed attacks
		Months	Rank				
4,5 (5)	75.4	48.5	10.4	3.3	.24	1.22	1.62
3 (2)	82.7	90.5	4.5	8.4	2.15	5.75	37.15
2,1 (5)	74.9	49.0	13.5	9.7	2.58	7.24	12.22

Communist states are excluded from these calculations. Voter turnout figures are for elections held between 1973 and 1977. Durability figures exclude the United States and Switzerland. Average months are based on Lijphart's preferred measure; average ranking reflects his summary of five different measures. All four measures of political unrest are numbers per one million population for the period 1948–77. For sources see note 3.

ends of the collegial–monocratic scale. Voter turnout, to be sure, is a relatively poor guide to overall participation rates; unfortunately, good comparative measures of the latter are not available for most of our nations. One serious obstacle to such comparisons is the fact that the profile of types or 'modes' of participation varies considerably from country to country. I know of no evidence, however, that suggests any consistent differences in overall participation rates between collegial and non-collegial countries.

Measures of more extreme forms of political participation are also often used as indicators of political stability. Taylor and Jodice have provided comparative data on the number of protest demonstrations, political strikes, riots, armed attacks, political assassinations, and deaths from political violence in their *World Handbook of Political and Social Indicators*. Here the more collegial nations, perhaps because of their accommodative cultures, appear to do substantially better than the monocratic ones. Another frequently used measure of political stability— the average durability of governments—does not appear to favour monocratic regimes, in spite of the frequency of coalitions among the more collegial polities. Durability, however, is an elusive concept—relatively frequent changes of government may conceal a good deal of continuity in the parties and personnel in power.

Overall, these data—with all of their limitations—give no support to Weber's suggestion that collegial regimes will perform less adequately than monocratic ones. On the other hand, it would be rash to assert that the generally higher scores of collegial systems on these performance indices conclusively demonstrate the superiority of collegial institutions. It is plausible that certain intervening variables, e.g., the presence of a 'culture of accommodation' or a neocorporatist structure of interest group representation, help to explain *both* collegial decision-making *and* relatively strong performance in the sectors considered in a number of countries.

NOTES ON CONTRIBUTORS

WALTER BAGEHOT was an economist, political analyst, and, as editor of *The Economist*, one of the most influential British journalists in the nineteenth century.

JOSÉ BATLLE Y ORDÓÑEZ served two terms as President of Uruguay (1903–7 and 1911–15) and was the editor of the newspaper *El Día*.

THOMAS A. BAYLIS is Associate Professor of Political Science at the University of Texas, San Antonio.

JEAN BLONDEL is Professor of Political and Social Sciences at the European University Institute, Florence.

SIMÓN BOLÍVAR was a leader of the Latin American independence movement and served as President of Bolivia, Colombia, and Peru.

The COMMITTEE ON THE CONSTITUTIONAL SYSTEM was organized in 1982 as a non-partisan organization for the study of the United States constitutional system.

The CONSTITUTIONAL REFORM COMMITTEE (SWITZERLAND) was the committee that prepared the 1848 draft constitution.

The CONSTITUTION DRAFTING COMMITTEE (NIGERIA) was the committee appointed in 1975 to prepare a new democratic constitution.

The COUNCIL FOR THE CONSOLIDATION OF DEMOCRACY was appointed by President Raúl Alfonsín of Argentina in 1985 to make recommendations for democratic reform.

ROBERT A. DAHL is Professor of Political Science at Yale University.

MAURICE DUVERGER is Professor of Political Science at the Sorbonne, Paris I.

CHARLES DE GAULLE was the first President of the French Fifth Republic.

J. P. A. GRUIJTERS was one of the founders in 1966 of the new Dutch political party Democrats '66.

ALEXANDER HAMILTON was a member of the 1787 US Constitutional Convention in Philadelphia.

DONALD L. HOROWITZ is Professor of Law and Political Science at Duke University.

The INTERNATIONAL FORUM OF THE ISRAEL-DIASPORA INSTITUTE consisted of Israeli and non-Israeli experts, including the editor of this volume, who met in 1989 to formulate recommendations for electoral and constitutional reform in Israel.

HARRY KANTOR was Professor of Political Science at Marquette University, Milwaukee.

BOLÍVAR LAMOUNIER is Professor of Political Science at the São Paulo Catholic University and a member of the 1985–6 Constitutional Study Commission that prepared a draft constitution for Brazil.

HAROLD J. LASKI was Professor of Political Science at the London School of Economics and Political Science.

AREND LIJPHART, the editor of this volume, is Professor of Political Science at the University of California, San Diego.

JUAN J. LINZ is Professor of Sociology and Political Science at Yale University.

SEYMOUR MARTIN LIPSET is Professor of Political Science and Sociology at Stanford University.

JAMES MADISON was a member of the 1787 US Constitutional Convention and the fourth President of the United States.

SCOTT MAINWARING is Associate Professor of Political Science at the University of Notre Dame.

CHARLES LOUIS DE SECONDAT, BARON DE MONTESQUIEU, was one of the foremost philosophers in eighteenth-century France.

CARLOS SANTIAGO NINO is Professor of Law at the University of Buenos Aires and served as chair of the Council for the Consolidation of Democracy.

G. BINGHAM POWELL, JR, is Professor of Political Science at the University of Rochester.

FRED W. RIGGS is Professor of Political Science at the University of Hawaii.

VASANT SATHE is a member of the Congress(I) Party and a former cabinet member in India.

ARTHUR M. SCHLESINGER, JR, is Professor of Humanities at the City University of New York.

DOUGLAS V. VERNEY is Professor of Political Science at York University.

A. JEYARATNAM WILSON is Professor of Political Science at the University of New Brunswick.

WOODROW WILSON was Professor of Jurisprudence and Political Economy at Princeton University and the twenty-eighth President of the United States.

GUIDE TO FURTHER READING

Since almost all of the selections in this volume are excerpts from longer works—articles, chapters, and books—my first recommendation for further reading is to turn to these articles, chapters, and books in their entirety. In addition, I would suggest the most important other works in the literature on parliamentary, presidential, and 'intermediate' forms of government. I organize these suggestions below, according to the division of this book, in five parts.

I. On the subject of definitions and classifications, Douglas Verney's 1959 work remains the best known and most authoritative, but the following two more recent books are also of special importance: Richard Moulin, *Le présidentialisme et la classification des régimes politiques* (Paris: Librairie Générale de Droit et de Jurisprudence, 1978), and Winfried Steffani, *Parlamentarische und präsidentielle Demokratie: Strukturelle Aspekte westlicher Demokratien* (Opladen: Westdeutscher Verlag, 1979). Of course, these books also deal with various other aspects, particularly the relative merits, of parliamentary and presidential government. Further treatments can be found as part of more general analyses of institutional differences among democracies in the following two books: Ivo D. Duchacek, *Power Maps: Comparative Politics of Constitutions* (Santa Barbara, Cal.: ABC–Clio Press, 1973), esp. ch. 7, and Le Mong Nguyen, *Les systèmes politiques démocratiques* (Paris: Éditions Ledrappier, 1987), esp. part 2. On different types of parliamentary and semi-presidential systems, see Werner Kaltefleiter, *Die Funktionen des Staatsoberhauptes in der parlamentarischen Demokratie* (Cologne: Westdeutscher Verlag, 1970).

As far as the British–American debate on parliamentary versus presidential government is concerned, the counterpart of the *Federalist Papers* is the work of the 'Antifederalists' who were opposed to the ratification of the US constitution. Although their arguments do not match the stylistic quality of the *Federalist Papers*, their objections and fears—including, for instance, their fear of an overpowerful and potentially arbitrary president—are well worth reading. A representative selection is W. B. Allen and Gordon Lloyd (eds.), *The Essential Antifederalist* (Lanham, Md: University Press of America, 1985). The two articles by Woodrow Wilson excerpted in this volume—both severely critical of the American separation-of-powers system—were originally published in 1879 and 1884. They were soon followed by his famous book-length critique *Congressional Government: A Study in*

American Politics (1885) of which several modern editions are available. A well-known exchange of opinions between prominent American and British scholars, Don K. Price and Harold J. Laski, took place under the title 'The Parliamentary and Presidential Systems' in the *Public Administration Review*, 3/4 (Autumn 1943), pp. 317–34, and 4/4 (Autumn 1944), pp. 347–63.

Since its foundation in 1982, the Committee on the Constitutional System has stimulated critical thinking about the US constitutional system. The Committee itself sponsored the publication of two books, respectively edited and authored by Donald L. Robinson: *Reforming American Government: The Bicentennial Papers of the Committee on the Constitutional System* (Boulder, Col.: Westview, 1985), and *Government for the Third American Century* (Boulder, Col.: Westview, 1989). Two other important books in the same vein, published by two of Washington's think-tanks, are James L. Sundquist (who is a member of the Board of Directors of the Committee on the Constitutional System), *Constitutional Reform and Effective Government* (Washington, DC: Brookings Institution, 1986), and Robert A. Goldwin and Art Kaufman (eds.), *Separation of Powers: Does it Still Work?* (Washington, DC: American Enterprise Institute, 1986). Both the Robinson and Goldwin–Kaufman edited volumes contain Lloyd N. Cutler's seminal article, first published in the journal *Foreign Affairs* in 1980, that can be regarded as the main catalyst of the American debate in the 1980s.

II. The article by Scott Mainwaring excerpted in this volume is a review article on the subject of presidential government in Latin America which covers both recent and older works in a well-nigh exhaustive manner. It is an excellent starting-point for further reading: 'Presidentialism in Latin America', *Latin American Research Review*, 25/1 (1990), pp. 157–79. Two valuable books with chapters on the operation of presidential government in several Latin American countries are Thomas V. DiBacco (ed.), *Presidential Power in Latin American Politics* (New York: Praeger, 1977) and the volume edited by Juan J. Linz and Arturo Valenzuela, *Democracy, Presidential or Parliamentary: Does it Make a Difference?* (Baltimore: Johns Hopkins University Press, 1992). Two other useful comparative surveys of Latin American presidential practices are Waldino Cleto Suárez, 'El poder ejecutivo en América Latina: Su capacidad operativa bajo regímenes presidencialistas de gobierno', *Revista de Estudios Políticos*, 29 (September–October 1982), pp. 109–44, and Humberto Nogueira Alcalá, 'Los regímenes presidencialistas de América Latina, Teoría y Practica', in Consejo para la Consolidación de la Democracia (ed.), *Presidencialismo vs. parlamentarismo: Materiales para el estudio de la reforma constitucional* (Buenos Aires: EUDEBA, 1988), pp. 125–68.

The classic analysis of the influence of the US model of government, including presidentialism, on Latin American and other foreign countries is Carl J. Friedrich, *The Impact of American Constitutionalism Abroad* (Boston: Boston University Press, 1967). A more recent and up-to-date treatment of the same theme is Klaus von Beyme, *America as a Model: The Impact of American Democracy in the World* (New York: St Martin's, 1987).

III. The most important comparative analyses of semi-presidential government are Maurice Duverger (ed.), *Les régimes semi-présidentiels* (Paris: Presses Universitaires de France, 1986); Humberto Nogueira Alcalá, *El régimen semipresidencial: ¿Una nueva forma de gobierno democrático?* (Santiago, Chile: Editorial Andante, 1984); and Stefano Bartolini, 'Sistema partitico ed elezione diretta del capo dello stato in Europa', *Rivista Italiana de Scienza Politica*, 14/2 (August 1984), pp. 223–43. The process of writing the Fifth Republic constitution is analysed by one of the members of the working group that prepared the text: Jean Foyer, 'The Drafting of the French Constitution of 1958', in Robert A. Goldwin and Art Kaufman (eds.), *Constitution Makers on Constitution Making: The Experience of Eight Nations* (Washington, DC: American Enterprise Institute, 1988), pp. 7–46. For an evaluation of French semi-presidentialism, see Ezra N. Suleiman's chapter in Linz and Valenzuela, *Democracy, Presidential or Parliamentary*, mentioned in section II above.

Another study of semi-presidentialism in Sri Lanka is H. M. Zafrullah, *Sri Lanka's Hybrid Presidential and Parliamentary System and the Separation of Powers Doctrine* (Kuala Lumpur: University of Malaya Press, 1981). Whether or not Finland is regarded as a case of semi-presidentialism, analyses of Finnish political institutions are all forced to treat the special relationship between president and prime minister. One recent example is Jaakko Nousiainen, 'Bureaucratic Tradition, Semi-Presidential Rule and Parliamentary Government: The Case of Finland', *European Journal of Political Research*, 16/2 (March 1988), pp. 229–49.

On the drafting of the 1848 Swiss constitution with its collegial executive, the classic source is William E. Rappard, *La constitution fédérale de la Suisse, 1848–1948: Ses origines, son élaboration, son évolution* (Neuchatel: La Baconnière, 1948). The operation of the Federal Council and its relationship with the legislature in the post-war period is discussed in Christopher Hughes, *The Parliament of Switzerland* (London: Hansard Society, 1962), esp. chs. 7 and 9; and in George Arthur Codding, Jr, *The Federal Government of Switzerland* (Boston: Houghton Mifflin, 1961), esp. chs. 5, 6, and 8.

Milton I. Vanger's political biography of José Batlle y Ordóñez gives an excellent account of the origin and early development of the concept of a collegial executive in an otherwise presidential system: *The Model Country: José Batlle y Ordóñez of Uruguay, 1907–1915* (Hanover, NH: University Press of New England, 1980), esp. chs. 10–16. The first, and only partial, experiment with a *colegiado* is analysed in Göran G. Lindahl, *Uruguay's New Path: A Study in Politics During the First Colegiado, 1919–33* (Stockholm: Library and Institute of Ibero-American Studies, 1962). The second *colegiado*, which operated from 1952 to 1967 and which matched Batlle's design much more closely, is discussed in Russell H. Fitzgibbon, 'Adoption of a Collegiate Executive in Uruguay', *Journal of Politics*, 14/4 (November 1952), pp. 616–42, and Alexander T. Edelmann, 'The Rise and Demise of Uruguay's Second Plural Executive', *Journal of Politics*, 31/1 (February 1969), pp. 119–39.

IV. The 1976 draft constitution for Nigeria provoked an avalanche of reactions, both critical and supportive. The most interesting of these—mainly editorial and readers' opinions in newspapers—were brought together in a single very useful volume, edited by W. Ibekwe Ofonagoro, Abiola Ojo, and Adele Jinadu, *The Great Debate: Nigerian Viewpoints on the Draft Constitution, 1976/1977* (Lagos: Daily Times of Nigeria, 1977). F. R. A. Williams served as chairman of the Constitution Drafting Committee and describes his experiences in his chapter on 'The Making of the Nigerian Constitution' in Goldwin and Kaufman, *Constitution Makers on Constitution Making*, mentioned in section III above. For further material on the possibility of a presidential system in India, see A. G. Noorani, *The Presidential System: The Indian Debate* (New Delhi: Sage, 1989).

In The Netherlands, the possibility of a 'directly elected prime minister', proposed by the new political party Democrats '66, was considered by a royal commission in 1969. After carefully reviewing all of the arguments for and against the proposal, the commission rejected it, but, by a slim majority, it recommended a somewhat weakened version; see the *Tweede rapport van de Staatscommissie van advies inzake de Grondwet en de Kieswet* (The Hague: Staatsuitgeverij, 1969), esp. part 3. On similar proposals in Israel, see Avraham Brichta and Yair Zalmanovitch, 'The Proposals for Presidential Government in Israel: A Case Study in the Possibility of Institutional Transference', *Comparative Politics*, 19/1 (October 1986), pp. 57–68. A recent detailed proposal was made by four Israeli members of parliament: David Libai, Uriel Lynn, Amnon Rubinstein, and Yoash Tsiddon, *Direct Election of the Prime Minister* (Jerusalem: Jerusalem Center for Public Affairs, 1990).

Another country in which a lively debate on presidential and parliamentary government has taken place is the Philippines. Its constitutional history has been mainly presidential, but there were two short-lived attempts at parliamentary government: the 1898 Malolos constitution, ended by the beginning of American colonial rule in 1899, and the 1973 constitution, which could not take effect because of the imposition of martial law. For an analysis of the 1973 constitution, see the special issue of the *Philippine Law Journal*, 48/4–5 (September–December 1973), esp. the historical survey by Irene R. Cortes, pp. 460–75.

V. Fred W. Riggs's evidence on the stability of parliamentary compared with presidential government in the Third World was presented in greater detail in his article 'Bureaucratic Power and Administrative Change', *Administrative Change* (Jaipur, India), 11/2 (1984), pp. 105–58; a revised version will appear as a chapter, entitled 'The Fragility of Third World Regimes', in the forthcoming book edited by Mattei Dogan and Ali Kazancigil, *Comparing Nations: The Pendulum Between Theory and Substance* (Oxford: Blackwell, 1992). A much earlier, but still quite valuable, systematic study of the viability of Third World democracies is Ledivina V. Cariño, 'Legislative–Executive Arrangements, Stability and Other Aspects of Political Development: A Comparative Analysis', *Philippine Journal of Public Administration*, 15/3–4 (July–October 1971), pp. 370–88. Finally, a new multi-authored volume edited by R. Kent Weaver and Bert A. Rockman presents a systematic attempt to assess the effectiveness of the American presidential system compared with several parliamentary systems in a series of specific policy areas: *Do Institutions Matter? Comparing Government Capabilities in the US and Abroad* (Washington, DC: Brookings Institution, 1991).

INDEX